"This volume approaches to a new fresh conception of the Local Development Policies on the 'non-physical' frontiers and helps to explain the complexity of two triangles: Informal Economy-Contraband-Drug Trafficking and Narco-Money Laundering-Other Illegal Activities."

Miguel Ángel Alarcón Conde, *Universidad de Castilla-La Mancha*

"Works like Blanes's, which deal with the illegal drug trafficking markets, must be recognized for their personal, intellectual and social value, because emotions and convictions go hand in hand with responsibility and risk. In addition, its approach from the concept of the border system provides a better understanding of these complex problems and measures the need, importance, and challenges to face it."

Sergio González López, *Universidad Autónoma del Estado de México*

"An essential book to understand the challenges that Latin American countries face due to the transnationalization of illegal activities."

Simón Pachano, *FLACSO Ecuador*

Bolivia's Border System

This volume demonstrates how Bolivia is part of a regional border system and intends to contribute to public policies, related to violence and distortions stemming from global illegal markets, specifically for vulnerable populations.

The book offers a multinational investigation on the changing and unknown image of the relationship systems that surround countries and, in particular, the structuring and functions of their borders. The chapters offer a reflection on how the lines of borders connect us to distant regions, which defines the real scope of the borders of globalization, while also impacting trade, labor flows, and organized crime. The book reveals how Bolivia has advanced from an image of borders, built through territorial disputes with neighbors, to today's conception of them. In doing so, it argues that underlying tensions have developed between the local and the global, namely, Bolivia inserting itself into the global system of illegal markets, thereby generating critical scenarios for various social groups.

Bolivia's Border System comprises the first research into Bolivia's border subsystem and illegal markets. It will be a vital resource for researchers of Bolivia and Bolivian history, international relations, security studies, border studies, and contemporary Latin America.

José Blanes Jiménez is the founder and current research coordinator of Centro Boliviano de Estudios Multidisciplinarios (CEBEM), in La Paz, Bolivia. He holds an MSc in Sociology from Pontificia Universidad Católica del Perú and has been a lecturer at several Latin American and Spanish universities. His research interests include population, development, border systems, and illegal markets.

Borders and Illegal Markets in Latin America

Beatriz Zepeda (Project Leader)
El Colegio de México

This series explores the strategic role that borders and borderlands play in the articulation of illegal markets to the south of the Río Bravo. Focusing on a variety of topics such as gender, contraband, migrant smuggling, drug trafficking, arms trafficking and human trafficking, and many more, the series sheds light on the particularities of illegal markets and the enabling role borders play therein, while providing – when taken as a whole – a more general and complete picture of how borders across Latin America are linked in ways that facilitate global illegal flows.

Latin America's Global Border System
An Introduction
Edited by Beatriz Zepeda, Fernando Carrión Mena and Francisco Enríquez Bermeo

Gender and Embodied Geographies in Latin American Borders
María Amelia Viteri with Iréri Ceja and Cristina Yépez Arroyo

Bolivia's Border System
Globalization of Illegal Markets
José Blanes Jiménez

Bolivia's Border System
Globalization of Illegal Markets

José Blanes Jiménez
Edited by Daniela Salinas

NEW YORK AND LONDON

First published in English 2023 by Routledge
by Routledge
605 Third Avenue, New York, NY 10158

and by Routledge
4 Park Square, Milton Park, Abingdon, Oxon, OX14 4RN

Routledge is an imprint of the Taylor & Francis Group, an informa business

© 2023 Taylor & Francis

The right of José Blanes Jiménez to be identified as author of this work
has been asserted in accordance with sections 77 and 78 of the Copyright,
Designs and Patents Act 1988.

Chief translator: Daniela Salinas.

Translation team: Katelin J. Reger and Paul Buffard.

All rights reserved. No part of this book may be reprinted or reproduced or
utilised in any form or by any electronic, mechanical, or other means, now
known or hereafter invented, including photocopying and recording, or in
any information storage or retrieval system, without permission in writing
from the publishers.

Trademark notice: Product or corporate names may be trademarks or
registered trademarks, and are used only for identification and explanation
without intent to infringe.

Published in Spanish by FLACSO 2017

ISBN: 978-1-032-06627-1 (hbk)
ISBN: 978-1-032-06628-8 (pbk)
ISBN: 978-1-003-20311-7 (ebk)

DOI: 10.4324/9781003203117

Typeset in Times New Roman
by Deanta Global Publishing Services, Chennai, India

This research is dedicated to the thousands of agents, people, and institutions working in Bolivia to help victims of violence resulting from the globalization of illegal markets. Faced with the great diversity of violence suffered in cities, in border areas, and, especially, in prisons, a group of actors today offer a portfolio of successful experiences in support of victims. These practices contribute to the learning of society in the absence of effective public policies. This work pays tribute to them, for their contribution to vulnerable populations.

Contents

List of figures	x
List of maps	xi
List of tables	xii
Series Preface to the English Edition	xiii
Preface	xiv
Preface to the Bolivian Volume	xvi
Acknowledgments	xix
Introduction	1

PART 1
History and Present of the Bolivian Border Subsystem — 3

1   The Bolivian Subsystem within the Global System — 5

2   Notes on the Evolution of the Concept of Borders in Literature and Politics — 17

3   Dimensions and Characteristics of the Borders — 32

PART 2
Illegal Markets — 67

4   Illegal Markets — 69

PART 3
Policies — 129

5   Public Policies and the Border Subsystem — 131

PART 4
Balance — 165

6   The Border Subsystem from Illegal Drug Markets — 167

Index — 179

Figures

1.1	Press Releases about Border Issues Compiled in the Newspaper Library	16
4.1	Press Occurrences of Drug-Related Seizures	77
4.2	Evolution of the Area under Coca Cultivation in Bolivia, Colombia, and Peru Total Hectares of Coca Cultivation	80
4.3	Production: Hectare/Price	82
4.4	Cartelization and Articulation of Roles in Drug Trafficking	87
4.5	Evolution of Nominal Coca Prices 2004–2014	95
4.6	Rationalization/Eradication of Coca and Area under Cultivation	100
4.7	Imports by Sector Evolution of CIF Imports in USD MM	106
4.8	Imports by Country of Origin	107
4.9	Gold Exports, Peru and Bolivia, in Millions of Dollars	113
6.1	Framework of Interaction of the Main Illegal Sectors	168

Maps

2.1	Territorial Loss	19
3.1	Bolivia's Border Cities and Their Counterparts in Neighboring Countries	37
3.2	Border with Brazil	43
3.3	Map of the cities of Guayaramerín (Bolivia) and Guajará-Mirim (Brazil)	48
3.4	Map of Puerto Suárez and Puerto Quijarro (Bolivia) and Corumbá (Brazil)	50
3.5	Border with Paraguay	51
3.6	Bolivian Border with Chile	58
4.1	Cocalera Basin: Colombia-Peru-Bolivia	78

Tables

3.1	Border Cities Mentioned in the Press	36
3.2	Main Smuggled Products from Peru	38
3.3	Population of Border Municipalities (2001 and 2012 Censuses)	40
3.4	Main Smuggled Products from Brazil	44
3.5	Main Products Smuggled from Paraguay	52
3.6	Main Products Smuggled from Argentina	54
3.7	Main Products Smuggled from Chile	58
3.8	Main Products Smuggled from the ZOFRI area in Iquique	59
4.1	Estimated Size of Illegal Markets	73
4.2	Evolution of the Informal Sector 1999–2007 (as a percentage of total employment)	76
4.3	Urban Informal Sector Contribution of the Urban Informal Sector (SIU) to the GDP of Each Sector of Economic Activity in the Urban Area (in percentage)	77
4.4	The Global Geography of Cartels Latin American Presence in International and Global Organizations (2009–2014)	86
4.5	Coca Cultivation in Bolivia, 2000–2015 (per hectare)	90
4.6	Quantification of Coca Cultivation by Region, 2004–2014 (hectares)	91
4.7	Area of Coca Cultivation within Each Protected Area	92
4.8	Estimation of the Potential Production of Sun-Dried Coca Leaf in the Monitored Regions (metric tons)	94
4.9	Average Prices of Coca Leaf 2013–2015	95
4.10	Summary of Coca Plantations Monitoring Results, 2015	98
4.11	Coca Seizures by Department, 2004–2014 (in kilograms)	101
4.12	Estimate of Smuggling 2000–2008 and Extrapolation 2009–2013	108
4.13	Bolivia: Complaints of Trafficking and Smuggling in Persons According to Management and Type of Related Crimes	116
5.1	Prison Population per Criminal Act	135
5.2	Related Cases Referred, Answered, Closed, and in Process	157

Series Preface to the English Edition

Four years have gone by since *El sistema fronterizo global en América Latina: un estado del arte*, the first volume of this series, was launched in Ecuador. Since then, the collection grew to include studies on the borders of eight Latin American countries and four themes that are central to understanding how borders in this region are interconnected and contribute to structuring global illegal markets.

As the first collection of academic works devoted exclusively to borders in Latin America, the series constitutes a valuable source of information on the geographic, economic, demographic, and social characteristics of the most important Latin American border regions and their relation to global illegal markets. Moreover, the analyses on illegal flows (drugs, contraband, arms, migrant smuggling, and human trafficking) that the country studies put forward, and which the thematic volumes go into in greater depth, offer a unique and comprehensive view of the ways in which illegal markets are organized in each country and how they connect across borders to create the global border system.

Thanks to Routledge's interest, it is now possible to make this series available to an English-speaking audience and share with the readers the findings of an international team of more than forty researchers from ten countries, who worked on this project over a period of three years.

While with the release of this collection we close a cycle, research on borders and illicit markets is more warranted than ever. Borders continue to gain importance not only in Latin America, but worldwide, and illegal flows evolve, almost by the day, creating new cross-border dynamics and global connections. We hope that this collection of works will contribute to illuminate the intricate relationship between the two of them not only in Latin America, but also on a global scale.

Finally, a note of thanks is due. In bringing these works to an English-speaking readership, no other person was more important than our editor, Natalja Mortensen. Natalja's permanent support since the publication of the series in English was but a proposal was essential to the completion of this work and the greatest encouragement we could possibly get. For this we are deeply grateful.

Beatriz Zepeda
Series Editor (English language edition)

Preface

The research project "Exploring the Political Economy of Violence in Latin American Border Systems: Towards a Comprehensive Understanding" was developed under the coordination of Facultad Latinoamericana de Ciencias Sociales (FLACSO Ecuador) and was made possible thanks to the support of the International Development Research Centre (IDRC), Canada. The project was carried out within a very far-reaching institutional framework, with the participation of El Colegio de la Frontera Norte, Mexico, FLACSO Guatemala, Fundación Paz y Reconciliación, Colombia, FLACSO Ecuador, the Catholic University of Peru, Centro Boliviano de Estudios Multidisciplinarios, Laboratório de Estudos e Pesquisas Internacionais e de Fronteiras, Brazil, Universidad del Litoral, Argentina, and Universidad San Francisco de Quito, Ecuador.

The study aimed at understanding the structure and characteristics of the global border system in Latin America, based on illegal economies and related crimes. In other words, it sought to elucidate how the cross-border relationship in Latin America is constituted on the basis of the actors (global crime network) and the "space of places" that structure the circuits, routes, and nodes of illegality.

The research was conducted under a collaborative arrangement of social production of knowledge, conceived from a perspective that attempted to go beyond case studies, in order to build a comprehensive vision of the borders in the region. It was further premised on the understanding that borders acquire a systemic condition of global reach, i.e., that the borders between countries are integrated over and above the territories of adjoining states.

With this objective in mind, two convergent methodological approaches were adopted: that of national border realities understood as subsystems (eight countries) and that of the themes conceived as cross-cutting (four themes). At the same time, the starting point was a conception of the boundary as a line that demarcates the territory of adjacent states – therefore, agreed between them – while the border is a region constructed from the confluence of interstate relations, which are born where neighboring states end or begin. This is why it can be said that boundaries are relatively immutable, while borders are social constructions that are in permanent change, for they reflect the dynamics of each state, and, nowadays, of the global economy as well.

Preface xv

This book marks the beginning of the second phase of the FRONTeras Collection,[1] consisting of a total of 12 volumes. The collection seeks to approach border studies in eight countries of the region (Argentina, Bolivia, Brazil, Colombia, Ecuador, Guatemala, Mexico, and Peru), as well as on four cross-cutting themes considered key to understanding the border system (illegal markets, gender, border cities, and comparative criminal legislation). Each one of the volumes constitutes a monographic study in its own right, while the reading of all the volumes of the collection offers the added value of providing a general panorama of the global border system in Latin America.

The name of the FRONTeras Collection comes from the plural of the Spanish word "frontera" (border). We conceive of it as a compound term between "front," which alludes to what lies ahead, and "eras," which refers to different historical periods marked by transcendental events. In other words, we think of it as a way to look positively at the eras ahead in the areas of integration – and not of walls – between states.

Fernando Carrión Mena   Markus Gottsbacher
Project Coordinator   Senior Program Officer, Inclusive Economies
FLACSO Ecuador   IDRC – Canada

Note

1 The first phase encompasses seven titles that can be consulted at FLACSO Andes: http://www.flacsoandes.edu.ec/.

Preface to the Bolivian Volume

This work is one of the products of the project "Exploring the Political Economy of Violence in Latin American Border Systems: Towards a Comprehensive Understanding." A collective research that has been developed among nine countries in the region.

As in the first publication of the series, in this work, I do not aim to achieve a finished product, nor close topics of discussion, but, on the contrary, I intend to show lines of work that feed the future work of the network of border studies. Our countries cannot be understood other than as members of a regional subsystem and its links with the global system. This existence as part of a network marks the reality of the countries of the region, their changes, tensions, and challenges in these years of globalization, and, especially, the global nature of illegal markets.

This work focuses on the Bolivian subsystem and aims to contribute to public policies related to violence and the distortive forces that influence its relationship with global illegal markets, particularly among populations in vulnerable situations. Because of the condition in which Bolivia is inserted into the global system of illegal markets, rather critical situations are generated for various social strata and groups. In turn, and in the same way, national sectoral policies face limits to address global problems.

It makes sense to call for multilateral, regional, or global mechanisms, as well as different forms of international, regional, or global cooperation, as these are problems that spill over border lines and form part of a regional subsystem that will have to be confronted within their framework.

Many of the political, economic, and social situations in our region will have to be confronted within the framework of these subsystems. Countries are transboundary in nature, so there are the issues of markets, economic blocs, integration, and cooperation institutions, multilateral and regional. This is not something new, since territorialities that cross countries and regions have been generated, from which fields of power that go beyond the scope of national action are created.

In order to address problems such as these, which are part of the globalization of illegal markets and forms of global crime, it is necessary to recognize their extent and influence on our countries, which actors are involved, and how local actors are linked to them. We are part of subsystems linked to other enveloping

Preface to the Bolivian Volume xvii

global systems that limit the sovereignty of States and local policies on issues such as citizen security, among others.

As a result of a year of discussion among a team of members from nine countries, interviews with experts with significant criteria and experience in the field, within a multidisciplinary teamwork environment, where primary and secondary information has been reviewed, some outlines or lines for future research relevant to public policies and action systems of our societies are presented.

In Bolivia, Mexico, Guatemala, Colombia, Ecuador, Brazil, Argentina, and Italy, we undertook an investigation on some questions related to the changing and unknown image of the relationship systems that surround countries and, in particular, the structuring and functions of their borders. We have reflected how the lines of our borders connect us to distant regions, which defines the real scope of the borders of globalization. The lines that divide and relate us at the same time tell us the current complex stories of how they have been structured and how they are understood today.

In Bolivia, we have gone from an image of borders, built through territorial disputes with our neighbors, to today's conception of them. We have reached an unsuspected level of relationship with the world through borders, with a global system. In the past, these lines were separating borders or passages that connected the country to the world by means of trains and carts. Today, they are hinges that open us to a very complex and unsuspectedly accessible but distant system. Trade is becoming increasingly distant; labor flows and the scope of organized crime work closely intertwined along the routes of these border systems that have been carved out during the decades of globalization.

But it is not about distant, inert, and soulless spaces, they are regions and fields of force from which the ways of linking the country with the world are conditioned. Global actors govern these fields of force and structure the flows between the country and the world, in the form of global networks. This conditions and modifies the way economic policies are made and the way productive priorities and social policies are established. Increasingly, individual countries find the exercise of policies more mediatized, more interdependent on distant scenarios, and many of the once local actors are now global. The spheres of action of cities have changed. For example, Oruro was a city that was understood by the mining, which was its organizing axis. Today, the cities of Iquique and Arica are the recognized passageways for the distant relations of trade with Asia, which is the current dominant axis of influence.

The conceptual change that has taken place regarding the functionality of borders, their opportunities and problems, is not homogeneous in the perception and practice of the population. For some, borders are their daily bread and butter. An army of thousands of workers in the so-called informal sector, *bagalleros*, and others make their living from borders and border cities. For other actors, borders are the foundation of their spaces of economic and social control, as in the case of coca growers, transporters and street vendors, police officers, hitmen, judges, prosecutors, and lawyers, those involved in cross-border business and especially

xviii *Preface to the Bolivian Volume*

in illegal markets. But there are also those who wield power in drug trafficking, smuggling, and other illegal markets. All of them live off borders. Obviously, the control that each of these actors has of distant borders is different and, therefore, their control of binational borders and dividing lines.

As a result of the collective work, we deliver products of reflection with which, despite the risk of many biases, we try to establish a future line of work. I am not chiefly concerned about the gaps or inaccuracies that this work might have since the goal is creating a scope for the research that will be opened through the formation of a large research network on the subject.

Acknowledgments

This research was made possible thanks to the joint work with the research team that accompanied me. Many thanks to Henry Oporto, sociologist and social researcher; Manuel Rebollo, engineer of systems and database manager of the Centro Boliviano de Estudios Multidisciplinarios (CEBEM); Andrea Rojas, political science graduate, expert on violence and gender issues; Rolando Sánchez Serrano, PhD in Sociology; and Rubén Ferrufino, MA in Economics from Arizona State University.

It is a pleasure to recognize the people and institutions that opened their agendas and listened to us, especially the Friedrich Ebert Stiftung Foundation (FES), which allowed us to share many debates on citizen security and drugs.

Of great value to the investigation has been the cooperation through interviews with experts involved in the subject, such as Colonel Gonzalo Quezada, former general director of the fight against drug trafficking in Bolivia; Colonel Alberto Echalar, director of the Crime Observatory; Diego Giacoman, former official of the crop substitution programs of the Vice-Ministry; Sabino Mendoza, general coordinator of the Consejo Nacional de Lucha contra el Tráfico Ilícito de Drogas (National Council of the Fight against Illicit Drug Trafficking) (CONALTID); Antonino De Leo, Representative of the United Nations Office on Drugs and Crime (UNODC); Timo Behrens, Associate Expert of UNODC; Carlos Díaz, UNODC Program Officer; L. Nicolaus Hansmann, European Union (EU) cooperation section in Bolivia; L. Benjamín Chimoy Arteaga, Ambassador of Peru in Bolivia; José Espinoza, EU consultant on integral development; Héctor Córdoba, former general manager of the Bolivian Mining Corporation (Comibol); Daniel Agramont, researcher at FES-ILDIS (Friedrich Ebert Stiftung-Latin American Institute of Social Research); and José Carlos Campero, specialist consultant in drug trafficking and international organized crime.

The English version of this book would not have been possible without the support of my editor Daniela Salinas, who also proofread and supervised the translation. Thanks to Katelin J. Reger, form the University of Maryland, for the first translation of this work from the Spanish, during her volunteering at CEBEM in 2019. Thanks to Paul Buffard, former UN official and economist, for his detailed reading of the English text. Thanks to Vicente Blanes Carpio, architect and MA

xx *Acknowledgments*

at Delft University of Technology, for helping me edit the maps. And finally, but not least important, many thanks to Charlie Baker at Routledge for his patience and understanding.

José Blanes, coordinator of the Bolivia research
La Paz, September 2022

Introduction

The following text aims to outline the broad strokes of a general global panorama that, at the risk of underestimating important holes and gaps, points out the forms and conditions of Bolivia's insertion in the illegal market scenario. We intend to show that this insertion of the country in global flows questions the way in which economic and social policies are made, especially those related to organized global crime, as if they were fields that could be operated separately. Many problems that can be observed in the country result from powerful distant actors and global agents with whom we are necessarily linked.

The global nature of the situations in which Bolivia is inserted is one of the factors of the current comprehensiveness of policies. Globalization is not an addendum to national policies; on the contrary, it is becoming an aspect to be considered with each passing day on pain of failure.

Therefore, border issues should not be considered superfluous; a reconceptualization of the subject is necessary. Due to the proximity in the constitution of our binational demarcation lines, the interpretation of borders as lines that divide and separate us from neighboring countries is maintained, as if that were the end of our borders.

The Study Comprises Four Parts

The first part contains three chapters. The first one is based on some considerations about the current importance of the borders for Bolivia and discusses the concepts and methodologies that have guided this work, which imply a reconceptualization of the subject, not only as abstract, but as a political concept and of actual practice. In the second chapter, the historical origins of borders are a briefly discussed, and it is highlighted that the conditions derived from the historical context are still reflected in literature and politics nowadays. Without attempting a review of the state of the art in literature and politics, several key moments in the construction of the borders of the globalization era are addressed. The third chapter aims to provide the reader – especially the non-Bolivian one – a general description of the diversity of situations on our borders and border lines, as well as of the traces of the global flows that can be glimpsed from them. This description

DOI: 10.4324/9781003203117-1

2 Introduction

is intended to provide a picture of the complexity of situations and challenges that the State has been dealing with, from its historically persistent centralist difficult position. The State needs unprecedented innovations to manage legal and illegal flows, which are ordered and structured by illegal markets, and in matters of citizen security, which occur and should be resolved at the local level.**

The second part tries to show the main features of the illegal markets that impact the Bolivian border subsystem the most. This part highlights the characteristics of drug trafficking as the main axis of the illegal markets and the smuggling sector. Some considerations are devoted to market sectors closely related to drug trafficking, such as smuggling, which is of enormous importance for the country, along with the human trafficking and smuggling, in order to land on the topic of legalization of the money obtained in each of the aforementioned illegal activities and their intersectoral and global flows. The general consideration of informality as a condition of efficiency for offenses, crimes, and the proper functioning of illegal markets is fundamental. This condition that affects the institutional life of the country is one of the main toxic residues that remain after the insertion of Bolivia in global flows, governed by illegal markets. It also provides a glimpse of the global and local actors of these markets in the country and in their relationship with neighboring countries and the world.

The third part is devoted to the policies with which the State faces the regulation of the main problems of illegal markets, with an emphasis on the topics covered in the second part of the book, regarding general and sectoral policies, such as drugs and human trafficking and smuggling, arms trafficking, and money laundering. This arises from the assumption that there is a huge gap between policy definitions – a deep development of laws, not always complete of laws – and serious problems with budgetary and institutional implementation of these policies to make them operational.

Finally, the fourth part discusses the main advances and the pending challenges, such as the policy integrity and attention to critical situations in the current moment. From there, strategic research studies focused on the trajectory of illegal markets and on the scenarios and options for State and societal action in the worlds of illegality can be perfected in the future.

Part 1

History and Present of the Bolivian Border Subsystem

1 The Bolivian Subsystem within the Global System

The evolution and consolidation of the five borders and the specificity of each one of them have occupied an important part of Bolivia's national life, in a permanent relation to what has happened in the region. Since the foundation of the republic, its dimensions have been subject to border delimitation processes with neighboring countries. The loss of bordering territories to each of the five countries shaped the dimensions and functions in the border system of the region, in a very different way in each case: rubber, oil, and minerals generated wars and defined the physical boundaries and their functions in the global border system. At the same time, Bolivia has been subject to the ups and downs of the global border system since its foundation. Today, when globalization comes hand in hand with the empire of illegal markets of drugs, smuggling, and organized crime, the border system acquires other connotations and challenges.

This chapter will try to show the general conditions of Bolivia's insertion into the global border system, its importance for national life, and Bolivia's contribution to the system. Why is the border issue important for Bolivia, and what role does it play in the global system? To this end, the conceptual framework of the work shared by other countries in the region, with which a regional border system is supposed to be formed, is presented.

The Importance of the Global Border System for Bolivia

Bolivia, while crafted by dependent relationships ingrained by the global border system and the flows that link it, is an important piece in the overall system. The ways in which Bolivia adapts to illegal markets play a structuring role in this phase of globalization, at all levels of its life as a country. For the same reason, Bolivia's importance in the global border framework is much greater than the one traditionally granted by its role as exporter of minerals or hydrocarbons. Clearly, its value seems to be much higher than that of its scarce participation in world trade and global GDP (gross domestic product).

DOI: 10.4324/9781003203117-3

6 *History and Present of the Bolivian Border Subsystem*

The Impact of Global Flows on Bolivia

The border issue and the changes that occur in it are of great importance for Bolivia. Although the country's current situation is closely related to the past, the profound and rapid changes that have occurred in the last few decades affect the country's internal capacity to manage them, posing important challenges. The border issue changes at the pace of globalization and according to the increase in flows that link Bolivia with its region and the rest of the world.

As a landlocked country and exporter of raw materials, Bolivia always depended on border fluidity with its neighbors, especially with the rest of the world. However, in the last few decades of globalization, the inclusion of the country in wider and more complex scenarios does not depend only on the flows that pass through them. The formation of force fields, created outside physical border demarcations, traces the trade flows that are defined in the global map. This is especially important for Bolivia when examining illegal markets that largely structure this map, from the globalization of the most distant borders. The incidences of these markets are especially important for the country, its policies, and the daily life of its population.

The changes that affect life along national borders demand new national policies, such as better adaptation to the conditions of each one of them and their areas of influence. There are few spaces in the country that are not linked to the impacts of the flows that constitute the border system. These change the opportunities and challenges of the border territories, in the new context of decentralization.

Generally, policies are lagging in relation to the great speed of changes occurring at the global level. The conditions in which Bolivia assumes its insertion in global networks and flows bring severe consequences on the economy, the State, and the life of its citizens. During the last 30 years and within the framework of the transition of the binational logic, built by the complementary asymmetries, the country's synchronization to the increasingly extensive, complex, and diverse external conditions has progressively deepened in all fields: economy, migratory flows, global culture, etc. The importance of its borders has been surpassed by the scope of exchanges and their functions within the framework of the new flows, structured by illegal markets. This has brought about changes in the nature and adequacy of the informal market sector, in the system of justice and the police, and, also, in the economy. The justification and legitimacy of illegal activities has changed; society must endure an increase of violence related to illegal markets, organized crime, and in citizen insecurity. It is no longer a matter of relations with lines that delimit sovereignties, as if they were fixed entities, since the flows with which the country is shaped are changing and depend on external forces and subjects of global scope, rather than on bilateral relations with neighboring countries.

Even though the flows of illegal activities begin to occur with increasingly distant countries, their impacts on the border are more profound. It is not only a question of flows of goods, but of symbolic universes and values. The depth of the border reaches farther and farther beyond its physical lines of separation and affects above all the main urban consumer centers.

The Bolivian Subsystem within the Global System   7

Since the second half of the twentieth century, the country has rapidly integrated into the world's road systems, surpassing the restriction of primary export of minerals, hydrocarbons, and some Amazonian primary products, such as rubber and chestnut, which structured the two main axes of connection with the outside. Each of the two trade routes – rubber and minerals, independently – facilitated the border flows in the early twentieth century, leading to the current economic system and to a pattern of external relationships with the exterior, more diversified and complex, though still featuring the extractivism that characterizes the different stages of the border conformation of these two routes.

The current link between Bolivia and contemporary global flows deepens the proportions of its primary export industry and the powerful aspects of current extractivism. The changes have occurred among the main exported products, the successive oscillations of minerals and oil prices, the boom in the coca-cocaine complex of the second half of the twentieth century, and monetary policy, which for more than two decades maintained the value of Bolivian currency, encouraging imports, smuggling, and its consequent link to drug trafficking.

The increasing importance of Bolivia's role as an exporter country of raw materials and semi-finished products leads to the expansion and development of a rentier economy, developing diverse tertiary and service sectors, as well as a gigantic, low-income informal army, mainly engaged in sales and transport. Drug trafficking and smuggling are nourished by these sectors since those facilitate the process of production, transportation, and stockpiling, which represent a small part of the illegal markets business and are usually the least favored within the criminal sector of the economy.

In the last decades, commercial activity on the border was what contributed the most to their fluidity, bringing together remote points of the interior of Bolivia with other regions and countries, such as Europe, the United States, and Asia. In the times when gas and minerals went through a rise in their prices, import flows grew with the increase in exports, reaching countries as far away as Japan and China. The pendulum movements, marked by the changing monetary policies of the region and the consequent relative price differences, emphasized the asymmetries with the neighboring countries, influencing and defining the directions and dimensions of flows and of negative trade balances.

However, beyond the changes in the flow of goods, the speed of the spread of global impacts stands out. The changes have short duration, and modernization of infrastructure has taken place at great speed. At unexpected speeds, Bolivia already belongs to ever-bigger global systems to ever-larger regions, which are, above all, discontinuous, distant, and pluralistic, extending the cross-border region to a system of integrated "global borders where political power is assumed by the local authorities, who then take on an international role, and the national powers that lose relevance to the regional blocs (they give up sovereignty)" (Carrión 2014, 3). The State's power migrates to non-state actors organized in global networks of illegal organizations. That is to say, it is a moment in which

8 *History and Present of the Bolivian Border Subsystem*

the powers are pluralized, the field of forces connects territories not only via the logic of complementary asymmetry, but also via the new logic of the administrative architecture of the "network of networks," typical of the illegal economies and the new global economy; thereby, the field of social forces amplifies, while the cross-border territory becomes global and transforms into a system.

(Carrión 2014, 2)

Bolivia's Importance in the Trade Flows of the Global Border System

Bolivia is important in the global border system, not so much because of the amount of its trade flows, but for the characteristics of these flows and the conditions of its border crossings. The importance of illegal markets in Bolivia's border flows can be shown as an element that defines Bolivia's significance as a contributor to the border system. It is a primary exporting country and origin of the coca leaf as a raw material, which is the first step in the production of cocaine base paste, along with the other two countries of the coca basin: Peru and Colombia. The southern end of the eastern slope of the Andes is the third largest producer of raw materials and supplies the world's coca-cocaine business. This region is also important in the refining of cocaine and functions under the control of Colombia's main cartels, principally. Bolivia is a transit country of cocaine base paste for the production of hydrochloride, to neighboring countries, mainly by air, on the way to the more distant markets.

With 6,834 kilometers of weakened borders and precarious border posts that are poorly connected to the country's main urban centers, Bolivia is an ideal setting for the functioning of illegal markets. Its border line links the country with its neighbors, through highly porous legal border crossings, complemented by a rate of clandestine crossings ten times greater in number. Five countries with their different economic and political regimes define the conditions of local, regional, and global flows with binational asymmetries that change from one stretch of border to another. This situation presents the country with different scenarios, in which national and local policies challenges are defined. To this map is added the physical geography, which intensifies the diversity of forms of coordination between the formal and the informal markets, with the latter comprising a wide range of illegal sectors, such as smuggling, drug trafficking, and human trafficking. In the regional border system, Bolivia's institutional weakness facilitates crime in land border areas.

The study of Bolivia's subsystem is relevant for understanding the role it plays in the system as a whole, which is considered a unit that constantly changes and updates its components, the subsystems of the countries. The roles that Bolivia has been playing in the global border system are important in several aspects: the various types of migration flows; the fact that it is a country in which drug trafficking routes are originated, but also it is a transit country; the role of an important destination in illegal markets, especially of smuggling. The Bolivian subsystem has been adapting to the asymmetries that characterize relations

The Bolivian Subsystem within the Global System   9

between neighboring countries, and with deeper ties over the course of the last few years.

Although a very important portion of drug trafficking – not yet well quantified – is exported from Bolivia by air, smaller quantities of base materials create significant impact when they reach land borders and come into contact with a large number of people. In this respect, borders show conditions that facilitate social, institutional, and legal laxity toward crime that seems to make Bolivia an illegal market paradise. This may be an important contribution by Bolivia to the functioning of the regional and global border system.

In this context, important institutional changes have affected the situation of border crossings, making them generally more functional for global flows. The territorial municipalization of the entire country has incorporated other actors and institutions that require new forms of governance from the central government. Border cities do not end up receiving the corresponding decentralized functions, which is detrimental to the development of corridors between the borders and the interior of the country. The modernization of the State, although uneven with respect to the expansion of the functions of the border line, deepens the lack of functionality and control of remote places, such as many border points that have developed border zones of commerce that link border countries: Chile with Brazil, Brazil with southern Peru, and Chile with Paraguay.

These flaws in the internal transformations go from being qualifiers to being substantive, to the rhythm of the globalization of flows. Substantive conditions are creating an increasingly functional context to the global functioning of informality. An enormous army of transporters, retail carrier smugglers (*bagayeros*), traders, brokers, and wholesale traffickers facilitate the informalization of the economy, deepening the institutional weakness of the customs system and the country's highly complex tax system. The legitimization of the illegal informality and corruption takes shape and makes the country an ideal paradise for the global system of illegal flows. For medium-sized flows of black money that originate and operate in Bolivia, the fissures in the legal economy facilitate money laundering. This flow of money has been consolidating and diversifying to the point of becoming a fundamental factor for a small economy, generating a buffer against the impacts of the vicissitudes of changes in export prices.

The change in border logic is also observed among social forces. There is a shift away from the traditional smuggler or drug trafficker, who was essentially a speculator moving goods from one side of the border to the other, to the consolidation of the presence of international networks incorporating a diversified and stratified army of actors. Many of the traditional actors now form part of a global army, attached to a global holding company under the forms of local outsourcing or franchising that control routes, nodes, and key points for the movement and consumption of illegal goods (people, weapons, organs, drugs). Aside from becoming a cross-border entity that imposes the rules of border trade, it has expanded its business to broader sectors. Indigenous communities, border peasants, and inhabitants of peripheral urban areas that have been incorporated into the production or distribution of drugs or contraband goods are already part

10 *History and Present of the Bolivian Border Subsystem*

of this global force that imposes the rules of illegality, with a high capacity for legitimacy. A growing part of the State apparatus itself is absorbed by these universal cross-border forces. Border lines have been adapted into functional places for global flows, gravitating in recent years toward the rhythm of the global economies.

In Bolivia, a growing importer of finished products and therefore a destination for goods, where smuggling increasingly dominates the economy, and, therefore, the main functions of border crossings, the institutional system reaches high levels of synchrony with the development of the informal, underground, and clandestine economy. The functions of border lines feed corruption, as well as the permissiveness toward noncompliance with norms, the legalization of the illegal, and the facilitation of conditions of efficiency in the functioning of illegal markets. The Bolivian border system offers great ease, even compared to those of neighboring countries, due to its fluidity within the country.

Bolivia is rapidly globalizing through a few central sectors, to which others are being added. The country plays a central role in the border system through the production and export of cocaine, gas, and minerals, particularly gold, as well as the import of contraband – especially automobiles – Chinese clothing, and used clothes. All this produces massive labor, generates aggregate demand, requests for services, and produces speculation; it also has led to the growth of the misnamed middle classes and to the emergence of a generalized feeling of well-being, which do not correspond to the capacity of internal production.

Flows reach further and further and become narrower with neighboring countries. The traditional incorporation of minerals into Asian markets in recent years has turned Bolivia into a country that sells fewer than 100 products to China in exchange for the import of more than 4,000 from that country. Small and large companies travel to China to obtain goods, and almost a hundred Chinese companies export machinery and military equipment to Bolivia. Many of these companies settle in the country by providing their services in the construction of roads, sugar factories, and paper mills. The most important mineral exports reach the Asian markets.

Finally, it can be concluded that the impacts in Bolivia originated from the distant fields of globalization deepen the country's adaptation to the functioning of illegal markets. A sort of closed circle from which it seems difficult to escape, and which has been closing for the last few years.

Conceptual and Methodological Considerations[1]

The project that gave rise to this research, *Exploring the Political Economy of Violence in Latin American Border Systems: Towards a Comprehensive Understanding*, proposed to work on a line of reconceptualization of Latin America's border system, taking into account eight national studies of their border subsystems and four cross-cutting sectoral themes that are supposed to influence the structuring of these subsystems.

The Bolivian Subsystem within the Global System   11

What Do We Mean to Convey by Border Subsystems?

In the first place, we intend to expand the concepts of border by overcoming its concept as a dividing line that links two countries. Secondly, we mean to analyze what is happening today with each country or subsystem in an atmosphere of globalization in an integral way, given that each is part of a global system, particularly concerning the global impact capacity of illegal markets.

There is not much research about borders that aims at identifying the connections among them, much less to illegal economic routes. The new functions that borders have in the world are not well understood and are not taken into account due to this. Crime is flexible in border regions as long as policies that govern those areas continue to be the traditional ones.

> The global border system not only allows to grasp the current reality, but also to contribute to the design of policies and strategies within the framework of the integration, prevention, development, and containment of the noxious results of the "balloon effect" of targeted policies.
>
> (Carrión 2014, 1)

Border is a concept that refers to actions and interactions rather than to objects, and we have gradually transitioned in that direction in Bolivia, even if it does not seem so in everyday language. We have been for many years involved in the definition of boundary lines, in territory losses, in losses of maritime access, etc., and it is difficult to dissociate oneself from this concept. But at the same time, amid globalization, we have – particularly newer generations – transitioned to other much accessible ways of conceiving relations with other countries and see cross-country business as something within the reach of many. Our products reach unimaginable places, and we get to know distant cultures. It would seem that the borders bring us closer to situations that were once considered to be far away.

In this research we start from the statement that borders are changing the way of conceiving the limits of Bolivia, the demarcations of the country's sovereignty. The concept of border that has gained ground is that of the "force fields," in which we are wrapped. We change because the world we relate to changes.

Carrión's study states that

> [t]he BORDER is a continuous space of alterity (hybridization), where various symbolic universes, communities, and economic realities encounter under the logic of the magnet, forming "force fields," which dimensions are directly proportional to the attraction-separation mass of the various social, economic, cultural, and political forces.
>
> (2014, 2)

Understanding the different concepts relating to borders becomes fundamental in order not to confuse the object of the policies, "since national security is linked to

12 *History and Present of the Bolivian Border Subsystem*

sovereignty contained within the fragmenting line (boundary); meanwhile, citizen security has to do with the guarantees that States provide for coexistence in the whole of an integrating region (frontier)" (Carrión 2014, 2).

The historical change of the border logic is also observed in the change of the social forces that conform and contain it. One goes from the traditional smuggler (*contrabandista*), who was essentially a speculator who moved goods from one side of the border to the other, taking advantage of the comparative advantages and ignoring the payment of tariffs – that is why they are a (bi)national actor, an isolated trader – to the trafficker, who is a global criminal attached to a holding company under the forms of local outsourcing or franchising that control routes, nodes, and key points for the movement and consumption of illegal goods (people, weapons, organs, drugs). Currently, this social subject is the one that imposes the rules of border trade, the one that expands the business to greater sectors thanks to extortion, kidnapping, and homicide – as forms of protection and promotion of this economy – and the one that guarantees its connection to the legal market (laundering) and to the State (corruption).

This double consideration territorial (universalization) and social (trafficker) allows us to understand that the transboundary region (field of forces) is sustained by in the fact that borders cease to be physical spaces and become a territory of flows. Manuel Castells says that "in this way, the economies of global borders are experiencing an economic boom, generating a gravitational mass of population attraction, in a context of growth both of violence and of links with other borders (border systems)" (quoted in Carrión 2014, 3).

The Structuring Axes of the Border Systems' Force Fields Are the Illegal Markets

As with the other national case studies, for Bolivia's research it has been assumed that the illegal markets are the main actors behind the country's global insertion, based on Carrión's proposal paper. These actors operating inside the illegal markets are true agents of globalization and play important roles in the structuring of border systems. Organized crime and illegal markets such as smuggling, drug and human trafficking, and money laundering have become a decisive factor in the globalization of relations between countries on various issues that make for sovereignty (Carrión 2014, 6).

Latin America's legal economy is inevitably linked to illegal activities – drug and human trafficking, weapons, etc. The presence of the illegal markets can be observed in the creation of illegalities, such as *presta diarios* (usury), *vacunas* (taxes), and violence (hitmen, kidnapping, reckoning). Due to the borders' transformation, these have become the preferred place where illegal economies and related crimes occur. World economy was dynamized by the openings and became a connection between the legal economy and the illegal one, thanks to *offshore logic* and to the strengthening of the services provided by tax havens (Carrión 2014, 5). With the scientific technologic revolution in the field of communications, new crimes were brought, such as cybercrimes or the illegal sale of human organs. The benefits and freedom the Internet brings have played an important role in the illegal markets on a global scale (Carrión 2014, 6).

> Borders become powerful dams to the physical mobility of the factors of production, but, paradoxically, they become strong nodes of integration of global networks of illegal economies (key links) and of promotion of their social actors (traffickers) as key forces in the continuous flow of illicit activities.
>
> (Carrión 2014, 3)

Border Violence: Another Structuring Axis

A specific type of violence is originated from the illegal markets' ability to structure borders and administer social, cultural, and economic asymmetries. This violence does not necessarily refer to the one that occurs at the border, but to those forms of violence that originate in countries that administrate different types of violence. According to Fernando Carrión, violence is considered historical and plural (2014, 6–7). In the first case, violence changes from *traditional violence*, which comes from social asymmetries, spontaneous cultures, and from strategies of survival to a *modern violence* that mainly originates from the illegal economies. It is important to highlight that today, modern violence is exercised with the objective of something; it is organized, creates networks and associations, and has a planning culture to decide the logic of the of their actions (Carrión 2014, 7).

On the other hand, Carrión mentions violence as plural. A set of social, economic, and political phenomena configure violence and illegalities with particular scenarios and logics. Some examples of these are urban violence, common violence, which originates in a public space, gender violence that arises from the inequality between the sexes and the relationship of power that one exercises over the other – among others (Carrión 2014, 4).

The management of illegality generates new forms of violence to penetrate territories far from the border. The increase in forms of violence and the cross-border crime – which not necessarily occur near the border – are being related to drug trafficking by the population. Illegality is spreading to different spheres of national life. This chapter will highlight how the dominion over the systems of administration of justice, the systems of extortion of judges and police officers, the emergence of the "protectors of crime" (hitmen), human trafficking and smuggling that transcends border boundaries, among others, impact Bolivia.

Although greater attention has been paid to violence in general, its focus has been only on certain types of it, while border violence has been ignored, since the concept does not attract much attention due to the rapid growth of other types of violence that affect large cities, mainly, or areas of illegal economy.

> Border violence is born of asymmetries between neighboring States because there resides its condition of existence. This leads to a second differentiation: violence at the border is different from border violence. While the first one

14　*History and Present of the Bolivian Border Subsystem*

refers to the concentration of violence in the cross-border region, the second relates to those arising from relations between States.

(Carrión 2014, 5)

The systems in charge of collecting information on the different forms of violence are partial and generally do not pay attention to border areas or to the analysis of the nature of some forms that derived from it and are related criminal activities. Moreover, when it comes to carrying out comparative studies, serious difficulties are encountered due to a lack of information and to the methodological construction of the available studies.

Public Policies and Border Problems

Fernando Carrión mentions that there are three situations that characterize the State's security policies. The first one is that they are unilateral – it is not considered that they take place in a transboundary reality and that borders are part of global systems. Secondly, they are designed homogeneously without distinguishing between the differences that exist along the length of the border, and, thirdly, they are conceived and implemented from national power centers, distant from the reality of borders (Carrión 2014, 9).

Current border policies are based on the traditional model of import substitution. Nowadays, new integration policies that attend the globalization needs are required. Border policies follow the lines of national and public security – prioritizing national security as the defense of the country's sovereignty from external enemies; migration, which grants visas and asylum; and economic, emphasizing restrictions like quotas and the collection of tariffs. "National security policies tend to produce barriers by building walls or by militarization, which create greater opportunities for illegal integration. At the same time, they lead to problems regarding legal activities and tend to boost transnational crime" (Carrión 2014, 8).

Deepening the Line of Research

Due to the nature of the subject, the results that have been observed focus on the need to "understand the structure and characteristics of Latin America's global border system – starting from illegal markets and related offences – in order to propose concrete recommendations to help shape safer and more prosperous regions" (Carrión 2014, 8).

This research proposes a line of work rather than a finished product, due to the changing and highly dynamic nature of structuring factors: illegal markets and the resulting forms of violence. These national studies are not intended to be comparative but to highlight the ways in which the national subsystems have been built within a framework of structuring determinations: **illegal markets** (narcotics, weapons, irregular migration, smuggling, money laundering), **gender-based violence**, **youth violence**, and **penal codes**. The eight national subsystems

The Bolivian Subsystem within the Global System 15

– Mexico, Guatemala, Colombia, Ecuador, Peru, Bolivia, Brazil, and Argentina – comprise Latin America's global border system. Complementarily, four cross-cutting investigations will be carried out which will make it possible to contextualize and understand the general problem.

Methodology

This research follows Carrión's methodology, which is based on two factors: national studies and sectoral studies. National studies analyze the eight countries that comprise Latin America's global border system mentioned above.

For the purpose of this book, it is important to address the **Andean countries** that are the principal producers of cocaine and that require the illegal import of chemicals and weapons. Their presence in the largest illegal markets of the world resides in the export of this narcotic. These Andean countries include Colombia, Peru, and Bolivia (Carrión 2014, 13).

On the other hand, **sectoral studies** seek to understand the context in which the global border system operates by researching the topics that are considered key for the subject: the normative (penal codes), the economic (illegal markets), and the social (gender and youth). "For methodological reasons, the research project confronts four cross-cutting sectoral studies, with the purpose of providing a general and contextual explanation of the problems of Latin America's global border system" (Carrión 2014, 14).

Basic Information

We have worked with information that has been gathered on a platform, as a database to be consulted by researchers and to give continuity to the aforementioned line of research:

- **Newspaper library**. In the case of Bolivia, the team collaborated with *El Diario*, a senior national publication and the only paper that retained digital records for the period chosen by all the countries in the study (see Figure 1.1).
- **Secondary information**. We reviewed and ordered documents, reports, and bibliography that has allowed "information to be generated (census data, homicides by borders, border crossings etc.), as well as to articulate recent interpretations" (Carrión 2014, 11).
- **Qualified informants**. With the identification of the correct officials and academics, we sought to both collect qualified information and establish the main lines of interpretation of the border issue.
- **Field reconnaissance**. Although not considered in the studies, this aspect of the research reflects in the Bolivian study data from several of the border crossings: Charaña, Tambo Quemado, and Chile. Observations have been made in several municipalities adjoining the borders of Peru and Chile, affected by being places where the passage of smuggled goods is administered and places of important passage in drug trafficking. Special attention

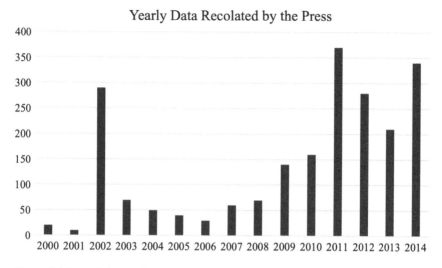

Figure 1.1 Press Releases about Border Issues Compiled in the Newspaper Library. Figure by the author with data from the newspaper library.

should be paid to the city of Oruro, the most important counterpart in terms of smuggling and legal flows of goods with the port of Iquique.

Figure 1.1 shows the form and dimension in which the variables or questions of the research have been reflected in the written press, operating on the assumption that this shows how a subject is seen as a relevant problem and originates in the very public institutions that, in general, qualify it or generate it.

The concept of border that defines Bolivia's relations with the rest of the world serves to understand to what extent national life is impacted by its insertion in the system of flows that define the border areas of globalization.

Note

1 This section presents a summary of the referential document for all the series participants in the project *Explorando la economía política de la violencia en los sistemas fronterizos de América Latina: Hacia una comprensión integral*. All the textual paragraphs refer to this document: Carrión (2014).

References

Carrión, Fernando. 2014. *Explorando la economía política de la violencia en los sistemas fronterizos de América Latina: Hacia una comprensión integral*. Unpublished Paper.

2 Notes on the Evolution of the Concept of Borders in Literature and Politics

The focus of border studies has changed in recent decades, but its principles are still lagging somewhat behind the evolution of the processes of insertion of the country into the flows of globalization; it still maintains the perception of borders as physical places distant from the main centers of development. Borders are abandoned places, devoid of the basic conditions of life, and the public servants assigned to them require incentives for their sacrifice.

It can be said that there is great ignorance of the current border reality of the country. Originally, the country's borders are explained based on the loss of sovereignty over natural resources. Bolivia's incapacity to appropriate and exploit natural resources led to the country losing territories, thus creating border demarcations with the neighboring countries. A brief and superficial review of the literature shows this situation as a foundational fact, which, although it took place in the past, continues to exist and influence the country's development policies.

It is striking that the border issue has not developed as the central element of the current development in a landlocked country, one that depends heavily on its policy of insertion into global economic flows, a state of dependence that would seem to imply going beyond the simple management of border lines. For most of the population, the issue that closely approaches a policy of insertion of the country into the globalized world is the maritime access dispute with Chile. Although the political collective imagination is not fully focused on that direction, the issue has become more of a political call for national unity. Border management is reduced to the policy of development of bilateral lines, its population and living conditions. These are very real and legitimate issues related to the occupation of the territories.

The following is a brief outline of the origin and evolution of the current borders with each of its neighboring countries, of the disputes over natural resources, the suitability of the territory for exports, and its suitability for a system of globalization. A review of the literature does indeed show this passive image.

Brief History of the Evolution of Borders

Three processes illustrate the evolution of the borders to the present day: Firstly, the foundational one took place from the Independence to the Chaco War

DOI: 10.4324/9781003203117-4

18 *History and Present of the Bolivian Border Subsystem*

(1825–1936) and is characterized by the dispute over natural resources at the borders and the consolidation of the definitive limits with each one of the countries. A second process, which overlaps in part with the first (from 1876 to 1970), is of the adaptation of the borders and the structuring of land communication networks to service exports and migration. The third and ongoing process also overlaps with the second, and it corresponds to the period from the end of the 1940s to the present day, characterized by the transformation and suitability of the function of the border in the context of globalization, due to the increase in trade flows, the movement of people, and, above all, the increasing operation of illegal markets.

The Starting Point: The Battles for Territory and Natural Resources

On August 6, 1825, Bolivia – twice the size it is today – initiated a process of consolidation of its physical borders through successive disputes with neighbors over natural forest and mineral resources. From the country's initial area, constituted of 2,363,769 square kilometers, Bolivia lost 1,265,188 square kilometers, a little more than half of its original territory, in only the first 59 years of its consolidation (see Map 2.1).

- Between a conflict for the exploitation of saltpeter and guano, during the War of the Pacific – which originated with the Chilean expansion toward Peru and Bolivia – Bolivia lost 1,265,188 square kilometers. Since the war, and after the signing of the Treaty of 1904, the country lacks maritime access.
- After the Acre War, through the Treaty of Petrópolis (1903), Bolivia ceded 340,000 square kilometers of territory rich in products to Brazil.
- When facing off against Argentina, through signing treaties in 1880 and 1925, Bolivia ceded 170,000 square kilometers of its territory in the Central Chaco region.
- Against Peru, in two boundary agreements of 1902 and 1909, Bolivia ceded 250,000 square kilometers of quinine trees and Brazil nut–producing agricultural land.
- After the Chaco War, also called "the War for Oil," Bolivia yielded 240,000 square kilometers to Paraguay, in the middle of the Great Depression. Even during those times, this has been a territory that contains the richest gas deposits (Mesa and Mesa 1988, 539–555; Klein 1982, 12–14).

Surely this story has influenced the collective imagination of border sites to this day: the story of dispossession that limits our development.

Connecting Borders through the Construction of Communication Networks

The other story is that of the structuring of the country to put the borders within the reach of exports. While Bolivia's borders were being consolidated, a process

Notes on the Evolution of the Concept of Borders in Literature and Politics 19

Map 2.1 Territorial Loss. Map by the author.

of road structuring, which started in the last two decades of the nineteenth century, took place, linking the country both to the Pacific ports and to the Paraná River. The two Bolivian networks that create terrestrial links between the country and the world – those of rubber and silver – consolidated their current structure during the first decade of the twentieth century. These networks were disconnected from each other until the 1940s, and, during that period, the most important changes of the territory, the processes of territorial integration, and productive diversification of the 1940s developed from them (Gómez Zubieta 2006, 9–23). The border route for rubber extraction from the Amazon East was projected toward Buenos Aires and from there to Europe, in addition to a moderate river exploitation. If it were not for the expectations aroused by the signing of the treaty with Chile in 1904, the river ports would have been developed further. Since then, the border cities of Puerto Suárez, Puerto Aguirre, and Puerto Quijarro – on the border with Brazil – live with the hope to be acknowledged because of their position at the beginning of the interoceanic corridor, which would link the Port of Santos in Brazil with the Pacific ports of Chile and Peru. The role of the eastern railway network that united this vast territory with Argentina toward the Atlantic cannot be ignored.

20 *History and Present of the Bolivian Border Subsystem*

The first border structure was created for the extraction of rubber in the Amazonian East; Casa Suárez traced the route to Buenos Aires and from there to Europe (Bismark and Araujo 2007, 7–13). This stage of the rubber industry reflects a project of a country from the Amazon region, from the borders with Brazil and Paraguay; a project that has been largely overshadowed because of the strong contrast with the country's vision of the Andes and its mining economy as the backbone of the country's economy, politics, most of the institutions, and the country's culture.

From an Andean and Bolivian perspective of minerals, the West has written much of the country's history. Its communication channels toward the global system were restricted to linking the Pacific ports through Peru, Chile, and Argentina.

The mining railway was the structuring engine of the West that was organized to export minerals, the main product of globalization, from Bolivia to the Pacific through Peru, Chile, and Argentina. This railway was the central instrument of the extractivist economy and of Bolivia's mono-exportive dependence. With the same extractive criteria, the border system was diversified by the expansion of the roads, forgetting for several decades what happened along the borders of the East (see Villegas 2013).

The two routes in the East and West – with no connection between them – separately structured the border flows of the early twentieth century. These flows gave way to today's more diversified and complex system. In the 1940s, communication was established by road between the East and West – Cochabamba and Santa Cruz – connecting the systems of Beni and Pando. In 1972, the first asphalted road joining the cities of Cochabamba and Santa Cruz was built, consolidating the so-called Central Axis of the country (CERES 2003, 167–223).

Henceforth, Bolivian communications advanced rapidly, although with a strong lag in time with respect to other countries. The land communications network between the country and its borders developed and densified, connecting every point in the country to global flows via Brazil, Paraguay, Argentina, Chile, and Peru. This is a very important step taken by Bolivia since it allowed the insertion of Bolivia into the globalized world.

The Border System of Globalization and Illegal Markets

Another important moment was the transition from dreaming of development toward an actual globalization. Starting in the 1970s, Bolivia undertook the definition of development policies with the support of the Instituto Latinoamericano y del Caribe de Planificación Económica y Social (Latin American and Caribbean Institute of Economic and Social Planning) (ILPES). This action is remembered as a commendable effort, recorded in many documents, among which the 1971–1991 Socioeconomic Development Strategy stands out. This document, prepared by a group of young intellectuals, defined the possible way to replace imports.[1] But, the country's great weakness to face import substitution policies prevented success in this endeavor, and the economic model was not changed; thus, Bolivia continued as a country that exported raw materials. Bolivia's agriculture and

Notes on the Evolution of the Concept of Borders in Literature and Politics 21

livestock achieved a relative self-sufficiency and managed to export a limited quantity of these goods from the East of the country. In the western side of the country, agriculture represented an important bastion in the self-sufficiency of traditional food crops. According to the Instituto Boliviano de Comercio Exterior (Bolivian Institute of Foreign Trade) (IBCE), today there is a growing trend to import food for daily consumption from neighboring countries, which signifies "a setback" in achieving the ideal of food sovereignty (Fundación Milenio 2011, 1–2).

This framework of an economy that is highly outward-oriented and increasingly dependent on industrialized foreign products determines the main current functions of the Bolivian border subsystem. Flows that articulate the country with the region are constantly changing, defining the functions of its border points, very sensitive to the impulse of factors such as monetary policies, productivity differences, and legal aspects that build the main factors of complementary asymmetries (Carrión 2014, 4). The volume and growth of contraband inside the global market shows the failure of the Bolivian import replacement model.

Of all the economic activities, trading has contributed the most during the last decades to mold the fluidity of the borders, bringing more and more remote points of the interior of the country closer to the global routes of Europe, the United States, and Asia. Cross-border trade is the axis of the conformation of the new border subsystem, which has incorporated Bolivia into the global system (Ferrufino 2015, 12–16).

Another issue of the globalization of the border system is that of migratory flows to neighboring countries, particularly to Brazil and Argentina, combining temporary and permanent migrations that have structured border routes for decades (Hinojosa 2008, 5). Since the middle of the twentieth century, Bolivian workers settled in territories near the border areas, benefiting from the advantages and opportunities in nearby areas, like northern Argentina, and even Buenos Aires. During the last 20 years, migratory flows have searched for new destinations beyond the traditional ones – Buenos Aires and São Paulo – continuing toward Spain, Italy, and the United States, where they contribute as a workforce in construction and agriculture. The number of Bolivians living in São Paulo and Buenos Aires together would add up to the equivalent of the largest Bolivian city. Migrations function as important artifacts of globalization, among which human smuggling and trafficking mimic (Hinojosa 2008, 2–5). Cross-border trade and migration are two sectors that generate changes in the character of the borders; territorial changes that have become part of a major global system.

Due to their volume and specific characteristics, the illegal markets gradually constituted one of the transformation engines, which nowadays model the functions of physical borders in their adaptation to the global system, with new impacts on the Bolivian economy. Illegal markets have used the routes and flows, operated by traditional commerce, and have connected the legal and the illegal along the same border line, extending it to the most remote places.

This evolution of the border system occurred in a little over a century, a period when social and economic reality imposed itself upon a concept that is still

22   *History and Present of the Bolivian Border Subsystem*

stagnant in the sense of physical limits and of problems related to administrative and tax collection. As it will be seen later, the ordering and structuring role of illegal markets has played a triggering role in a strong process of the globalization of these markets.

Borders in Intellectual Production

In the following paragraphs, the image of the border concept in the intellectual production will be summarized in a very brief way. This concept is closer to the first stage of the Bolivian borders, that is to say, to the foundational border, in which the concept of delimitation of a binational dividing line predominates. This corresponds to the first decades of the twentieth century. With great changes in the border functions, dimensions, and characteristics of the border areas, it is strange that the concept of border itself has not changed in the same manner, and there is still a persistence of a vision of the borders as physical sites and dividing lines. Conceptual production, which has been unequal over time, incorporates diverse formats, including diplomatic documents, novels, chronicles, and journalistic columns.

The stage of territorial consolidation and the definition of border areas from Bolivia's independence until the end of the twentieth century produced many documents, some of which were oriented toward the study of territorial limits with its neighbors, from the perspective of geopolitics and economics. General history textbooks about Bolivia describe the circumstances in which borders were consolidated – from wars and territorial losses to an active foreign policy. Until the middle of the twentieth century, the history of the nation's territory walked in the footsteps of the dispossession of its territories, followed by three decades of extractive industries like mining and the cultivation of rubber, and the years of the Chaco War (1932–1935) (see Mesa 1988; Klein 1982; Vásquez 1990; Valencia 2000; Felman Velarde 1967).

Since the 1950s, the construction of road infrastructure and the consolidation of the railways defined borders as areas that join the extraction of raw materials with the foreign market. Today, these places have become some of the main channels of globalization flows and are documented in studies on the constitution and development of the national territory (Blanes et al. 2003; Villegas Nava 2013). The still vivid memory of the territorial losses in the Chaco War kept alive the concept of State security in the definition of border issues and the primacy of the State as a central and almost exclusive actor in border discourse. Until today, policies assign to the national government the central role of guardian of resources against external predators, despite more than 20 years of political and administrative decentralization (ADEMAF 2015).

Territorial losses impacted the entire country equally, but the Chaco War represented a national catharsis. Participation by all the country's social sectors, particularly peasants and indigenous peoples, had a deep impact on the collective consciousness of a territorially, socially, and ethnically disjointed country. Borders challenged the sectors of the economy, politics, and culture by demanding

Notes on the Evolution of the Concept of Borders in Literature and Politics 23

changes that led to several stages of nationalism. Its first impact was the transition from the old liberal and conservative parties to the new nationalist, indigenist, and revolutionary parties. A kind of refoundation of the country was set in motion as Nicolás Richard well describes (see Richard 2008). A remarkable amount of literature –especially novels –about the war and its consequences for the country was produced, including *Aluvión de fuego* (1935) by Oscar Cerruto and *Crónicas heroicas de una guerra estúpida* (1936) by Augusto Céspedes, as well as a great systematization written by Siles Salinas in 1969.

Several decades earlier, the War of the Pacific and the subsequent treaties generated the issues that, years later, would put Bolivia's sovereignty over the sea on the national discussion table. These issues, which remained latent in the imaginary, established the factors for a conceptual political change that nowadays is turning to see Bolivia's borders. Bolivian claims on access to the sea seek access to the Pacific flows that are of great importance in the twenty-first century (Carrión 2014, 4). Bolivia's characteristic as a landlocked country, excluded from access to the Pacific, is a strong counterpoint in a world which is already accessible through increasingly important long-range flows. Its high profile in politics is because Bolivia feels today that the loss of its maritime status is very important in global trade flows. In this field, the largest number of studies oriented toward the exercise of international relations and the construction of a deep sense of patriotic social unity have been carried out.

More than a century of literature inspired foreign policy proposals that were unprecedented in the history of the Republic and, above all, of Bolivia's imaginary of relations with Chile and the world. An exponent that sums up a century of historical analysis and construction of sociopolitical imaginaries is the *Libro del Mar* (Book of the Sea) (2014) that the Bolivian government distributed along the national territory and even at international levels, motivated by its case before the International Court of Justice in The Hague. After abandoning the trial of the Treaty of Peace and Friendship (1904), which mainly concerned geographical boundaries, Bolivia's lawsuit before the International Court of Justice – which brought together for the first time all former presidents, former foreign ministers, and political personalities – focused on the moment of the globalization of trade flows. Bolivia resorted to dialogue with Chile, and, on 48 separate occasions, the latter promised Bolivia access to the Pacific, to solve its problems as a landlocked country, which would improve the country's position in the border system to which it is linked as never before in its history. The *Libro del Mar* is a good account of the evolution of the concept of borders, used by Bolivia for the communication and information campaign in the international sphere on an issue concerning the State.

The current primacy of the sea issue has been the shepherd of a rich bibliography on Bolivia's relationship with neighboring countries. The main focus of Bolivian foreign policy with Chile, Peru, Argentina, and Brazil is the history of border delimitation (Abecia 1979; Fernández 2013; Ministerio de Relaciones Exteriores 2004; Moreira 1972; Vásquez 1990).

The issue of Bolivia's communication routes to the Atlantic via river, as opposed to access via the Pacific, has not been ignored; the river connection via

24   History and Present of the Bolivian Border Subsystem

the eastern borders to the Atlantic is now very important. The presence of Asian interests on the continent, particularly China's, and the possibility of exploiting the largest iron deposit in this region give the interoceanic corridor a strategic importance for the passage of soybeans from neighboring countries to the Pacific ports. In this way, the programs for the Integration of Regional Infrastructure in South America (Integración de la Infraestructura Regional Sudamericana) (IIRSA) have developed a vast amount of literature for the national political debate, to which the integrationist proposals and programs of the international organizations and the incipient national discussion forums are added (Carbone 2014; Gómez García 1997; Villegas 2013).

The border issue has also recently advanced regarding the State's territorial policies and the processes of decentralization and municipalization of public management. During the last 20 years, the country's territorial management introduced new visions, which implicitly touch on the issue of borders, to the extent that administrative decentralization generated new relations between the central government, the municipalities, and the regions (Blanes 1989; FES - ILDIS 2004; Quiroga 2003; Urenda 2007). Since the municipalization of the country, which began in 1993, almost half of the territory has been occupied by border municipalities. Eight of the nine departments are border departments; however, there is not much consideration of the border, despite the fact that the issue is present in many of them, as reflected by José Carlos Campero (2012) in his work. Nonetheless, these 72 municipalities are considered as a new type of actor intervening in the world of global flows.

While border areas are changing in their nature, as required by the dynamics of international trade, public policies are not yet moving in the same direction. The last 20 years have seen setbacks with respect to the law of decentralization (Galindo 2013, 12). Trapped by the return of centralism, these border territories are struggling with the need to adapt the conditions of the borders to the framework of the advances of globalization. The most critical issues of the borders – violence, corruption, and administrative inefficiency in the cities and border posts – are not so much the responsibility of the municipalities and regions as of the national government.

The functioning of illegal markets has generated a series of general scenarios such as large-scale smuggling, drug trafficking, corruption, and the informalization of society, as well as critical intergenerational and gender scenarios at specific locations (Miranda 2016). Along the same lines (Campero 2012; Miranda and Agramont 2015), each of the border regions and points is experiencing precarious situations, especially in some of their most critical scenarios: drug trafficking, violence, and smuggling, which characterize some borders, turning them into red zones (Courtis 2010).

The general issues that condition and characterize global flows as the transmission axes of the country's globalization are drug trafficking, smuggling, money laundering, and human trafficking. These sectors of the illegal markets use the corridors and infrastructure of legal import and export activities in a changing and creative way due to the possible legal and police difficulties they may encounter.

Notes on the Evolution of the Concept of Borders in Literature and Politics   25

The weight of these sectors of the illegal markets in the structure of global flows is very important; the so-called new borders have reached faraway places. There are few and incomplete studies that address these illegal flows, and they mainly refer to critical scenarios or partial aspects. In the aspects described in reports and monographs, we highlight some issues that continue to predominate nowadays and will be addressed in later chapters:

- The annual monitoring reports of the United Nations Office on Drugs and Crime (UNODC 2015) and the Consejo Nacional de Lucha contra el Tráfico Ilícito de Drogas (CONALTID 2014a, 2014b) on coca leaf production, eradication, and drug seizures.
- On corridors (PIEB 2012); on organized crime (Campero 2011, 2014); on smuggling (CEPB 2009; Ferrufino 2009, 2015; Jemio 2013; Vidaurre Andrade 2005).
- Customs evasion on imports (Bonilla 2014).
- On the conditions of informality (Valencia and Alcides 1998).
- On the legal production and exporting of gold (Valencia 2015).

Borders in National Policies

This study, still very preliminary, aims to contribute to a global and comprehensive treatment of the issues of illegal markets. The interest is to take the discussion beyond sectoral policy considerations to the role that these sectors play in the globalization process and in Bolivia's role in illegal global markets.

The absence of border issues in national public policies is a major gap between the evolution of market globalization and the governance that these markets demand in the country. To begin with, there has been a clear absence of comprehensive approaches to sectoral policies in recent decades. This process is parallel to the deterioration of planning in the face of the progress of neoliberalism.

Policies Related to Illegal Markets

The two traditional sectors that link Bolivia to globalization – gas and minerals – are joined by those of gold and drug smuggling, as well as import smuggling. The latter compete in terms of size and impact on the economy as a whole and cannot be addressed through sectoral policies alone. Smuggling and drug trafficking, along with other sectors of the criminal economy, are consolidating as the backbone of globalization and, consequently, of Bolivia's link with the global world, requiring global and comprehensive policies.

Today, although there are information and management systems of the global market, there are no studies that conceptualize the situation of Bolivia in the global border system. It is true that progress has been made in information on international trade, but there is still a lack of indicators to facilitate comparability between countries that reflect their role and place in the global concert. This aspect is clearly deficient and has been felt as a great void in research.

26 *History and Present of the Bolivian Border Subsystem*

Borders in Development Strategies

The issue of borders has not been considered as a priority in the national development plans, which are mainly sectoral documents with enormous weaknesses regarding territorial planning. The planning has been mainly focused on departmental and municipal levels, but even in these two levels of the State's territorial planning, borders are not considered important; instead, they focus on the improvement of communication networks geared toward the borders. The last truly global vision of the country, which sought to overcome the sectoral visions, was the development strategy of the early 1970s. The book *Desarrollo Nacional 1971-1991* (National Development 1971–1991), recently reissued in La Paz, recalls what the government dreamed 45 years ago. The long period of time that has elapsed and, at the same time, the topicality of the subject show how the State was not able to implement the domestic development. The development strategy proposed aimed

> to overcome the situation of backwardness and dependence in which they found themselves, proposing a bold change in their model of "inward growth," which implied introducing profound changes in economic and institutional policy, as well as in the behavior of economic and social actors.
>
> (Machicado 2016, 5)

Machicado notes that one of the basic points of the strategy was to deploy an essential effort to obtain – internally and in the short term – the maximum generation of economic surplus, by placing products on the external market, giving priority to projects that were short term and had relatively assured markets. Through the internal market, the aim was to make greater use of natural resources and capital goods that remained idle, incorporating marginal groups into the productive apparatus and the consumer market. The underlying idea, in this regard, was to generate internal surpluses that would make it possible to finance, in later phases, larger projects, so that external financing would play a complementary role. The proposal was that only in this way could the objective of freeing the country from dependency structures become effective in economic terms.

While import substitution was being considered as the basis for inward development, the economy was shifting to the borders in large proportions, either by exports or by imports. Meanwhile, efforts related to territorial management policies emphasized physical and communication co-responsibility, which links Bolivia more intensely to the system of global flows. Although not in discourse, the practice reflected in the policies is closely related to the border system and its growing importance. In conclusion, there is a great deficit in the field of integral policies and a focus on programmatic approaches of a sectoral nature.

The Centralism of Decentralization and Border Policies

In the last ten years, the border issue has tried to move toward a decentralized political trend, but it has not been possible due to the many weaknesses and

Notes on the Evolution of the Concept of Borders in Literature and Politics 27

inconsistencies in its implementation. Actually, centralized policies and institutions – as is the case of ADEMAF, which is oriented toward the development of large regions and has a centralist orientation, and the Ministry of the Presidency and the Armed Forces – have controlled borders. Against the backdrop of pressure from the multimember democratic processes, tension is moving toward the strengthening of centralism. The discussions on the social pact, in which the central government claims the execution of more than 80% of the national budget, are an example. This situation contrasts with the nature of border problems, which require local consideration and the strengthening of local management conditions. A vision of this problem is established in several of the social policy sectors, such as education and health, where the oxymoron of centralization of decentralization is described (Galindo 2013, 19–22).

Despite the involution of decentralization policies, the municipalization process has affected border issues. Changes in territorial management policies have evolved over the last 20 years and have affected the characteristics and functionality of land borders. This has also changed the areas closer to the border crossings. Border municipalities ceased to be the isolated spaces of previous decades and began to be built by local society. From 1994 onward, state bodies were established, with fiscal revenues defined by law and regulated by various social and political laws. The municipalities became important actors at the subnational level and therefore in the border areas, classically orphaned by the State. As a result of the application of the Washington Consensus measures, the political and social participation – which promoted the decentralization process, aimed at deconcentrating fiscal expenditures – was a milestone in the dynamism of the border areas, especially, because of the relief role played by the external sector in the long international price crisis (1982–2005). With great differences from one place to another, the municipalities invested in infrastructure, schools, health centers, streets, and squares. Border programs were organized to support capacity building and infrastructure development.

Decentralization led to a long-standing confrontation, particularly in the eastern part of the country, between local leaders (in many cases caciques) and the national government. These tensions changed with the municipalization promoted by the Popular Participation Law, the Law of Administrative Decentralization, and the reform of the Political Constitution of the State in later years. Although implemented in a vertical manner, and, even though these decentralization policies focused mainly on administrative and political aspects, they generated demands for participation and consequent gaps that are still difficult to resolve today, as well as a relative loss of control by the central government in many aspects. This situation has led in the last ten years to promote, as a reaction, controls and restrictions in the granting of competences and resources to decentralized governments (Galindo 2013, 19–22).

In recent confrontations, the border territories are possibly the most active, perhaps because of the greater development of the border economy and the uncontrolled way in which the opportunities offered by the asymmetries between countries at the border crossings have been taken advantage of, especially when

28 *History and Present of the Bolivian Border Subsystem*

the relative prices of the products of exchange have suffered strong imbalances. Borders have been the main arena for the promotion of illegal economies. The local level began to take shape and influence national life from there.

Seventy-two border municipalities – equivalent to more than the third part of the national territory – became, in many cases, actors in opposition to national policies, actors at the subnational level and, therefore, in the traditionally State-orphaned border areas. The political and social participation promoted by the decentralization process was a milestone in the political change of the border areas, which were more complex due to the presence of local governments; mayors, councilors, and administrations joined the multiple preexisting actors.

Border areas acquired a life of their own and promoted social, political, and state leaderships that served as a means of dialogue with the actors of the flows, incorporating the neighbors of the migrants in a more active way. The border population grew and living conditions improved. The presence of police and control mechanisms increased, despite the persistence of their dependence on the central levels of the State. With great differences between some places, the municipalities invested in infrastructure, schools, health centers, streets, and squares. However, after more than two decades of decentralization and municipalization policies, there is still a long way to go before municipal institutions appropriate to the border issue will have been consolidated. In many cases, institutional informality, corruption, and the politicization of the border economy have expanded.

Border areas require special attention, given their relative physical and administrative distance from the central government. Local problems have acquired new characteristics and dimensions in terms of citizen security, gender violence, criminality, corruption, and economic informality. These problems require very specific approaches, and most border municipalities today follow the logic of national policies and are unable to deal with these very special border situations. These municipalities generally do not control the police, which remains national, nor the education and health policies, or citizen security; customs also depends on national-level administration. The easiest action for municipalities in general has been to invest in roads and urban infrastructure, education, and health. Border programs have been organized to support the development of capacities, but mostly from a national security perspective; most of them are operated from national-level mechanisms implemented at the local level. Even the implementation of nationally defined programs is often carried out by floating teams dependent on central government mechanisms.[2]

But, above all, the contradictions between this centralized management, which remains almost entirely monopolized by National Customs and depending on the increasingly centralist agenda of the Ministry of Finance, have been decreasing. In the border areas, all actors face each other: the municipal government, the governor's office, the National Police, and the special police forces dependent on National Customs.

In these confrontations, the conditions for resolving the problem of the country's growing incorporation into regional and global flows have shaped a broader and more complex web of relations. The importance of physical borders, their

Notes on the Evolution of the Concept of Borders in Literature and Politics 29

functions, and role in the face of rapidly changing communications has changed. It is also important to mention that tax revenues are increasingly receiving support from both tax policies and a thriving parallel economy burgeoning within the framework of the borders.

Notes

1 Plan Decenal 1962–1971 (Decennial Plan), the Estrategia socioeconómica del desarrollo 1971–1991 (Socioeconomic Strategy for Development), the Plan quinquenal de Hugo Banzer Suárez (1976–1980) (Five-Year Plan of Hugo Banzer Suárez), the Plan de desarrollo 1984–1987 de Hernán Siles Suazo (the Development Plan 1984–1987 of Hernán Siles Suazo), the Plan de todos de Gonzalo Sánchez de Lozada (the Plan for All of Gonzalo Sánchez de Lozada), and the Plan nacional de desarrollo (PND) 2006–2011 (National Development Plan).
2 Twenty years after decentralization in 2014, ADEMAF assigns a generous budget for the implementation of programs and projects in the municipalities and territories of several of the governorates. Macro-regions of planification, superimposed on the decentralized territorial administrations, were designed. Most of that budget was allocated to emergency situations and was executed directly from the Ministry of the Presidency, with the logistical support of the Armed Forces (ADEMAF 2014, 25–57).

References

Abecia Baldivieso, Valentín. 1979. *Las relaciones internacionales en la Historia de Bolivia*. Cochabamba: Los amigos del Libro.
ADEMAF. 2014. *Macroregiones y Fronteras*, Vol. 1, No. 4.
———. 2015. *Agencia para el Desarrollo de las Macroregiones y Zonas Fronterizas Memoria 2014*. Bolivia: La Paz.
Blanes, José. 1989. "Cocaine, Informality, and the Urban Economy in La Paz, Bolivia. Bolivia economic aspects state participation statistical data." In *The Informal Economy. Studies in Advanced and Less Developed Countries*, edited by Alejandro Portes, Manuel Castells, and Lauren A. Benton, 135–150. Baltimore and London: The Johns Hopkins University Press.
Blanes, José, Fernando Calderón, et al. 2003. "Formación y Evolución del Espacio Nacional. Cuaderno de Futuro 18." In *Human Development Report*. La Paz: Plural Editores.
Bonilla, Claudio A. 2014. "Análisis de la evasión aduanera en las importaciones." *Paper for the Undersecretary of the Treasury*, October 20, 2014.
Campero, José Carlos. 2011. "El crimen organizado (vinculado al narcotráfico) en Bolivia." In *Crimen organizado y gobernanza en la región andina: Cooperar o fracasar*, edited by Catalina Niño. Quito.
———. 2012. "Estudio exploratorio sobre Problemáticas de seguridad en ciudades frontera. Caso: Ciudad de Cobija." In *Regional Security Forum, FES Bolivia, Policy Papers 03*. La Paz.
———. 2014. "Los retos para Bolivia ante un nuevo marco mundial de política de drogas." In *Unpublished Manuscript for Parlamentary Disscusion About the New Drugs Act*. La Paz: CEBEM.
Carbone, Daniel and Mariano Frutos. 2014. *Corredores interoceánicos, análisis bibliográfico para su aplicación*. Argentina: Universidad Nacional del Sur, Departamento de Ingeniería.

30 History and Present of the Bolivian Border Subsystem

Carrión, Fernando. 2014. "Explorando la economía política de la violencia en los sistemas fronterizos de América Latina: Hacia una comprensión integral." In *Research Project*. Mimeo.

CEPB. 2009. *Comercio Exterior Ilegal en Bolivia. Estimaciones: 2000–2008.* Confederación de Empresarios Privados de Bolivia.

CERES. 2003. *Formación y evolución del espacio nacional. Cuadernos del Futuro. Inform on Human Development*, December 2003.

CONALTID. 2014a. *II Estudio Nacional 2014 sobre Prevalencia y características del Consumo de Drogas en Hogares Bolivianos de las Nueve Capitales de Departamento, más la ciudad de El Alto, 2014*. La Paz: Consejo Nacional de Lucha Contra el Tráfico Ilícito de Drogas.

———. 2014b. *Informe Institucional 2012–2014*. La Paz, Bolivia: Consejo Nacional de Lucha Contra el Tráfico Ilícito de Drogas.

Courtis, Corina. 2010. *Migración y Salud en zonas fronterizas: El Estado Plurinacional de Bolivia y la Argentina*. Santiago de Chile:CELADE.

Felman Velarde, José. 1967. *Memorándum sobre política exterior boliviana*. La Paz: Editorial Juventud.

Fernández Saavedra, Gustavo. 2013. *Memorando Bolivia-Brasil 2012*. La Paz: Plural Editores.

Ferrufino, Rubén. 2009. *Comercio exterior ilegal en Bolivia: Estimaciones 2000–2008. Confederación de Empresarios Privados de Bolivia.* Unpublished Paper. La Paz.

———. 2015. "La economía transfronteriza de Bolivia: Aproximación a los flujos económicos ilegales." *Unpublished Paper Prepared for the Centro Boliviano de Estudios Multidisciplinarios.* La Paz: CEBEM.

FES-ILDIS. 2004. *Municipalización Diagnóstico de una década. 1 and 2.* La Paz.

Fundación Milenio. 2011. "Seguridad alimentaria en Bolivia." *Coloquios económicos*, No. 22 (July).

Galindo, Mario. 2013. *Construcción de Agenda Pública Alternativa Oxímoron: Las Autonomías Centralistas de Bolivia o de las Autonomías a la Heteronomía.* La Paz: CEBEM.

Gómez García, Vincent. 1997. *Corredores interoceánicos e integración en la economía mundial Bolivia ante los desafíos de la globalización económica, la competitividad internacional y el desarrollo humano sostenible.* La Paz: UDAPEX, ILDIS.

Gómez Zubieta, Luis Reynaldo. 2006. *Políticas de transporte ferroviario en Bolivia 1860–1940.* La Paz: Bolset.

Hinojosa, C. Alfonso. 2008. *La visibilización de las migraciones transnacionales en Bolivia*11 (25). La Paz: PIEB, Tincazos, Tinkazos.

Jemio, Luis Carlos. 2013. "Comportamiento de las importaciones en Bolivia." *Cámara Nacional de Comercio*, 14. La Paz.

Klein, Herbert S. 1982. *Historia general de Bolivia*. La Paz: Editorial Juventud.

Lima Bismark, Manuel, and Abraham Cuellar Araujo. 2007. "El Norte Amazónico: Entre el aislamiento y la globalización." In *El Norte Amazónico de Bolivia y el Complejo del río Madera*. La Paz: FOBOMADE.

Machicado, Flavio. 2016. *Desarrollo nacional 1971–1991*. La Paz: UMSA.

Mercado Moreira, Miguel. 1972. *Historia internacional de Bolivia*. Bolivia: Editorial Don Bosco.

Mesa, José de Teresa Gisbertm, and Carlos D. Mesa Gisbert. 1988. *Historia de Bolivia*. La Paz: Editorial Gisbert.

Notes on the Evolution of the Concept of Borders in Literature and Politics   31

Ministerio de Relaciones Exteriores. 2004. "Raíces de la doctrina internacional de Bolivia. La Paz." In *Enciclopedia geográfica de Bolivia*, edited by Ismael Montes de Oca. La Paz: Ministerio de Relaciones Internacionales/Academia Diplomática Rafael Bustillo.

Miranda, Boris. 2016. "Etnografía de la Vulnerabilidad: Escenarios Críticos del Narcotráfico en Bolivia." In *Seguridad Regional en América Latina y el Caribe. Anuario 2015*, edited by Catalina Niño, 38–44. Bogotá: Frederich Ebert Stiftung.

Miranda and Agramont (Eds.). 2015. *El rostro de la (In) seguridad en Bolivia. Siete crónicas sobre circuitos delictivos*. La Paz: Frederich Ebert Stiftung.

PIEB. 2012. *Corredores Ilícitos entre Bolivia-Perú. ¿Rutas escondidas y extrañas?* Cochabamba, Bolivia: Puente Investigación y Enlace.

Quiroga, J. Antonio. 2003. "Descentralización y reconfiguración territorial del Estado boliviano." In *La descentralización que se viene: Propuestas para la (re)constitución del nivel estatal intermedio*. La Paz: Editorial Plural.

Richard, Nicolás (Ed.). 2008. *Mala guerra. Los indígenas en la guerra del Chaco (1932–1935)*. Asunción/París: ServiLibro-Museo del Barro/CoLibris.

UNODC. 2015. *Estado Plurinacional de Bolivia. Monitoreo de Cultivos de Coca 2014*. La Paz.

Urenda, Carlos. 2007. *Autonomías departamentales. Un aporte a la Asamblea Constituyente boliviana*. Santa Cruz de la Sierra: La Hoguera.

Valencia, A., José Luis, and Justo Alcides Casas. 1998. *Contrabando e informalidad en la economía boliviana*. La Paz: FUNDEMOS.

Valencia, Lenin. 2015. *Las rutas del oro ilegal. Estudios de caso en cinco países. Programa de ciudadanía y asuntos socioambientales*. Lima: SPDA.

Valencia Vega, Alipio. 2000. *Geopolítica en Bolivia*. La Paz: Editorial Juventud.

Vásquez, Humberto. 1990. *Para una historia de los límites entre Bolivia y Brasil*. La Paz: Editorial Juventud.

Vidaurre Andrade, Gonzalo M. 2005. *Impacto de la importación de ropa usada en Bolivia*. Santa Cruz de la Sierra: Instituto Boliviano de Comercio Exterior.

Villegas Nava, P. 2013. *Geopolítica de las carreteras y el saqueo de los recursos naturales*. Cochabamba: CEDIB.

3 Dimensions and Characteristics of the Borders

Bolivian borders stand out because of their dimensions and characteristics, as well as the differentiated impact of each one on national life. The structuring presence of illegal markets determines the roles of each of them in the border subsystem and the conditioning of the national territory to exercise those roles, which involves differentiated accessibility and distances, among others.

It is important to make a brief tour of the borders of each of the five countries from the departments that manage them.

General Aspects of Land Borders

There are five neighboring countries with which Bolivia must relate because of the shared borders. These countries represent differentiated challenges for which local approaches are normally insufficient to handle. This is due to the specificity of each location and its challenges, and the limitations of a purely centralist perspective. The construction of the border functionality has been complex, involving the population and the conditioning of transit corridors and border crossings according to the specificities of the exchanges between neighboring countries. Each border has its own history and development, defined by the flows of migrants, the different trafficking of goods, smuggling activities, the habitability of border centers, and the construction of clandestine routes. This process involved flows of migrants, smugglers, police, cooperation programs, neighborhood organizations, criminal gangs, mayors, state programs, the armed forces, cross-border cooperation programs, and non-governmental organizations (NGOs). A long army of actors – each building a different thing, depending on the country – are the borders today (Sánchez 2011, 34–35).

Statistical Geography: Borders with Other Countries

The total perimeter of the borders reaches 6,834 kilometers. The following list of Bolivia's borders with its neighboring countries depicts the regions of each country that limits Bolivia, according to the National Institute of Statistics (INE).

DOI: 10.4324/9781003203117-5

Dimensions and Characteristics of the Borders 33

- **Border with Argentina (773 kilometers)**: This international border comingles at Cerro Zapaleri and ends at Esmeralda (tripartite border point between Argentina, Paraguay, and Bolivia). The main border points are Cerro Panizo, Cerro Malpaso, Villazón, Bermejo, Fortín Campero, Yacuiba, and Fortín d'Orbigny on the Pilcomayo River.
- **Border with Brazil (3,423 kilometers)**: This international border is the most extensive. It starts in Bolpebra and ends in Bahía Negra (tripartite border between Brazil, Paraguay, and Bolivia). The main border points are Brasiléia, located in front of Cobija; Fortín Manoa, near the Madera River; Villa Bella, at the confluence of the Beni and Mamoré Rivers; Cerro Cuatro Hermanos; San Matías and the La Gaiba, Mandioré, Cáceres, and Puerto Gutiérrez Guerra lagoons, on the Paraguay River.
- **Border with Chile (850 kilometers)**: The current limit between Bolivia and Chile was defined by the Treaty of Peace and Friendship of 1904. The document stipulated the cession of sovereignty of the Bolivian coast to Chile, leaving the country without sea access. The border begins in Visviri (tripartite landmark between Chile, Peru, and Bolivia) and ends in Zapaleri (tripartite landmark between Argentina, Chile, and Bolivia). The main points of the border are the Licancabur and Ollagüe volcanoes and the Payachata hills. The border cuts off some natural water flows such as the Lauca River; thus, conflicts have arisen over the use of its waters.
- **Borders with Paraguay (741 kilometers)**: Begins in Esmeralda and ends in Bahía Negra (tripartite landmark between Paraguay, Brazil, and Bolivia), on the Rio Negro that flows into the Paraguay River. The main border points are Cerro Ustares, Palmar de las Islas, Chovoreca milestone, and Cerrito Jara.
- **Borders with Peru (1,047 kilometers):** Begins in Bolpebra (tripartite milestone between Peru, Brazil, and Bolivia) and ends in Choquecota (tripartite border between Peru, Chile, and Bolivia). The most important border points are Puerto Heath on the Madre de Dios River, Nudo de Apolobamba, Puerto Acosta from where the border line begins to be drawn in Lake Titicaca, Copacabana peninsula, and Desaguadero.

As already mentioned, the borders with the five neighboring countries show a great difference between zones, and the variety of challenges that Bolivia's relationship with the global border system assumes are built on different variables: ecological and environmental conditions, the history of each border, economic functions, flows, and the rearticulation of both national and international routes.

The dynamism and densification of the border system are common to all five neighboring countries, in which there are some aspects that are worth emphasizing.

- **The borders with Peru**: The arrival of raw materials for the manufacture of hydrochloride in Bolivia predominates, with the role of transit to the main neighboring countries. The exchange of gold and cocaine, complementary with the advance of smuggling, constitutes a little studied area of money laundering.

34 *History and Present of the Bolivian Border Subsystem*

- **The border with Brazil**: It is the exit route for drug trafficking and the import route of a large amount of smuggled assets for industry and modern agriculture.
- **The border with Paraguay**: Its role as an important smuggling passage has been complemented by its current role as the main supplier of the marijuana that travels via Bolivia to the main regional consumers – Argentina and Chile – and, from these countries to consumers outside the region.
- **The border with Argentina**: It has been shifting rapidly toward the complementarity of the traditional black market of smuggling and the transit of drug dealers, using not only the "informal army of land" in the customs posts, but also the flights to the north of Argentina from Bolivia and large land transports.
- **The border with Chile.** Depending on its origin, it functions as the first or second gateway to the distant markets of Europe and Asia for drugs, taking advantage of the modern transport infrastructure, provided by mining operations.

It is necessary to emphasize the close relationship that has been consolidated between these borders, which are diverse and complementary to the internal transport system and increasingly functional to the requirements of the border system as a whole. The construction of border functionality has been complex since the population and the conditioning of border corridors and crossings have been carried out in accordance with the specificities of the exchanges between neighboring countries.

Between 2001 and 2012, the intercensal changes in size and population density of the 72 border municipalities show a trend of higher-than-average growth compared to the numbers as the country as a whole and closer to the rates of the largest cities. The 72 border municipalities increased from 713,661 inhabitants in 2001 to 909,899 in 2012. These 196,238 people represent a higher growth than the country's average urban population (INE 2002, 2013).

The growth, however, was differentiated, according to the characteristics of the border. In some cases, there are still inhospitable places, wide jungle, lake, highland, Chaco, and river borders, which are very easy for certain types of smuggling and drug trafficking and very active in the complex and changing border world, where legal activities are combined with illegal and clandestine ones. In some cases, there was a strong increase in densification and urbanization. Both now fulfill different and very active functions in the complex and changing border world, where legal activities are combined with informal and clandestine ones. What stands out is the consolidation of "hot spots" on each country border. They serve to define and structure the route map, which, although ever-changing, maintains an important hierarchy. In some municipalities, such as Cobija, growth was over 100% between the last two censuses.

Such a broad system full of changing conditions is ideal for illegal activities such as drug trafficking. In the case of the Balloon Effect, it is ideal since control is reinforced at one border when the traffic moves to the other. Contraband enters from the Brazilian, Argentinian, and Chilean borders. On the other hand, drug trafficking uses the all five borders, entering through Peru or Paraguay and leaving from Brazil, Argentina, and Chile. This does not include flights in from Peru and flights out to Brazil, Paraguay, and Argentina.

It is necessary to stress that a border cities system is important either they exist or not, as reflected in the press. The research in a 14-year newspaper archives shows that Bermejo, Yacuiba, and Villazón are the borders that most attract attention and make headlines. They are not the most important in terms of volume of products, but they do speak to the importance that Buenos Aires and northern Argentina play in the Bolivian border system, not only as destinations, but also for being the traditional route to the Atlantic.

The proximity and cultural continuity between Bolivia and its neighbors partly explain why the towns of Desaguadero, which link cities in southern Peru with the cities of El Alto and La Paz, are another area that makes headlines. This is a gateway to Chile and Argentina, via Lake Titicaca, when it comes to drugs, and to the cities of western Bolivia, when it comes to the exchange of other products. The urban set that governs this enormous territory is Quechua and Aymara, with the cities that go from Cuzco, Arequipa, Puno, and the cities of Oruro and La Paz.

Urbanization processes are specific to each country. For comparative purposes we must agree on a few parameters, which allow us to better understand the general urban phenomenon. If we speak of large, medium, and small cities, many of the urban centers on Bolivia's borders are no more than towns, with more or less developed systems of urbanization. Many border points are no more than demographic clusters with little urban construction proper, such as services and living conditions.

On the Bolivian borders we find three categories: (1) cities related to their peers on both sides of the borders and that constitute a binational urban whole in a contiguous way, separated or united by roads or bridges; (2) small and dispersed population centers that sometimes only constitute a border crossing, with urban centers relatively distant from each other, but that exercise influence as centers of origin and destination nearer to the border flows; and (3) systems of peer cities, which are distant from the border line but, still, sustain important commercial relations between them.

It is important to consider the aforementioned conditions of the Bolivian border because of the relationship between the processes of urbanization with reference to the functions of the border (see Map 3.1). In the first group, the cities of Cobija, Guayaramerín, Puerto Suárez, Puerto Aguirre, Yacuiba, Bermejo, and Villazón can be considered the set of intermediate size cities for the Bolivian average, which define very important urban functions for the border system. San Matías, Desaguadero, Copacabana, and Bolpebra constitute groups are linked to relatively important urban centers in their respective countries and that exist along the border, not so much in urban functions as in the exchange systems controlled by the respective major urban centers. Finally, in the third group, there are three clearly defined cases of city pairs carrying out border exchanges between cities, without much friction with customs border crossings, beyond the administrative

Table 3.1 Border Cities Mentioned in the Press

	2002	2003	2004	2005	2006	2007	2008	2009	2010	2011	2012	2013	2014
Bermejo	18	0	2	2	1	0	2	2	8	5	2	6	6
Boyuibe	1	0	2	0	0	1	0	0	0	0	1	0	1
Charaña	4	1	4	1	0	1	3	1	5	0	1	1	3
Cobija	5	1	0	4	2	1	7	11	4	5	5	4	12
Desaguadero/Copacabana	12	5	3	1	3	10	9	6	12	17	8	4	15
Pisiga	3	5	4	3	0	3	0	6	4	6	1	0	8
Puerto Suárez/Puerto Quijarro	2	1	1	1	0	0	0	0	0	4	2	2	2
San Matías	3	0	1	1	0	0	2	1	0	1	5	2	3
Tambo Quemado	3	0	1	2	3	2	0	5	2	3	2	4	5
Villazón	15	0	2	0	0	3	2	3	0	6	1	5	3
Yacuiba	37	1	2	5	0	3	2	2	3	6	3	4	8

Source: Compilation of information from the newspaper library.

Map 3.1 Bolivia's Border Cities and Their Counterparts in Neighboring Countries. Map by the author.

level. The relations between Arica, in Chile, and the city of La Paz are practically direct since they are 350 kilometers away; the same occurs between Iquique and Oruro, between Boyuibe and Mariscal Estigarribia. The pairs, Iquique in Chile and Oruro in Bolivia, Arica in Chile, and La Paz-El Alto in La Paz, do not share an urban life, despite the density of their flows. In an intermediate situation would be San Matías and Cáceres, with similarities like Cobija with the city of Río Branco; although the model that best explains them is that of northern Chile with Bolivia.

Regardless of border cooperation activities between contiguous partners, projects originating in neighboring countries should be studied toward border areas, aiming at the incorporation of neighboring countries through specific cooperation. But this type of project – like the one that starts in northern Argentina and moves toward Bolivia – is not so much based on urban projects as on regions of border development in which local urban systems play important roles.

38 *History and Present of the Bolivian Border Subsystem*

Land Borders with Five Countries

The following describes the dimensions and characteristics of the borders between Bolivia and each of the five countries, establishing differences in several cases according to the sections that run through each department. This aspect is important, given that these are different government administrations on a country's border: Peru borders the departments of La Paz and Pando; Brazil borders the departments of Pando, Beni, and Santa Cruz; Paraguay borders Santa Cruz, Chuquisaca, and Tarija; and, finally, Chile borders Potosí, Oruro, and La Paz.

Bolivia–Peru Border

Bolivia shares with Peru the country's second largest border. In addition to its two main border posts (Yunguyo and Desaguadero) in the lake area, there are many other points of infiltration from Peru through the western mountains and the tropical zone, which goes down to the Bolpebra post on the tri-national border. This is one of the most difficult borders to control because of the large number of unregistered border crossings between Peru and Bolivia, used in the flow of contraband, human trafficking, and gold, among the main exchanges (see Table 3.2).

Table 3.2 Main Smuggled Products from Peru

The Ten Main Illegally Imported Products from Peru Values calculated by the difference method (2006–2008) (in millions of USD)	*Accumulated Value between 2006 and 2008*
Mineral fuels, mineral oils, and products of their distillation. Bituminous materials, mineral waxes	8.13
Boilers, machines, devices, and mechanical devices and their parts	6.35
Cereals	5.96
Fine natural or cultured pearls, precious or semiprecious stones, plated precious materials, costume jewelry	5.92
Pharmaceutical products	2.56
Clothes and accessories	2.31
Essential oils and resinoids, toilet or cosmetic perfumery preparations	2.17
Vehicles: automobiles, tractors, velocipedes and other land vehicles and their parts	2.13
Plastics and their manufactures	1.86
Iron and steel foundry	1.80
Total	39.19

Source: Ferrufino (2009).

There are three border sections, and they are very different from each other, which makes the task of controlling the passage very complicated. Except for the lake area near Copacabana and Desaguadero, the rest are not very accessible. The border population of the 31 municipalities of the country considered for this analysis shows an inter-census stagnation; that is, they have not attracted population as have other border areas (see Table 3.3). In any case, it is important to observe a couple of cases: those municipalities in the mountainous area and in the semitropical zones and those closer to the border have received more migration, which would mean that there has been an important increase in their activity as they are important crossings for the transportation of goods.

Other types of municipalities, close to large cities, such as La Paz and El Alto, have lost migration to these centers. This situation persists without major changes, which may mean that this is a traditional activity and that the recent years of increased drug trafficking and smuggling were not new trends or forms of commerce to these areas.

The lake side of the border is the most populated area and only a political demarcation. There is ethnic-cultural continuity between the two countries, which is expressed in forms of family organization, production, and cultural characteristics. Dozens of small islands in the lake are cultivated by Peruvians and Bolivians, making this entire area a territory that facilitates contraband and drug trafficking.

The mountainous zone descends from the lake Altiplano to the semitropical zone, with heights that exceed 5,000 meters. It is the land of the Kallawaya; however, not many populated stops are recorded along this route.

The unpopulated and remote **semitropical zone**, which has countless border crossings along the rivers that separate the two countries, is easily used as a route for smuggling cocaine and gold. In addition to being a zone expansion and colonization of coca fields, the most precious locations for the search of alluvial gold are there. Far from the state's control, the smuggling of gold from Peru is mimicked. Thus, in addition to the clandestine exploitation of gold, gold from Peru and Colombia is also smuggled and re-exported as Bolivian gold through Peru to the United States, by air. This business is fed by cocaine trafficking and of Bolivian fuels (gas and gasoline) that are smuggled into Peru.[1]

The areas near the border with the department of Pando, where the urban centers of Bolpebra and Cobija are located, meet all the conditions for the transit of cocaine, contraband, and especially gold, between Peru, Bolivia, and Brazil to the United States, as the main destination. They are far from state control, and there is significant border violence. Frequent murders, including those of police and military, are attributed to coca leaf producers. It is said to be the preferred place of movement for guerrillas of the Revolutionary Armed Forces of Colombia (FARC) and the Sendero Luminoso (Shining Path) (Farfán 2013).[2]

Of the three areas, the lake is the most frequented and is characterized by a very high historical cultural continuity, similar to what can be seen in Argentina. The large influx of people transiting from and to Peru facilitates the weakness of migration control and the functioning of the informal economy, both small trade and illegal trafficking (El Deber 2013). Peru's border with northern Bolivia is an

Table 3.3 Population of Border Municipalities (2001 and 2012 Censuses)

	Department	Province	Municipality	2001	2012	Intercensal Increase
1	Chuquisaca	Luis Calvo	Macharetí	7,386	7,418	32
2	La Paz	Omasuyos	Achacachi	70,371	46,058	−24.313
3	La Paz	Omasuyos	Ancoraimes	15,1999	13,136	−2.064
4	La Paz	Omasuyos	Huarina		7,948	7.948
5	La Paz	Omasuyos	Santiago de Huata		8,562	8.562
6	La Paz	Omasuyos	Huatajata		3,927	3.927
7	La Paz	Omasuyos	Chuacocani		5,003	5.003
8	La Paz	Pacajes	Calacoto	10,336	9,879	−457
9	La Paz	Pacajes	Charaña	3,005	3,246	241
10	La Paz	Camacho	Puerto Acosta	2,823	11,29	8.467
11	La Paz	Camacho	Mocomoco	14,541	13,154	−1.387
12	La Paz	Camacho	Puerto Carabuco	18,827	14,589	−4.238
13	La Paz	Camacho	Escoma		7,186	7.186
14	La Paz	Camacho	Humanata		5,342	5.342
15	La Paz	F. Tamayo	Apolo	13,271	20,308	7.037
16	La Paz	F. Tamayo	Pelechuco	5,115	6,780	1.665
17	La Paz	Ingavi	Tiahuanacu	11,309	12,189	880
18	La Paz	Ingavi	Guaqui	7,552	7,278	−274
19	La Paz	Ingavi	Desaguadero	4,981	6,987	2.006
20	La Paz	Ingavi	San A. de Machaca	6,299	6,145	−154
21	La Paz	Ingavi	Jesús de Machaca	13,247	15,039	1.792
22	La Paz	Ingavi	Taraco	5,922	6,603	681
23	La Paz	Los Andes	Pucarani	24,57	28,465	3.895
24	La Paz	Los Andes	Batallas	20,925	17,426	−3.499

Dimensions and Characteristics of the Borders 41

25	La Paz	Los Andes	Puerto Pérez	7,83	8,157	327
26	La Paz	Abel Iturralde	Ixiamas	5,625	9,362	3.737
27	La Paz	B. Saavedra	Juan José P. (Charazani)	6,203	13,023	6.820
28	La Paz	Manco Kapac	Copacabana	14,586	14,931	345
29	La Paz	Manco Kapac	San Pedro de Tiquina	6,093	6,052	−41
30	La Paz	Manco Kapac	Tito Yupanqui	2,213	6,261	4.048
31	La Paz	J M Pando	Santiago de Machaca	4,402	4,593	191
32	La Paz	J M Pando	Catacora	1,735	2,881	1.146
33	Oruro	Sajama	Curahuara de Carangas	5,278	4,184	−1.094
34	Oruro	Sajama	Turco	4,16	5,207	1.047
35	Oruro	Atahualpa	Sabaya	4,684	8,018	3.334
36	Oruro	Atahualpa	Coipasa	616	903	287
37	Oruro	P Mejillones	La Rivera	390	509	119
38	Oruro	P Mejillones	Todos Santos	387	727	340
39	Potosí	Sur Chichas	Tupiza	38,337	44,814	6.477
40	Potosí	Nor Lípez	Colcha "K"	9,645	12,997	3.352
41	Potosí	Nor Lípez	San Pedro de Quemes	815	1060	245
42	Potosí	Sur Lípez	San Pablo de Lípez	2,523	3,371	848
43	Potosí	Sur Lípez	Mojinete	716	1180	464
44	Potosí	Sur Lípez	San A. de Esmoruco	1,666	2,284	618
45	Potosí	Daniel Campos	Llica	2,901	415	412
46	Potosí	M. Omiste	Villazón	36,266	44,906	8.640
47	Tarija	Aniceto Arce	Padcaya	19,26	18,681	−579
48	Tarija	Aniceto Arce	Bermejo	33,31	34,505	1,195
49	Tarija	Gran Chaco	Yacuíba	83,518	92,245	8.727
50	Tarija	Gran Chaco	Caraparí	9,035	15,366	6,331
51	Tarija	Gran Chaco	Villamontes	23,765	39,867	16,102

(Continued)

Table 3.3 Continued

	Department	Province	Municipality	2001	2012	Intercensal Increase
52	Tarija	Avilés	Yunchará	5,173	5,52	347
53	Santa Cruz	Velasco	San I. de Velasco	41,412	52,362	10.950
54	Santa Cruz	Cordillera	Charagua	24,427	32,186	7.759
55	Santa Cruz	Ángel Sandoval	San Matías	13,073	14,470	1.397
56	Santa Cruz	Germán Busch	Puerto Suárez	15,209	19,829	4.620
57	Santa Cruz	Germán Busch	Puerto Quijarro	12,903	16,659	3.756
58	Beni	Vaca Diez	Guayaramerín	40,444	41,814	1.370
59	Beni	Mamoré	San Joaquín	5,452	6,917	1.465
60	Beni	Mamoré	San Ramón	5,927	4,955	-972
61	Beni	Mamoré	Puerto Siles	1018	945	-73
62	Beni	Iténez	Magdalena	9,908	11,377	1.469
63	Beni	Iténez	Baures	5,264	5,965	701
64	Pando	Nicolás Suárez	Cobija	22,324	46,267	23.943
65	Pando	Nicolás Suárez	Porvenir	3,713	7,948	4.235
66	Pando	Nicolás Suárez	Bolpebra	1,194	2,173	979
67	Pando	Nicolás Suárez	Bella Flor	2,305	5,756	3.451
68	Pando	Manuripi	Filadelfia	3,145	5,756	2.611
69	Pando	Abuná	Santa Rosa del Abuná	2,097	2,395	298
70	Pando	Abuná	Ingavi	899	1.654	755
71	Pando	F. Román	Nueva Esperanza	740	1.654	914
72	Pando	F. Román	Santos Mercado	509	8,663	8,154
Total Border Population				713,661	909,899	196,238

Source: Own elaboration using data from INE (2002, 2013).

important land corridor for moving cocaine to Argentina and Brazil and is used for clandestine departures from the country by persecuted politicians, Sendero guerrillas, and the FARC.[3]

The border, but especially the lake side, is subject to the presence of agents from the drug trafficking cartel system. Despite the coordination efforts made by the Bolivian and Peruvian governments, the prolific activity of the gangs and their auxiliaries seems to have security that facilitates their operation (Página Siete 2016).

The news reports reflect an intense activity in which smuggling – a considerable proportion of which comes from Chile – is predominant, and it is not just small-scale smuggling, but large amounts of transport that cross the country from one end to the other with relative ease (La República 2015). There is no system of border towns as there is on the Argentine border. The border system connects cities like Puno and La Paz; both are about three hours away from the borderline and connect a series of towns and small intermediate cities on both sides of the border socially and economically.

Bolivia–Brazil Border

The longest border is with Brazil (2,655 kilometers) (see Map 3.2), which has few border controls, probably because of the border's great distance from Brazilian urban centers. In this case, not only the enormous extension of the borders stands out, but, above all, the geographical difficulties that condition the life of its people,

Map 3.2 Border with Brazil. Map by d-maps.com (http://d-maps.com/carte.php?num_car =4844&lang=es).

44 *History and Present of the Bolivian Border Subsystem*

the lack of communication routes, and the distance from the population centers – two big ones on both sides. This long border runs through the departments of Pando, Beni, Santa Cruz, and Chuquisaca.

Among the most important border points are the twin cities of Guayamerín/ Guajará-Mirim and, to the south, Puerto Suárez and Puerto Quijarro/Corumbá, which are equipped with physical and administrative infrastructure, with a long tradition of shared urban life that could facilitate spaces for collaboration. Recent constructions, such as Puerto Evo to the north, also stand out.[4]

The problem of drug trafficking is very sensitive throughout this border, as it is an important corridor from Colombia and Peru to Brazil, Argentina, and Paraguay. In response to these flows, which have increased over the last ten years, Brazil has periodically displaced military contingents equipped and prepared to intercept drug trafficking. Brazil not only became a major consumer destination for various forms of Bolivian cocaine, but also a transit country for cocaine on its way to Europe. There are more than 700 clandestine airstrips in this area for drug flights to Brazil and Paraguay (Ciudad del Este) (on smuggling, see Table 3.3).

Department of Pando

The city of Cobija, with 46,267 inhabitants and the highest relative population growth in the whole country, is followed in that part of the northern border by Porvenir, with 7,948, a growth rate of more than 100% (see Table 3.3). The importance of this place lies in the fact that it is a center of communications with Peru and Brazil, with which it has traditionally maintained more relations than

Table 3.4 Main Smuggled Products from Brazil

The Ten Main Illegally Imported Products from Brazil	*Accumulated Value between 2006 and 2008*
Values calculated by the difference method (2006–2008) (in millions of USD)	
Footwear, leggings, and similar articles and parts of these articles	60.67
Boilers, machines, and mechanical devices and their parts	46.63
Iron and steel foundry	42.71
Plastics and their manufactures	36.69
Cotton	34.25
Rubber and its manufactures	29.95
Aluminum and its manufactures	26.83

Source: Ferrufino (2009).

with Bolivia. There is not yet an adequate land route with the main urban centers of Bolivia.

This city has experienced rapid growth due to several important factors such as the decentralization reforms of the 1990s, but, above all, due to the dynamism achieved by the smuggling of goods. Many of these arrive from the distant ports of Arica or Iquique, traveling more than a thousand kilometers from these ports; this territory is the worst connected to the center of the country. It is an extreme example of the process of population densification caused by economic activities favored by asymmetries in legal, political, and economic terms.

The dynamism of other small municipalities that have also doubled their population in recent years is worth noting. These nine municipalities – located on the northern border with Brazil – have benefited from the territorial development policies of the national State since the 1990s. They have gone from being dispersed riverine populations to urban centers with growing commercial dynamism, mainly due to being among of the important passages or corridors for drug and gold trafficking and smuggling between Peru, Bolivia, and Brazil. The latter is linked to first-class urban centers such as Rio Branco. A point close to Cobija is the small but important Bolpebra, a tri-national population center that brings together Bolivia, Peru, and Brazil. This border point is an example of the combination of factors that facilitate illicit activities and crime: it is an inaccessible area, and at the same time it is close to illegal economic spaces, such as the clandestine extraction of gold. It is also a natural passage for smuggling and drug trafficking from Peru, which, together with the Bolivian goods, go to the large and distant Brazilian cities such as Rio Branco and Manaus. In this border zone predominates weakness and, in some cases, the absence of State mechanisms. On the other hand, there is the dominance of local gang leaders and their forms of social control. It is the area with the fastest population growth in the whole country due to government-induced migrations in the last ten years. All these factors have constituted an environment that has facilitated organized crime. This border is considered one of the most important hot spots of the five national borders, not so much because of its size, but because of its low institutionalization.

Cobija: Illegal Markets and Insecurity

This corner of the Pando region on the Bolivian-Brazilian border – a continuation of the stretch that descends from the Bolivian and Peruvian mountains to Bolpebra (Bolivia, Peru, and Brazil) – is a territory open to the movement of all kinds of goods, without much state control given the inaccessibility from both sides of each of the three countries. However, an enormous number of unregistered border crossings between Peru and Bolivia play a very important role in the operation of smuggling, drug trafficking, and other activities related to organized crime. On the Peruvian side, this area has developed a good road infrastructure, due to its extension and the absence of roads on the Bolivian side and border posts along rivers such as the Madre de Dios and others. It has become one of the most fertile areas for the smuggling of cocaine and gold. The Bolivian side, an

46 *History and Present of the Bolivian Border Subsystem*

important zone for the cultivation of coca fields – formerly a traditional and now not so traditional activity – is today the main zone of gold prospecting among river deposits.

José Carlos Campero describes how homicides and murders increased by 500% during the last seven years since 2005; rapes and physically violent crimes increased by 267%; robberies increased by 287%, and carjackings by 1,263%. All of this is without counting the increase in Peruvian cocaine trafficking to Brazil through the streets of Cobija, in addition to the smuggling of wood and gold. The capital of the department of Pando, Cobija, is becoming the second most insecure city in Bolivia, after Santa Cruz, which leads the ranking of citizen insecurity (Campero 2012).

This space near Cobija plays an important role in the development of the illegal economy and in the violence with the presence of groups of the FARC, of Sendero, and others of Brazil, over the control of territory. Territory considered out of the control of the Bolivian State has been the scene of confrontations resulting in the death of Bolivian military personnel, police, and civilians. In its nearby spaces, there are the most precious places for gold prospecting, generally without state control, and which accounts for the mimicry of smuggling from Peru. There are approximately 1,700 registered cooperatives in the country, of which 800 exploit gold, in addition to several times that number of clandestine or nonformal "cooperatives."

Department of Beni

In the Bolivian East, specifically in the department of Beni, there are several urban centers of historical importance that are developing exchange activities, in the form of mirror cities between Brazil and Bolivia. Among this, Guayaramerín and its counterpart in Bazil, Guajará-Mirim, stand out (see Table 3.3).

Unlike Cobija, Guayamerín has a history of development as an export center since the colonial period, especially from the middle of the nineteenth century. From centers in that area, among which are Riberalta and Cachuela Esperanza, a very important role has been developed in the construction of the local societies of great importance during the development of the rubber, quinine, and chestnut era, by which the region is linked to the flows that occurred with the old continent before and after the first war. Gum, quinine, chestnuts, cattle, and wood are the economic bases of the families that founded the wealth of the area, which built the other pole of Bolivian exports and functioned in total disconnection with the mining activities.

From very early on, this Bolivian Amazon area was related to the world market, and powerful families had their interests in what was then the center of the world. In that time, it was a Bolivia that was not very visible to the Altiplano and valley regions. It was the region that was linked by the Atlantic, parallel in its development with the Altiplano and the valleys that were connected to the Pacific, via Peru and Chile, together with the railway branch that entered through Villazón toward Buenos Aires.

The current border is organized by this pair of intensely active cities on both sides of the border, far-removed from the circumstances that gave rise to them. Today the main activity of the municipality is commerce, which is active due to the currency changes of recent years. Three years ago, Brazilians bought goods in Bolivia for half the price that they costed in Brazil. In 2016, the opposite happened. Nowadays, the transformation industries are few.

Guayamerín and Guajará-Mirim communicate through the Mamoré River, on which a construction debt has been pending from Brazil since 1905. A binational bridge that would connect the two was planned for 2012, when local authorities from Guayaramerín and private Bolivian businessmen met and began a tour of the Bolivian Amazon to learn about the region's potential. To date, its construction is still under negotiation.

Although the area is apparently not classified as critical in terms of drug trafficking and smuggling, data indicates that 95% of Bolivians arrested in Brazil are for drug trafficking. This area is on the road leading to the Amazonian haciendas, where a good part of the hydrochloride crystallization laboratories is located.

The exploitation of natural resources is the main source of employment and economic income: chestnuts, rubber, wood, and native palm hearts; gold exploitation continues today as one of the main items along with trade. This originates the current modest patterns of life in that city, compared to other municipalities in the region. Even so, the municipality is a place of passage and origin of migrants to other Bolivian cities and to countries such as Brazil, Europe, Japan, and the United States.

Trials of cooperation between cities on both sides are necessary in border cooperation programs. Equipment and institution-building have been important following the decentralizing reforms of the 1990s. Along the river, which serves as a natural border, there are crossings between the two countries, without any customs system or police control. In the city of Guayaramerín, however, the control of crime and insecurity is more contained because it has been done by local organizations themselves. For more than a century, they have made up for the absence of the central government through local forms of control.

Department of Santa Cruz

In this long stretch of the border there are two very different situations. First, there is San Matías, a small town connected to the distant city of Cáceres in Brazil, that has currently become one of the axes of cocaine trafficking and smuggling out of minerals. It is closely linked to the Bolivian Precambrian where semiprecious stones abound. San Matías is one of the points where in the last few years, deaths of traffickers and police officers have been recorded, documented as reckonings. The other more complex border point is the area where Puerto Suárez and Puerto Quijarro are located.

San Matías – located at 830 kilometers from the city of Santa Cruz de la Sierra, at the eastern end of the department of Santa Cruz – is a very active center, and, although it is not the most important along this border, it is the one that stands out

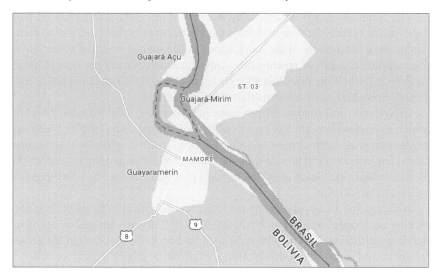

Map 3.3 Map of the cities of Guayaramerín (Bolivia) and Guajará-Mirim (Brazil). Map by the author with data from Google Maps (https://www.google.com/maps/@-10.7797921,-65.3558914,12.87z).

for the news of citizen insecurity and for being a place of smuggling and poorly controlled drug trafficking. Information from the anti-narcotics police frequently mentions San Matías, due to the proximity to crystallization laboratories and the absence of infrastructure and low police presence; it is probably the place with the highest rates of violence and crime in the country (see Vargas 2016).

San Matías has no specialist doctors, and the hospital is in poor conditions. It is also isolated due to the lack of roads to Santa Cruz. Inhabitants at San Matías have been asking the government to build a road that would connect the town to San Ignacio, but their requests have been ignored.[5] Cattlemen and merchants take between 12 and 18 hours to travel to Santa Cruz, while they only need one hour to reach Brazil.

Puerto Suárez, Puerto Aguirre, and Puerto Quijarro

These three border towns and their river accesses stand out as the most important crossing points to Brazil, via Corumbá, and they make up the best communication nodes to the center of Brazil and to Bolivia in the interoceanic corridor.

The municipality of Puerto Suárez is the capital of the Germán Busch province in the department of Santa Cruz, in the far east of the country, with a population of 19,829 inhabitants, according to data from the INE (2013) (see Table 3.3). It is located along the border with Brazil in the so-called Bolivian Pantanal, on the shores of the Cáceres Lagoon, connected with the Paraguay River through the Tamengo Channel.

There is good communication with San José de Chiquitos and Santa Cruz de la Sierra in Bolivia and with Corumbá in Brazil; it has roads, railways, and a port. At the beginning of the twentieth century, it was Bolivia's main river port; however, Cáceres Lagoon is not currently navigable by larger vessels due to the cutting of its river tributary, the Tuyuyú Channel. A few kilometers from the city, there is the Mutún Iron Reserve, the largest in the world, which, like the city, has generated great expectations for growth in the Bolivian Pantanal region, an aspiration supported by a civic movement with great capacity for mobilization.

Puerto Quijarro and its free zone is an important gateway between Brazil and Bolivia. With its Tamengo Channel – a main waterway that links the city to the Paraguay River – it has been declared the Port Capital of Bolivia. The 2001 census showed 12,903 inhabitants in that region; 12 years later, in 2012, it reached 16,659 (INE 2002). In other words, it has one of the highest population growth rates in the department of Santa Cruz (5.23%). Most of its population is of Chiquitano origin, a good proportion of immigrants from the West, and more than one floating presence of Brazilians. The rest of the northern border is practically abandoned by these population centers, due to the distance and lack of communication routes to the interior of the territory. Its inhabitants study in the schools of the neighboring country. Puerto Quijarro regularly makes the daily news for similar issues to those of San Matías and Cobija.

This section of the border is of great importance for the future of the exports from Bolivia via river. Uruguay has offered access to port facilities; two ports are being planned, and it is a good exit route for soybeans controlled by the company Gravetal,[6] as well as the iron route from the Mutún complex. Some negotiations between the countries have suggested the creation of an interoceanic corridor that would, by various modes (river, train, road) connect the posts of Santos and others of the Paraná River with the Chilean and Peruvian posts of the Pacific, improving their communication. With this, Bolivia would reaffirm its role in the region as a transit country.

Bolivia–Paraguay Border

Bolivia and Paraguay, distanced after the Chaco oil war of the 1930s, share a border of approximately 700 kilometers, with less dynamism in comparison with the borders between Bolivia and Peru or between Bolivia and Argentina. The greater population concentration operates the opportunities generated by asynchronies, especially in trade issues, which certainly represents high degrees of complementarity for the populations. This circumstance goes parallel to the problems of terrestrial communication and, above all, to the fact that the most important populations are far from the border areas. This situation has changed favorably over the last 20 years, as both countries have greatly improved land connection; however, there is still a lack of significant border populations. Charagua is the municipality that could be considered as a border point; however, it is not, because of the distance that exists from the city to the border. In the case of the Bolivia–Paraguay border, there is not something similar to the twin cities that neighbor Brazil.

50 *History and Present of the Bolivian Border Subsystem*

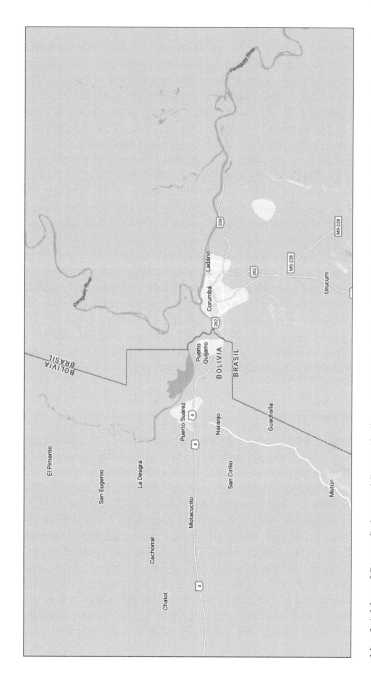

Map 3.4 Map of Puerto Suárez and Puerto Quijarro (Bolivia) and Corumbá (Brazil). Source: Google Maps (https://www.google.com/maps/@-18.9690618,-57.6809776,11.25z).

Dimensions and Characteristics of the Borders 51

Physically, the border comprises the departments of Tarija, Chuquisaca, and Santa Cruz, the region belonging to the Gran Chaco in Bolivia, and the regions of Alto Paraguay and Boquerón in Paraguay. The international border begins in Esmeralda, the tripartite border between Argentina, Bolivia, and Paraguay, and reaches the mouth of the Paraguay River, forming the tripartite landmark between Bolivia, Brazil, and Paraguay.

Bilateral trade between Bolivia and Paraguay, although quite irregular and lacking a strategy from both countries, has grown rapidly and continues its ascent today, thanks mainly to the increase in smuggling, marijuana trafficking, and the overvaluation of the Bolivian currency. Even so, as it will be seen below, imports/exports are among the lowest in the region.

Although interconnection routes have improved greatly, the main entry for formal trade is from the Argentine side: the Yacuiba border (Bolivia) from Pocitos (Argentina). The rout passes through Villamontes and heads to Santa Cruz and other Bolivian cities. Most of the trade is destinated for the two great metropolitan cities: Asunción and Santa Cruz de la Sierra. There is, without a doubt, an exploitable potential in the commercial relations between both countries that can be enhanced, including the closest populations of the borders that are in the Gran Chaco of both countries. To this end, protocols have been signed within the framework of the Southern Common Market (Mercosur).

The destinations and routes marijuana are Argentina and Chile, and it is sometimes listed as coming from Peru (see Endara Sánchez 2016). The ultimate destinations of cocaine on its way to Paraguay are not being adequately reported, though it is assumed that they continue their way to Argentina and Brazil. Aerial flows of hydrochloride are detected via Ciudad del Este (see Table 3.5).

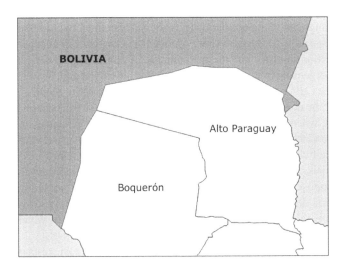

Map 3.5 Border with Paraguay. Map by the author.

52 *History and Present of the Bolivian Border Subsystem*

Table 3.5 Main Products Smuggled from Paraguay

The Ten Illegally Traded Products from Paraguay Values calculated by difference method (2006–2008) (in millions of USD)	*Accumulated Value 2006–2008*
Tobacco and manufactured tobacco substitutes	7.11
Miscellaneous chemical products	6.17
Boilers, machinery, mechanical appliances, and their parts	2.67
Animal and vegetable fats and oils and their cleavage products; animal or vegetable waxes	2.52
Electrical machinery (apparatus and equipment, recording and sound reproducing apparatus, TV and TV parts and their parts)	1.01
Cotton	0.90
Vehicles, automobiles, tractors, velocipedes, velocipedes and other land vehicles and parts thereof	0.85
Wood, charcoal and articles of wood	0.70
Miscellaneous food preparations	0.62
Glass and its manufactures	0.60
Total	23.14

Source: Ferrufino (2009).

Bolivia–Argentina Border

According to the extensive references found in the written press, this is the oldest, most active, and important border in the country, both in terms of the amount of goods and population flows, as well as for being one of the most traditional regarding forms of organization, infrastructure, and equipment. This border was a traditional route for migrants to the northern sugarcane harvest and a road to both intermediate cities, especially to Buenos Aires. Among the activities migrants perform are the construction industry and the manufacture of clothing. Bolivians in Argentina are highly organized in several of the villas in the big capital city, but they are established in cities all over the country such as Mendoza, Rosario, Santa Fé, Córdoba, and all over the north. In areas quite far from the border, like Cochabamba and the Chapare area, where the coca leaf is produced, a significant percentage of the population born in Cochabamba has at some time gone to Argentina, and a significant number of their children have Argentinean birth certificates (Blanes 1983, 29–32). In times of crisis, temporary migration is an important survival mechanism.

This border is composed of 14 municipalities, with 320,075 people, according to the 2012 census, and differs from the other border municipalities in its relative prosperity; it maintains inter-census growth rates of around 2.5% per year, which indicates normal average urban growth (Table 3.3).

Three pairs of border cities in the departments of Tarija and Potosí, respectively, deserve special attention. These cities have populations that share not only an economy, but also a culture, with enormous possibilities for integration and

Dimensions and Characteristics of the Borders   53

border cooperation. This situation makes the two departments and some of the main municipalities case studies on the difficulties and opportunities for establishing cooperation programs and decentralized development models.

This border shows the very different ways in which border populations can establish businesses of different magnitudes by taking advantage of the asynchronies between the two countries. Given the great exchange rate instability of the last few years, when the prices of products on the Argentine side collapsed, there was a movement to buy dollars on the Bolivian market, which was a great attraction for the black market of the dollar, money laundering, and "ant" smuggling (individually hauled) products into Bolivia. There are more than 30 department stores that wholesale food products in Salvador Mazza (Argentina) (Datos 2014).

It is along this border that much of the drug trafficking, smuggling, and human trafficking take place, taking advantage of the enormous complementarity between illegal markets. Periodically, textile workshops, employing semi-enslaved Bolivian labor, are discovered in Buenos Aires and other cities. Food and drink contraband accompanies the drug trafficking that is increasing on this border. This situation is reproduced along the border, although with important differences at various border points from Potosí to Tarija.

Large quantities of coca leaves are smuggled into Argentina by trucks or trains, which has turned many places in northern Argentina into producers of cocaine base paste, adding to the already traditional passage of pure cocaine to the two consumer markets: Argentina and Brazil. These countries are also a bridge to Africa and Europe.

On both sides of the border areas, there is a good development of agroindustry and livestock that could serve as a basis for border cooperation, facilitating the strengthening of the formal economy. This important border is divided between Tarija and Potosí, the latter being key due to its railway importance. With the enormous diversity of activities, illegal activities are mimicked (see Table 3.6).

Department of Tarija

Good road and rail communications have generated the most frequented traditional border crossings equipped with all the administrative requirements. Two important cities, Yacuiba and Bermejo, are also the centers of the country's border economy. Although all these municipalities are considered borderlands, the crossing between the two countries is concentrated mainly through Yacuiba and Bermejo from the Bolivian side. Bolivian migrants and the border trade in food and beverages have built these crossings, which today are used by drug traffickers, who move products including cocaine and coca leaf. Large stores on both sides show the development of the border infrastructure, where wholesale trade is taking place, supplying a very important part of the small formal and informal trade in the country's cities.

The city of Yacuiba has a population of 91,998 inhabitants, making it the second most important city in the department, after the city of Tarija. It represents 55.5% of the total population of the province. It is the most densely populated center within the Gran Chaco, one of the lowest-density regions in the country.

54 *History and Present of the Bolivian Border Subsystem*

Table 3.6 Main Products Smuggled from Argentina

The Ten Main Illegally Imported Products from Argentina *Values calculated by the difference method (2006–2008) (in millions of USD)*	*Accumulated Value 2006–2008*
Preparations made of cereals, flour, starch, or milk; pastrycooks' products	23.80
Boilers, machines, and mechanical devices; parts for these machines or appliances	11.30
Vehicles, automobiles, tractors, velocipedes, and other land vehicles and their parts	9.62
Various products of the chemical industries	9.19
Sound, recording, image, speakers, television, and parts thereof	6.39
Optics, photography, cinematography, and medical-surgical instruments or apparatus	2.83
Iron and steel foundry	2.59
Sugars and confectionery	2.17
Manufactures of cast iron or steel	1.40
Inorganic chemicals, precious metal compounds, radioactive elements, isotopes	1.40
Total	70.69

Source: Ferrufino (2009).

In the last intercensal period it registered 80.1% of the population growth of the whole province (that is, 33,699 of 41,706 inhabitants) (see Table 3.3).

The history of Yacuiba is linked to those of Pocitos[7] and Salvador Mazza, Argentine towns that, in the late 1940s, developed commercial activities from both sides of the border through the Sauzal and Aguas Blancas streams that trace the path between the two republics. Trucks with fuel and wooden logs passed through there. These cities became a transitory passage and storage place of merchandise that was transferred from the Argentine Republic to Bolivia, adapting their road networks and equipment.

Yacuiba gradually adapted to its role as passageway through stages such as the Chaco War, the Agrarian Reform, and the National Revolution, as well as its current participation in hydrocarbon exploration, which provides it with extremely important royalties for investments in infrastructure and road networks that allowed it to improve its arrival with goods to and from Argentina.[8]

The formation of power groups with relative decision-making capacity with respect to the central government, the constitution of the civic committees in the mid-1950s, the Regional Development Corporation of Tarija, and the municipal and departmental decentralization marked important stages in the management of border issues in the late 1990s, when a better articulated relationship with national policies was consolidated.

At present, investment in infrastructure has accompanied the growth of exports to Argentina and of imports with growing trade deficits for Bolivia, due to the deepening of competitive conditions in agricultural and industrial production. The border trade sector is the one that establishes the basis of Yacuiba's urban economy, which implies the development of mobility, storage, and administration infrastructures. At the same time, the predominant form of "ant" trade – with *bagalleros* or *bagayeros* and small-scale transportation – has generated a grassroots economy of enormous proportions. As a result of the fluctuations in the Argentine currency, many products have been brought into Bolivia and, above all, the search for dollars by Argentinians has developed the informal exchange market in the city (La Razón 2016).

Its population has doubled in the last ten years, which implies the development of services according to important commercial movement, an effect of its strategic border location, crossroads of road corridors of continental importance, and the fact that it is seen as a future city of services for Mercosur. It mixes the charm of a young and rural city with the pragmatism of modernity, with its traditional restaurants, places of entertainment, spas, discos, excellent hotels, and, in its surroundings, an incredible Chaqueño landscape: the humid Aguarague mountain range, the Chaco plain, and the dazzling sun.

The commercial activity and the dense informal sector that transports goods on this crowded border bridge and its surroundings conceal an important sector of the illegal economy: drug trafficking, smuggling, and human trafficking.

The city of Bermejo, with 34,505 people (based on the 2012 Census), belongs to the province of Aniceto Arce de Tarija and is twinned with the Argentine city of Aguas Blancas, a little further from Oran. Founded on December 7, 1952, this border town is characterized by dynamic growth, but, also, by great instability. In 1920, the Bolivian government granted the U.S. firm, Richmond Levering Co., a huge extension to exploit the oil deposits located in the departments of Santa Cruz, Tarija, and Chuquisaca. With the Bermejo well, the first in Bolivia, a local economy of great impact was inaugurated. With the second drilling, the aspirations of Standard Oil doubled, and the construction of four more wells followed. From Oran (Argentina), machinery and equipment were moved 53 kilometers along difficult roads, with carts pulled by mules transporting hundreds of tons consisting of boilers, drilling towers, drills, and other metal implements.

The settlement of oil workers and their families and the camps on the bank of the Bermejo River, back in 1918 to 1924, formed the historical cradle of the city. A considerable flow of migrants followed the establishment of an organized camp, numerous wells drilled, and the already-settled families.

In the last few years, tourism projects and the important sugar industry have been developed with the expansion of sugarcane crops and the prosperous trade with Argentina through the Aguas Blancas border post and the large number of clandestine crossings that can be found by crossing the Bermejo River. All of this

56 *History and Present of the Bolivian Border Subsystem*

is making this city a recent favorite spot for drug traffickers, smugglers, and the ever-present army of *bagalleros* (porters), as well as the bureaucracy that facilitates legal and illegal business.

Its original name is Pozo del Bermejo. It is an area rich in hydrocarbons (oil); it has four important economic bases: the hydrocarbon industry, the trade system, the sugar industry, and agricultural and livestock production. The agricultural production of approximately 600,000 tons of cane guarantees the production of more than 1,500,000 quintals[9] of sugar and eight million liters of alcohol, which are commercialized in the interior of the country and exported to the world market. This activity generates more than 8,000 direct jobs and thousands of indirect jobs. The sugarcane industry has a significant weight within the economy of this municipality; a minor part of the land is dedicated to fruits (citrus, papaya, and banana) in the cities of Bermejo and Tarija. The trade of clothes, groceries, home utensils, and others coming mainly from Argentina predominates. Bermejo, a tourist destination on the border with Argentina, is located 208 kilometers from the city of Tarija.

Department of Potosí

The Western Altiplano and valleys of Bolivia are linked to the northern cities of Argentina and Buenos Aires through a railway and an important road infrastructure. Since its foundation, Villazón has been an important railway point and has been considered the first station toward Bolivia or the last one leaving it, which joins the railways that transport minerals and goods to and from Buenos Aires.

Villazón is a city in the southern area the department of Potosí, province of Modesto Omiste, which shares a single culture and field of economic activity with the city of La Quiaca in Argentina. With its 44,906 inhabitants, it is the largest city in the south (INE 2013). It is a cosmopolitan city, inhabited by people from all over the world.

From the eight municipalities of Potosí considered to be border towns, an important flow of people and merchandise converges in Villazón. Although it is the second city of this border group, Villazón is a unit linked to the city of La Quiaca, Argentina (see Table 3.3). With this entry and exit of goods and people, Argentina receives a double flow from Bolivia: from the south, the one that arrives from the Eastern network to the border of Tarija; and from the north, through Villazón, the network of the Altiplano; thus, the two Bolivian networks are articulated toward the distant Atlantic.

Villazón is located 347 kilometers from the city of Potosí and at an altitude of 3,400 meters above sea level. It was founded on May 20, 1910, during the government of Eliodoro Villazón, from whom it takes its name. Its population increased from 36,266 in 2001 to 44,906 in 2012, which shows a moderate growth of secondary city.[10] Also known as the folkloric capital of the south of the country, it was formerly known as "La Quiaca Boliviana," a commercial city with infrastructure built by the municipality and the people, with commercial shopping centers offering electrical appliances and clothing.[11] The intense commercial movement between the two cities is infiltrated by the lure of smuggling, whereby tons of goods moved by an enormous army of shippers and vendors cross daily, between one direction and the other, through an "ant" trade in food, electronic products, and beverages, partially controlled by customs. This scenario confirms that the main characteristic of traffic on this border, which comes from the Paraguayan border itself and moves along the entire Tarija border, is carried by porters in small quantities. As a result, large numbers of men and women, who usually work together, get arrested by the police, and quantities of merchandise are seized almost daily on the buses.

Mobile anti-narcotics police posts have been set up in different parts of the region, mainly because of the recurrent violence that affects anti-narcotics police and customs agents, and which manifests itself in battles between traders and carriers. Colombians and Peruvians have been accused by passersby in Villazón of extortion in smuggling cases and robberies of free traders. It has been claimed that this route is also being used for the transfer of synthetic drugs.

Bolivia–Chile Border

The border with Chile comprises 850 kilometers (see Map 3.6). It is a sparsely populated area due to the extremely arid nature of the territory, but it is through this passage that most of the imports enter. The ports and warehouses in the free trade zones of northern Chile, Iquique, and Arica process imports into Bolivia from all over the world, but especially from Asia and the north, via the Pacific, and to a lesser extent from Chile itself. Compared to Brazil and Argentina, the transit of people through this border is lower, but it is the most important border in the flow of goods, not only in quantity but also in value. It is the trade connection with Asia par excellence, while the other four borders are dominated by products from neighboring countries.

This border is connected to the rest of the country through the most modern road network. The rail network between Arica and Charaña was rehabilitated and a connection between the most important lead, silver, and zinc mine, San Cristóbal, with the southern railway network has been extended. In addition, a large road supplies fuel to the mine through the department of Potosí. Although there are three important border crossings (Pisiga through Oruro and Tambo Quemado, and Charaña through La Paz), which have the usual mechanisms for the control of merchandise and migration, more than 100 more have been discovered in the last 30 years, through which smuggling and drug trafficking operate due to the absence of state control in both countries (see Table 3.7).[12] From the Chilean side, the free zones, especially the ZOFRI area of Iquique, facilitate the transit of goods to all Bolivian cities and other border areas of several of the neighboring countries. A distinction is made between imports from Chile and those from overseas, which are more significant. Among the latter, thousands of tons of used clothing stand out, which approximately 30 large wholesale importers distribute through thousands of sellers located in all the cities of the country, at prices highly competitive with domestic garments.

58 *History and Present of the Bolivian Border Subsystem*

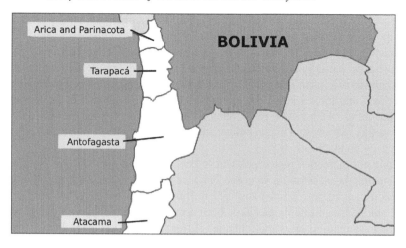

Map 3.6 Bolivian Border with Chile. Map by the author.

Table 3.7 Main Products Smuggled from Chile

The Ten Main Illegally Imported Products from Chile Values calculated by the difference method (2006–2008) (in millions of USD)	*Accumulated Value 2006–2008*
Boilers, machines, mechanical devices, and their parts	69.20
Vehicles, automobiles, tractors, velocipedes, and other land vehicles and their parts	47.70
Manufactures of cast iron or steel	24.15
Electrical machines (apparatus and material), recording apparatus, sound reproduction, TV, and its parts	23.12
Beverages, alcoholic liquids, and vinegar	13.50
Man-made or synthetic staple fibers	13.30
Paper and cardboard, articles of cellulose pulp of paper or cardboard	12.15
Essential oils and resinoids, toilet or cosmetic perfumery preparations	11.55
Preparations of fish or crustaceans, mollusks, and other aquatic invertebrates	10.60
Organic chemicals	9.72
Total	234.99

Source: Ferrufino (2009).

Cars that arrive on cargo ships generally come from Asia, dock in Chilean ports, and are commercialized in Bolivia, Peru, Argentina, or Paraguay. In total, it is estimated that more than 30% of cars are illegally obtained in Bolivia;

Dimensions and Characteristics of the Borders 59

Table 3.8 Main Products Smuggled from the ZOFRI area in Iquique

The Ten Smuggled Products in ZOFRI Values calculated by difference method (2006–2008) (in millions of USD)	*Accumulated Value 2006–2008*
Vehicles, automobiles, tractors, velocipedes, and other land vehicles and their parts	450.00
Electrical machines (apparatus and material), recording apparatus, sound reproduction, TV, and its parts	318.00
Boilers, machines, and mechanical devices and their parts	148.70
Man-made or synthetic staple fibers	86.90
Footwear, leggings and similar articles, parts of these articles	82.20
Toys, games, articles for recreation, or sports and their parts	65.02
Garments and clothing accessories, except knitted	45.51
Knitwear and accessories	43.16
Other made-up textile articles	37.50
Plastics and their manufactures	28.00
Total	1,305.00

Source: Ferrufino (2009).

approximately 50% of these have managed to comply with the requirements of the law shortly thereafter. From this border, stolen or used cars, home appliances, and electronic products – among the most important – head for the free zones in other parts of the country, including faraway Pando, which is located more than 1,300 kilometers away, where they enter Brazil. When it comes to used cars – now restricted or stolen – they usually cross the vast plains of the Lauca River delta that extend from the Chilean border near Pisiga to the city of Oruro.

The network of national routes has grown in quantitative terms and has also improved in its conditions of the flexibility required by the changing routes of illegal markets, such as drug trafficking, contraband, and illegal exports of gold. In the free zones on the Chilean side, especially the ZOFRI of Iquique, taxes are suspended, facilitating the transit of goods to Bolivia and from there to other countries (see Table 3.8).

Regarding the role played by the large free zone of the ports of Iquique and Arica in northern Chile, the only precaution taken by the Chilean police is to deal with stolen cars, which – as on the borders of Brazil, Paraguay, and Argentina – arrive in considerable numbers and are nearly identical to the rest of the undocu-mented cars. Since 2012, Bolivian law prohibits the entrance of unregistered cars and used clothing, but corporate associations have been formed with a high degree of social and political pressure to "make legal" what is illegal. Customs control is relatively easy to circumvent, with products often being seized hundreds of

60   *History and Present of the Bolivian Border Subsystem*

kilometers from the Chilean border. This border offers one of the most enlightening examples in which drug trafficking and smuggling are closely linked, both penetrating through the most diverse fissures in the legal economy.

The most frequent acts of border violence are lynching of informants of smuggling activities and problems of smuggling and drug trafficking, often including police who turn over drugs or seize cars. Indigenous populations in the area are involved in these criminal activities, but in no way the violence reaches the numbers of the borders with Argentina and Brazil.

The cities on the Chilean border bear no resemblance to those in other countries, as they are twin cities, closely linked to each other, but at a great distance. The city of Iquique operates normally with the city of Oruro and Arica with the city of La Paz, across distances superior to the 500 kilometers. Along the route, important centers that play a role in the flows do not exist, outside that of small services to the transport. Between these cities, there is hardly any accommodation or commercial activity on the two most modern roads in the country. However, there is an intense activity of smuggling and drug trafficking, which, although it is small, has nothing to do with the transporters from the Argentine border. Specialized people cross the pampas of the Lauca delta with great ease, generally at night, moving mostly via used vehicles. Information and support services for rural populations are often used. Larfe trucks are also used to transport smuggled goods under the form of sub-declarations to customs. The latter frequently reports the seizure of smuggled trucks.

Departments of Oruro and La Paz

Six important crossings stand out on this border, which are not located in cities, but only in places where customs and police administrations are. The most important are Portezuelo del Cajón, Portezuelo de Chaxas, Chungará-Tambo Quemado, Colchane-Pisiga, Salar de Ollagüe, and Visviri (La Paz).

Chungará-Tambo Quemado is located on the axis from La Paz to the port of Arica in North Chile, on the Brazil–Bolivia–Chile interoceanic route, across the Snowy Sajama on the Bolivian side. It reaches the border along the Chungará Lagoon and an altitude of 4,680 meters above sea level. It is the second most important border crossing point with customs on the border with Chile, permanently enabled and suitable for all types of vehicles.

Colchane-Pisiga is the main crossing, in terms of volume and value of goods. It connects the city of Oruro with the port and Free Zone of Iquique (ZOFRI), on the Bolivian side, the town of Pisiga, and on the Chilean side Colchane, at an approximate altitude of 3,700 meters. Access to customs services is similar to that of Tambo Quemado.

On the Bolivian side and past the Coipasa salt flat to the plains of the municipality of Chipaya, inhabited by the Uru Chipaya population, the zone is accessible. There are dirt roads, which are only navigable by the most expert, and run parallel to the international highway, where the large transports that pass through customs circulate. This road is sought by many smugglers until it blends in with the car caravans on the main road. The "bells" that warn of the presence of the

Dimensions and Characteristics of the Borders 61

police and specialized people guide smugglers and other agents of a major underground economy. There are other minor crossings such as Portezuelo del Cajón, Portezuelo de Chaxas Salar de Ollagüe, and Visviri-Charaña.

Multimodal Routes: Air, Land, and Water

In recent years, the main concern of Brazil, Argentina, and Paraguay regarding drug and arms trafficking has been focused on the problem of air routes, which are in constant change and have become unpredictable, and through which smugglers move enormous quantities of cocaine, arms, and gold between countries, avoiding the difficult and narrow land routes, which do not necessarily adapt to the conditions of drug trafficking. The land borders have gone through a long history of adaptation based on the traditional functions of short- and medium-range merchandise flow; however, due to the volumes and demands of the confrontation between cartels changes have taken place in order to adapt to the new conditions of the global drug market, with air traffic growing considerably.

Small, modern, and versatile aircrafts can land on any road or on temporary clandestine runways that do not require large infrastructure. There have been official reports of stolen airplanes in the United States that operate between Bolivia and Peru, moving drugs from the United States to Brazil and Paraguay using more than 70 clandestine runways in the Amazon department of Beni to refuel. This is evidenced by the frequent accidents and captures of small planes with cargoes of around 350 kilograms of cocaine.[13]

Finally, it has been discovered that the market uses the Jorge Chávez airport in Lima to export Peruvian gold from Bolivia, with volumes close to 35 tons per year. Until recently, the export was done directly from Bolivia in the form of amalgam and industrial waste to the United States. Now, it is exported in the form of metallic gold ingots, clandestinely traveling the Peru–Bolivia–U.S. route, passing through airports in Peru; thus, Bolivia contributes to tax evasion in Peru. Other flights stop at the cities of Guayaramerín and Riberalta in the northwest, the Pantanal area (Puerto Suárez and Puerto Quijarro), and other minor points.

Bolivia is not a country with a fully structured network of land roads, which is supplemented by an air transport system that moves products and people to and from the cattle ranches in the Amazon. Today, this system is being used for the transfer of illicit goods (gold, cocaine paste, and hydrochloride) and serves as a transit base to other neighboring countries due to the characteristics of the transportation used. The data ranges from 700 to 2,000 clandestine routes, which cannot be either verified or dismissed. It is assumed that every cattle ranch has its own route. There are others that are not on farms.

There have been no major changes in the five land borders in the last 30 years, except for the intensity of the flows. Since the beginning of the century, the increase of the importance of illegal and long-range markets, both in migration and in merchandise, as well as the articulating capacity of these flows on the society and the economy of the country, has led to the articulation of all means of transport in the field of drug trafficking. The historical circuits and their respective routes were

62 *History and Present of the Bolivian Border Subsystem*

Bolivia–Argentina, Bolivia–São Paolo, Bolivia–Peru, and Bolivia–Chile. These continue to operate and have become more significant in volume, but they are not always direct routes, such as Paraguay–Bolivia–Argentina or Paraguay–Bolivia and from here to Chile and Peru.

But in the last 20 years the routes and their respective stages have diversified. The traditional ones have intensified, and many clandestine passes have been added to each of the routes. What has changed? The flows are longer, more global – a phenomenon driven by illegal markets. Formal crossings have been combined with clandestine crossings, personal and small-scale transport with high-tonnage transport and land transport with air transport. These multiple combinations make the market flexible and efficient, allowing for the changes required at any given time. An example of this is expressed in the case of Peru with the transfer of gold or base paste to Bolivia. When bombing the airstrips in the Amazon ramped up, the loaders that cross the forests and the mountains began to operate, permanently looking for trails.

The land borders have gone through a long history of adaptation based on traditional functions: flow of short- and medium-range goods. The roads drawn by the traditional flows of people who used them for decades and the density generated in each of them contributed to it. The fact is that the physical borders between countries are a social, economic, and political construction that consolidates a reality: informality, which in Bolivia involves everything. A fundamental element of this informality is the legitimization and extensive development of the crime of widespread corruption and unprecedented levels of extortion.

Despite progress in adapting the borders to the functioning of the informal economy, they are still not enough to handle the volume or adapt to the new conditions of the global drug market. The submarines in Lake Titicaca remain an anecdote, while the reality of the discovery of hundreds and hundreds of clandestine tracks operating from both sides of the physical borders predominates. Small air vessels of fantastic versatility can land on any road or on runways that do not require a large infrastructure. The air routes should be studied as expressions of the expansion and flexibility of traffic, overcoming the limitations and roughness of land borders, but at the same time deepening without precedent the scope of informality in daily life.

Bolivian government authorities repeatedly insist on the presence of a large amount of traffic via Bolivia; almost 50% of the drugs seized are Peruvian. They claim that in 2012 there were approximately 36 tons of base paste and hydrochloride. There are no official data on how much cocaine Bolivia produces, although the UN has estimated that it was around 115 tons per year and that the country is the world's third largest cocaine producer, after Peru and Colombia (UNODC 2021). Bolivian and Peruvian cocaine have as their main destination markets Brazil and Europe, according to the international entity (Bartolomé and Barreiro 2019).

Conclusion

The border system, referring to binational lines, is very complex, especially if it is governed by national policies. For Bolivia, each country represents a very different nexus with domestic politics. The physical accesses are very different, from the classic ones with Argentina, Chile, and Peru, to the most depopulated and distant from the urban centers, such as those of Brazil and Paraguay. The types of markets that characterize each border are similar, but the dimensions are very different. In each case, legal and illegal trades are combined, so the concentration of violence in each of them, among other aspects, implies a differentiated policy. In conclusion, such a complex system and a lack of local policies to address border issues are fertile ground for informality, weak state presence, and the porosity of the illegal economy. The illegal markets, under this new dynamic, are a complex reality, where there is a plurality of products, actors, and countries that have acted together throughout the history (Carrión 2015, 35).

Notes

1 As fuels are subsidized in Bolivia, they are sometimes sold up to five times their price. In Bolivia, the amount of fuel that can be purchased in the border strips – up to 50 kilometers from the borderline – is under control.

2 In mid-October 2014, in an ambush against military coca eradicators near the Peruvian border, coca farmers killed 4 soldiers and left 14 wounded. The government said that the ambush was organized by foreign drug traffickers, mainly Peruvian, to prevent the destruction of crops (Farfán 2013).

3 According to the United Nations Office on Drugs and Crime (UNODC), more than 1,000 tons of cocaine transit from Colombia, Peru, and Bolivia to Brazil and Argentina (Aliaga 2013).

4 At the end of April 2007, the town of Montevideo (200 kilometers away from Cobija) suffered a fire that forced its inhabitants to re-establish the town under the name of Puerto Evo, a free trade zone, a destination for smuggling routes arriving from the Chilean and Argentinean borders (Cortez Torrez 2008).

5 The violent situation in San Matías is not recent. The departmental director of Citizen Security of the Santa Cruz Governor's Office, Enrique Brun, revealed that approximately ten years ago, drug trafficking took hold in the town (El País 2016).

6 Gravetal Bolivia S.A. is a company engaged in the production of different soybean products: crude oil, soybean meal, and pelletized soybean hulls. It was established in 1993, in Santa Cruz de la Sierra. It exports its production to all countries in the world.

7 Named after its counterpart in Argentina, the Bolivian Pocitos was founded on March 19, 1949, which is the day of San José, thus assigning this saint to its name: San José de Pocitos. Currently, it has more than 16,000 inhabitants. They depend on the economic movement that is generated in the international bridge and proximities where an important commercial sector has been installed. There are about 20 retail trade unions and 4 of *vivanderas*, associated to the Federación Especial de Trabajadores Gremiales (Special Federation of Union Workers). The Asociación de Bagalleros 27 de Mayo groups around 1,000 people who work moving goods from Argentina to Bolivia: cab cooperatives, a cargo transport union, two handcart unions, and various service institutions.

8 More than 45% of the province's fiscal income comes from the oil industry: an approximate annual income of 300 million extra dollars since 2011. To this income is added the development of agriculture and livestock (Honorable Alcaldía Municipal de Yacuiba 2001).

64 *History and Present of the Bolivian Border Subsystem*

9 One quintal is equivalent to 100 pounds, or approximately 45 kilos.

10 In the department of Potosí, secondary urban centers form an important group and break the urban primacy of the other departments in which the capital city accounts for more than 50% of the departmental total.

11 Since 1936, its first well-shaped streets were laid out where buildings were erected and named after places like Tupiza. The commercial centers, squares, and the House of Culture were distributed in them. The market and the first transport terminal of the country was built in the 1970s, facilitating the commercial activity and modern services required by the increase of passengers and the rise of smuggling, which benefits as an important activity to the local population and the floating population coming from Argentina and Bolivia. Today it is one of the most important import and export points for Argentina.

12 According to sources from Carabineros de Chile, "the two countries share between 106 and 114 clandestine border crossings that are used by smugglers and drug traffickers." In Chile, they facilitate the transfer of *chuto* (undocumented) vehicles to Bolivia (El Deber 2014). According to the General Customs Law (Law 1990) of 1999, Law 3467 and its regulations of 2006, and Law 133 of 2011, in Bolivia *chuto* vehicles nationalization is no longer allowed, but the entry continues.

13 Approximately 700 clandestine runways are located in different points of the border.

References

Aliaga, Javier. 2013. "La ONU ve riesgo de violencia en Bolivia por trasiego de cocaína hacia Brasil." *La Razón (Bolivia Edition)*, April 13, 2013. https://www.la-razon.com/nacional/2013/04/13/la-onu-ve-riesgo-de-violencia-en-bolivia-por-trasiego-de-cocaina-hacia-brasil/.

Bartolomé, Mariano, and Vicente Ventura Barreiro. 2019. "El papel de Bolivia dentro de los esquemas del tráfico de cocaína." *Real Instituto Elcano*, November 8, 2019. https://www.realinstitutoelcano.org/analisis/el-papel-de-bolivia-dentro-de-los-esquemas-del-trafico-de-cocaina/.

Blanes, José. 1983. *De los Valles al Chapare. Estrategias familiares en un contexto de cambios*. Cochabamba: CERES.

Campero, José Carlos. 2012. "Estudio exploratorio sobre Problemáticas de seguridad en ciudades frontera. Caso: Ciudad de Cobija." *Regional Security Forum, FES Bolivia, Policy Papers 03*. La Paz.

Carrión, Fernando. 2015. *La Red Global del Narcotráfico. Perspectivas de una corte penal regional en el marco de la UNASUR*. Ecuador:Friedrich Ebert Stiftung/ILDIS - Fiscalía General del Estado. http://works.bepress.com/fernando_carrion/688/.

Cortez Torrez, José Antonio. 2008. "Puerto Evo. Una plaza cuestionada del comercio con Brasil." *Comercialización Agrícola*, December 21, 2008. https://comercializacionagricola.blogspot.com/2008/12/puerto-evo-una-plaza-cuestionada-del.html.

Datos. 2014. "Bajan los precios en frontera y hay alto recelo por el dolar." January 30, 2014. https://datos-bo.com/express-capital/banca/bajan-los-precios-en-frontera-y-hay-alto-recelo-por-el-dolar/.

El Deber. 2013. "La ONU ve riesgo de violencia por trasiego de cocaína hacia Brasil." April 13, 2013. https://eju.tv/2013/04/la-onu-ve-riesgo-de-violencia-por-trasiego-de-cocaina-hacia-brasil/.

———. 2014. "Identifican más de 100 vías ilegales en fronteras de Bolivia-Chile." July 13, 2014. https://eju.tv/2014/07/identifican-ms-de-100-vas-ilegales-en-fronteras-de-bolivia-chile/.

El País. 2016. "San Matías, pueblo cruceño sin ley y olvidado por el Estado." January 4, 2016. https://www.elpaisonline.com/index.php/noticiastarija/item/200349-san-matias-pueblo-cruceno-sin-ley-y-olvidado-del-estado.

Endara Sánchez, Lubomir. 2016. "Narcos usan Bolivia para llevar marihuana a Chile." *El Día Digital*, April 6, 2016. https://www.eldia.com.bo/noticia.php?id=195709&id_cat=1.

Farfán, Williams. 2013. "Diputado afirma que hubo emboscada a erradicadores." *La Razón (Bolivia Edition)*, October 31, 2013. https://www.la-razon.com/nacional/2013/10/31/diputado-afirma-que-hubo-emboscada-a-erradicadores/.

Ferrufino, Rubén. 2009. *Comercio exterior ilegal en Bolivia: Estimaciones 2000–2008*. Unpublished Paper. La Paz: Confederación de Empresarios Privados de Bolivia.

Honorable Alcaldía Municipal de Yacuiba. 2001. "Plan Desarrollo Municipal Distrito 8 Yacuiba." *Estado Plurinacional de Bolivia*. https://es.scribd.com/document/327106366/plan-desarrollo-municipal-Distrito-8-yacuiba.

INE. 2002. "Censo Nacional de Población y Vivienda 2001 y 2002." La Paz, Bolivia. https://www.ine.gob.bo/index.php/censos-y-banco-de-datos/censos/.

———. 2013. "Censo Nacional de Población y Vivienda 2012." La Paz, Bolivia. https://www.ine.gob.bo/index.php/censos-y-banco-de-datos/censos/.

La Razón. 2016. "Policía reporta bloqueo del Puente Internacional en Yacuiba por manifestación de "bagayeros"" May 4, 2016. https://www.la-razon.com/economia/2016/05/04/policia-reporta-bloqueo-del-puente-internacional-en-yacuiba-por-manifestacion-de-bagayeros/.

La República. 2015. "Incautan 18 camiones con mercancía de contrabando proveniente de Bolivia." September 6, 2015. https://larepublica.pe/sociedad/880144-incautan-18-camiones-con-mercancia-de-contrabando-proveniente-de-bolivia/.

Página Siete. 2016. "Bolivia y Perú alistan operación 'sandwich' contra los narcos." May 28, 2016.

Sánchez Serrano, Rolando. 2011. "Las fronteras importan: Una aproximación conceptual." *Revista Estudios Fronterizos* 1(1) (July–December): 1–26.

UNODC. 2021. Estado Plurinacional de Bolivia. In *Monitoreo de Cultivos de Coca 2020*. La Paz: UNODC.

Vargas, Nona. 2016. "Gobierno: La "matanza" en San Matías es por el narco." *El Deber*, October 21, 2016. https://eju.tv/2016/10/gobierno-la-matanza-en-san-matias-es-por-el-narco/.

Part 2
Illegal Markets

4 Illegal Markets

Illegality and Informality

About the Concepts

As it was seen in the previous chapters, the illegal markets – a dimension of the informal economy in Bolivia – are one of the articulating factors of the border subsystem. Their importance lies in their close connection with transnational criminal networks and illegal trade flows in the world, as well as their relationship with the formal legal economy and the massive economies of the so-called urban informal sector. In recent decades, this sector has acquired significant weight in the structure of the economy, given its cross-cutting influence on various economic sectors. Although it may seem inadequate, we will include all these different situations insofar as they have the same systematic relationship with the principle of profit.

> The informal economy is then not an individual condition, but a process of income-generating activity characterized by one main fact: it is not regulated by the institutions of society in a social and legal environment where similar activities are regulated.
>
> (Carrión 2015, 15)

The absence of institutional regulation in the informal economy may relate to different elements of the labor process: the status of the worker or the form of management of enterprises, for example, fraud. In other cases, some economic activities may be called informal by their very nature because they are defined as criminal by institutions or society. However, sociologists know that

> the categories normal/abnormal, legal/criminal are social patterns subject to change. When required, these categories often represent sources of economic opportunity outside the palliative of institutional regulation.... The so-called criminal categories specialize in the production of goods and services that are socially defined as illicit.
>
> (Castells in Blanes 1990, 23–24)

DOI: 10.4324/9781003203117-7

70 *Illegal Markets*

On the other hand, the basic distinction between formal licit and illicit activities does not emphasize the final product, but the way in which it is produced and exchanged.

We include within the concept of illegal that of criminal, not only because of the way it is produced, but also because of the final product that is harmful to citizens. This is the case with drug trafficking, murder, legal extortion, and the many forms of violence. Finally, the usefulness of including this whole set of different activities is that they have some points in common, related to society and regulatory frameworks, to the validity of laws, or to the impulses of individuals or groups that profit from the violation of rights and from crime.

The important role of the informal economy in the border system began to take hold in the 1980s – in the context of structural adjustment and opening up to foreign trade – when the informal sector, especially the urban sector, began to emerge vigorously under the impetus of growing trade in border areas with neighboring countries; this was a precarious, informal, and small-scale trade – basically smuggling – as reflected in the study by Napoleón Pacheco and José Luis Evia (2010). Since then, and progressively, the informal economy has become intertwined with legal and illegal trade at the borders, where the most varied goods (clothing, food, appliances, vehicles, spare parts, machinery, construction material, and many other goods) transit, so that the lines of demarcation between informal trade and smuggling have become tenuous, relative, and volatile. Moving from informal to contraband and vice versa is a common phenomenon in Bolivia. Smuggling gravitates to the entire popular economy, mostly informal, and its ramifications extend to all other economic sectors, including formal private and public activities.

In turn, the expansion of smuggling comes hand in hand with drug trafficking and its entire production chain (coca cultivation, production, trade, and export of cocaine), that is, the activities that make up the coca-cocaine complex and that include the import of precursors. On the other hand, there are many indications that drug trafficking injects capital into smuggling, while, at the same time, it is a vehicle for money laundering.

In 2012, illegal exports were estimated to be over $1,806 million – 6.7% of that year's GDP – with drug trafficking accounting for the largest share; meanwhile, smuggling mobilized resources of approximately $1,889 million, suggesting that this activity is financed to a significant extent by the foreign exchange generated by drug trafficking and is, therefore, the main channel for money laundering.

When we speak of illegal markets, we include this set of interrelations under the mantle of informal, illegal, and criminal, which has shown a high capacity to structure many aspects of the economy and society. But, above all, they condition the ways in which Bolivia is inserted in the global border system of Latin America and the world. Thus, Bolivia has structured a dense system of interactions from the informal sector with smuggling and drug trafficking, with a growing impact on various spaces of national life.

Informality is fed by businesses that can be openly criminal, and these, in turn, can be subsumed into the informal behavior of the economy, especially the domestic and foreign trade sectors. That is why it is so difficult to establish

Illegal Markets   71

clear boundaries between the informal economy and the illegal and underground businesses, which also operate within it. The more difficult the separation is, the greater the overall efficiency of money laundering and the greater the redistributive impact on their levels of influence will be. There are sectors of the economy that are at this level, such as public bank bonds, the real estate economy, and commerce – considering smuggling as such. One sector of the market that facilitates this porosity is the huge informal army of workers, such as street vendors, service providers, transporters at border posts, and input suppliers.

It is known, on the other hand, that drug trafficking – and perhaps some of the contraband – is linked to the action of criminal groups (national and foreign), but its dynamics transcend these actors and are spread over a wide population and a variety of economic agents; many of them operate in the border areas, although not only there. This is also the reason for the enormous complexity of the criminal world operating in Bolivia, immersed in a variegated social fabric, territorially dislocated, and with connections in other countries, mainly neighboring ones.

Following the strategies of business diversification, in Bolivia, the mafias linked to drug trafficking make their presence felt in many other criminal actions, such as kidnapping, trafficking in persons and organs, arms trafficking, illegal exploitation, exports in mining, and, particularly, gold smuggling.

> A central fact is the omnipresence of illegal economies stemming from drug trafficking: (between $500 and $800 billion a year), arms ($12 billion), smuggling ($40 billion tax losses), human trafficking ($15 billion). All of this has an impact on the expansion of consumption and on the insertion into the legal economy (tourism, construction, trade).
>
> (Carrión and Alagna 2016, 4–6)

All of these intricate set of businesses, criminal activities, and social relations ultimately configure a complex web of socioeconomic relations around the triangle: informality-contraband-drug trafficking, whose incidence reaches other spheres of the economic structure and also the political and institutional system, and, of course, the country's border relations, in a context of precarious state presence at the borders, weakness of border control institutions (Customs, Migration, Police), official corruption, and lack of action by the organs of justice. All of this happens because the culture of informality and illegality is deeply rooted in the Bolivian society.

The institutional precariousness of the State is a result of not only informality in a global sense, but also to a condition of the social and political institutional system, derived from the action of the mafias that put pressure on law and order institutions. There are many actors who adapt institutional weakness to their needs, even though it is a process that apparently lacks visible actors and is more the result of the hidden laws of illegal markets and crime. But a fundamental relational context is generated, without which illicit and criminal activities would not have an expeditious path to operate. This institutional precariousness was not necessarily created on purpose because the daily reality takes care of it, either by

72   *Illegal Markets*

economic pressures that legitimize it or by the incidence of public actors that turn it into a fundamental piece of the vicious circle that facilitates the good functioning of crime and criminality, and not only informality that simply alludes to institutional controls. It is a reality that, despite the contradictions, develops in daily life, acquiring a high degree of legitimacy.

For example, since the formal economy does not supply the foreign exchange demands of drug trafficking and smuggling flows, it is easy to assume that a significant contribution of this money comes from the illegal markets, from the underground economy of corruption and laundering. This interrelationship is critical to the operation of smuggled imports. Drug trafficking and smuggling combine and gain space and legitimacy, as well as visibility; they maintain internal demand, the image of growth of the middle classes consuming cars and departments, and the highly stratified informal trade sector. Small business sectors – articulated and dominated by power groups, distributors of products of legal and illegal imports – drive the development of these relational spaces.

Our thesis regarding illegal markets refers to the fact that these structure the border system in a leading way, together with the legal markets and certainly above them. It is even possible to think that illegal markets are highly structured, due to their great capacity to stimulate networks of diversified economies with a high level of legitimacy. The broad layers of the population, who benefit from significant welfare, give the benefit of the doubt to the existence of these illegal and even criminal sectors. Low-income popular sectors access their economic benefits in processes of crisis of the formal economy, considering it as an opportunity, as a saving cushion in the narrowness of the formal sector. There are times when the opportunities of the informal economy are higher than in the formal economy, since they do not require graduating from university to have a job, which most of the time is necessary in the formal sector. A mining engineer can earn less than half as much as a cooperative worker or gold-panner with no university education.

Money laundering occurs naturally without the need to migrate to tax havens, given the multiple forms of porosity generated in these networks between the informal and the formal. When the illegal informal economy was a small sector, banks were used to launder money. Now, the illegal sector has grown enough for the gold smuggler or the drug trafficker, who handles medium capital, to invest in smuggling. This way, the sector circulates illegally, but with thousands of opportunities to launder itself on the road, or rather in the labyrinth of the illegal economy circuit. When the volume of this illegal economy is greater, it is also more difficult to discover the line of separation. A detailed example of the informal/formal networks can be seen in the study by the Social and Economic Policy Analysis Unit (UDAPE) (Ramírez 1996, 16).

Pontón (2015, 138) speaks on the dimensions of the illegal economy, based on data from international agencies, and develops some hypotheses to establish the value of illegal markets. Rather than the accuracy of his data separating and distinguishing some markets from others, it is worth the effort to consider the dimension of these markets in relation to the legal economy. When reading these data, it is necessary to avoid the temptation to establish lines of separation between them and with respect to the legal economy because reality shows that there is a deep relationship between both and the porosity of the legal economy, facilitated by informality. Economies with diluted or even invisible dividing lines between them characterize the conditions of implementation of policy mechanisms. It is difficult and unproductive to try to dimension them as if illegal markets could be differentiated in practice. The goal of illegal markets is to become legal activities. Table 4.1 may serve to illustrate the global dimensions and sectors that in practice establish flows that are difficult to measure among themselves.

In this chapter, special emphasis is made on the case of drug trafficking, as it is the sector that is, by far, the most predominant in computerized illegal markets and about which the most information is available. This structuring role is mainly due to its globalized nature, since it is based on demand that extends beyond borders. It is the most dynamic sector of the economy, due to its agility since it does not require certain legal and institutional conditions like the legal economy. Drug trafficking is elusive and knows how to occupy the empty spaces of the economy.

This chapter also emphasizes two important points of drug trafficking: first, because of its economic and social dimension that feeds many more sectors of the legal and illegal economy, it penetrates all sectors of the order; and, second, because it is organized by a very powerful sector that is the manufacture of cocaine hydrochloride, the central engine of the coca-cocaine complex that articulates the sectors that manage the largest part of the value and, consequently, the main connections of the other illegal sectors.

Table 4.1 Estimated Size of Illegal Markets

Illegal Market	Accumulated Value (in millions of dollars)
Drug trafficking	320,000
Counterfeit electronics	50,000
Human trafficking	31,600
Trafficking of wildlife and natural species	19,000
Oil trafficking	10,800
Fish trafficking	9,500
Wood trafficking	7,000
Trafficking of art and cultural propriety	6,300
Counterfeit cigarettes	2,600
Gold trafficking	2,300
Organ trafficking	1,200
Small arms trafficking	1,000
Gemstone trafficking	860
Counterfeit medicines	40
Total	651,000

Source: Own elaboration, based on UNODC 2015 reports.

74 *Illegal Markets*

Informal/Illegal Sectors

In South America today, it is very difficult not to feel the presence and the weight of the illegal economies that come from drug trafficking, arms, smuggling, or human trafficking. Within this complex, it is drug trafficking – particularly cocaine – that has the gravitational weight of the structure of illegal economies. All of this would not be possible without globalization, the development of new communication technologies (ICTS), and the reform of the State (privatization), insofar as they generate a new economy on a global scale, to which the illegal one is integrated (Carrión 2015, 10).

This chapter deals with the sectors that are included in the set of "illegal markets." It starts by defining that condition common to all of them, the absence of institutions and the obtaining of their profits precisely because they are illegal. Even though its performance penetrates other sectors of the legal economy, it is not only about the economy of the illegals but about the illegal economy and in criminal cases. The main features that define the size and dynamics of each sector are outlined, keeping in mind the gaps in information related to these types of economic activity. We posit that drug trafficking plays an important role in all of them. Some of the relationships and interactions between the four major sectors include the following:

The unregulated sector – also called informal – of the self-employed, the unemployed, the so-called urban informal sector that makes up a very high percentage of the economically active population (EAP). This sector participates in various stages of the cycle of illicit activities. Its informality mostly consists in not being registered as formal and a part of it is fundamental in smuggling and drug trafficking.

The drug trafficking sector, to which we have just referred, shows a series of stages in which a de facto army of economic actors provides services. It is a very broad and diverse sector that is present with its organizational capacity in all sectors of the economy, administration, and services.

The import and export smuggling sector involves dimensioning and locating countries and border points. A significant number of the informal sector are inserted in this one too.

Gold smuggling, within illegal mining, is a sector that has been little explored, but we will concentrate on an evaluation of its volume and performance in recent years.

Despite the fact that the State has a complete statistical system for **human trafficking and smuggling**, it is possible to establish some ideas about its size and form of operation.

Finally, **the sector of money laundering or legitimization of profits** can be considered the most important of all of them and about which we lack adequate information. We will reference partial information that allows us to suspect its importance.

The informal sector in employment. Household surveys show that those workers who are self-employed, family workers or apprentices who are not

Illegal Markets 75

paid, employers and workers, or employees in organizations with less than five employees make up almost two-thirds of the EAP. Data from 2011 shows that these people represented 61.7% of total employment. It is also important to note that these numbers do not vary over time.

This sector, not being registered as an employee or an employer, evades taxes and is not affiliated to any sector of social security; the companies, mostly family-run, evade labor regulations.

Among the small businessmen and workers who do not comply with public records required for the exercise of their economic activity, a very broad sector is established that plays a fundamental role in the distribution and commercialization of contraband and drug trafficking products. The importance of this sector for the porosity of the legal economy favorable to the drug trafficking and smuggling economy is not usually considered. Its importance relies on the global demand, especially that of the middle classes, another important aspect.

On the visibility of the predominant sector in the illegal markets, Figure 4.1 reflects the perception of the importance of each phase of production through the written press in Bolivia, where hydrochloride plays a predominant role.

If the news in the press represents the knowledge that the average population has, it can be said that it is abundant but decreasing, and that the issue of hydrochloride is positioned at the center of the issue of drug trafficking.

Drug Trafficking

Drug trafficking is the structuring axis of illegal markets; thus, more attention will be paid to it. Since its emergence, it has been a complex market, geographically, sectorial, economically, and politically speaking.

The start of drug trafficking occurs on a slope that unites three countries. The eastern slope of the Andes, which runs from Colombia to Bolivia, is the cocaine basin and the origin of the great global cocaine business, from which it establishes close links between Bolivia, Peru, and Colombia. Bolivia shares with Colombia and Peru its status as a coca producer. All three share the most favorable ecosystem for the coca leaf production, with altitudes ranging from 1,500 meters to the foothills of 200 meters. This part of the eastern slope of the Andes, where the coca basin is constituted, forms a regional corridor of international scope and is the beginning of the global flows of drug trafficking.

But it is not the similarities in the physical characteristics of the three countries that condition the role of the multinational coca basin, but rather the organization imposed on it by the global drug trafficking market. There are differences and complementarities between each of the three sub-basins since the beginning of the drug trafficking cycle. For the shifting logic of drug trafficking, this type of space is ideal: three countries with multiple complementarities, as is the case with other drugs.

The most important variations between the three countries lie in the way they are connected to the different phases of the cocaine-cocaine circuit: production of the leaf, processing of the base paste and hydrochloride, organization of

Table 4.2 Evolution of the Informal Sector 1999–2007 (as a percentage of total employment)

	1999	2000	2001	2002	2003	2004	2005	2006	2007	2011
Formal Employment	33.7	35.2	36	33.6	33.9	33.9	41.8	39.6	38.8	36.26
Informal Employment	63.2	60.7	58.8	62.5	61.4	61.4	54.4	56.2	55.6	61.72
Domestic Employment	3.1	4.1	5.2	3.9	4.7	4.7	3.8	4.2	5.6	2.02
Total	100	100	100	100	100	100	100	100	100	100

Source: Own elaboration, based on data from INE (2007).

Table 4.3 Urban Informal Sector Contribution of the Urban Informal Sector (SIU) to the GDP of Each Sector of Economic Activity in the Urban Area (in percentage)

Year	2005
Manufacturing	15.5
Construction	20.3
Trade	22.7
Transport and Storage	36.4
General Services	18.8
Restaurants and Lodging	22.6
Personal Services	15.5

Source: Own elaboration, based on data from Martínez Cué F. et al. (2009).

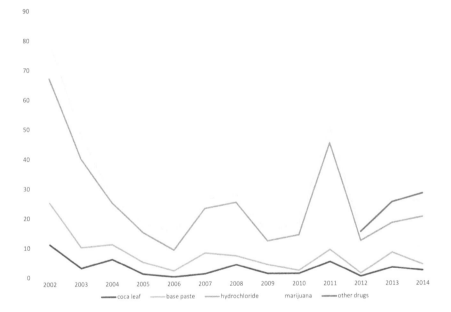

Figure 4.1 Press Occurrences of Drug-Related Seizures. Figure by author with data from the newspaper library.

production, storage, and transport, as well as control of the destination and money laundering. This economic circuit is cartelized; Colombia occupies a structuring role in comparison to Peru or Bolivia, which function relatively subordinated to the role of producers of the base activities.

These differences are important for understanding the subsystem that begins in this basin. The first difference is noticeable in the initial phase of drug trafficking with the type of leaf produced. Whether for cocaine production or for chewing, in Peru and Bolivia there are both, and it is in Bolivia that the second

78 *Illegal Markets*

Map 4.1 Cocalera Basin: Colombia-Peru-Bolivia. Map by Mallette J. et al. (2016).

difference stands out most. There are specific areas for the cultivation of both and a law that estimates the amount allowed for personal use, both for chewing and for other rituals. Other differences lie in the participation of global production, eradication policies, forms of production, technologies and forms of social organization, and political importance of producers at their respective national levels.

Illegal Markets 79

These are three basins, three countries, and national systems (see Map 4.1). Considering the size of the production area, the three countries have participated with varying scales. Peru became the second largest producer in the last 20 years, with Colombia disputing the place at some times, while Bolivia remained the third largest. But differences in the forms of production may be important in distinguishing the differentiated role of these primary actors in the circuit. In Colombia, production takes place on large- and medium-sized land areas, in some cases reaching crops of more than ten hectares, while in Peru and Bolivia, it is predominantly in the hands of small producers. Within this category, the difference in Bolivia is the way in which production permits are granted and the consequences of this on development and crop substitution programs and on State policies in this regard.

At the southern end of the coca-growing basin – in the Yungas of La Paz and in the department of Cochabamba – Bolivian coca growers are highly organized in unions, central unions, and federations with rules that control their status as producers. This organization, although not homogeneous in all the Bolivian territory, is very important because it has constituted a social sector with a high capacity for organization and demand in the face of state policies and cooperation in the drug trafficking matters. The producers of the Chapare, department of Cochabamba, are organized based on the "legal" concession of a *cato* of land (1/6 of a hectare = 1,600 square meters) per member, generally family; although, in some places, it has been opened to several members of the family.[1] Approximately, two-thirds of the total coca cultivation originates from the eastern slopes of the Yungas of La Paz, which are steeper and higher than in the Chapare; its main purpose is chewing. Although they are also organized into trade unions, these are not as structured or related to political life as the former.

The three areas of the great eastern slope of the Andes are linked by national inter-basin flows and intra-basin flows. Among neighboring zones, cases such as the Peru–Bolivia flows are worth mentioning. Flows between Bolivia and Colombia have occurred during the Medellín cartel phase, when large shipments left for Colombia. In the current phase, Colombia's role lies in the transfer of technology and organization of major cartels. In the last 20 years, the flows between Peru and Bolivia have stood out, which, depending on changes in cocaine routes, smuggling, and, particularly, the flow of gold facilitate large shipments from Bolivia to Brazil, Paraguay, Argentina, and Chile to the Pacific and Europe. Bolivia has become a country of transit and stockpiling; Peru contributes with part of the supplies to complete the necessary quotas, stockpiling of base material for crystallization and flows of people at critical moments of the Revolutionary Armed Forces of Colombia (FARC) and the Shining Path (Sendero Luminoso), for example. Colombia provides Bolivia's cocaine with the highest-quality brand in the international market. In Bolivia, there are two large areas in the basin that connect Peru from the Wilcabamba and Amboró corridors in Bolivia. The area of coca destined for chewing or traditional use is mainly produced on the higher slopes and the area destined mainly for cocaine production on the plains near the foothills. In Peru, there is a similar division as in Bolivia, the Valle de los Ríos

80 *Illegal Markets*

Apurímac, Ene y Mantaro (Valley of the Apurímac, Ene, and Mantaro rivers) (VRAEM) and the Valle de la Convención y Lares.

It highlights how from this first territorial association, Bolivia's links to the system of global flows and the functions of national borders are structured. The evolution of drug trafficking in Latin America is changing the position of the Andean countries in the geopolitics of drugs. In turn, the changing characteristics of the global drug market are a key factor in explaining some new trends in the region.

Among the conditions of the global market is the phenomenon of emerging drug markets, such as Brazil – and, to a lesser extent, Argentina and Chile in the regional setting – and many countries in Europe, West Africa, and Oceania. This means greater demand, opportunities, and facilities for cocaine production and export from the Andean countries. On the other hand, technological innovations, both in coca cultivation (more crops per hectare) and in processing and refining (higher yields of crystallization), generate increases in productivity and, therefore, greater volumes of cocaine for its entry into the markets, in addition to other innovations in the modalities of transportation, packaging, marketing, inputs, and precursors.

The increasing trafficking of cocaine base to Bolivia from Peru[2] for refining in disjointed laboratories in different Bolivian regions would be a phenomenon that responds, at least in part, to competitive market conditions and, more specifically, to disparities in production costs between the two countries. Thus, unofficial data refer to a lower cost of base paste production in Peru, estimated at around $800 per kilogram, compared to the $1,000 and $1,200 in Bolivia.[3]

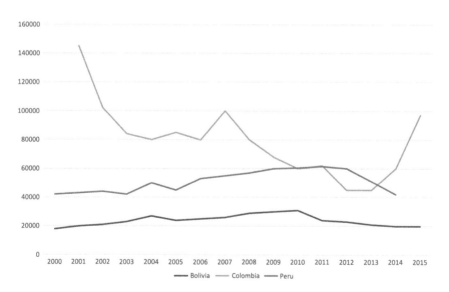

Figure 4.2 Evolution of the Area under Coca Cultivation in Bolivia, Colombia, and Peru Total Hectares of Coca Cultivation. Source: Own elaboration, based on UNODC 2015 reports.

Illegal Markets 81

However, it is essential to highlight that the three countries, in particular Peru and Bolivia, are inserted into the subsystem as suppliers of raw materials and at different levels of the processing. The other phases of the coca-cocaine circuit are no longer totally under their control, and this is where most of the profit from the business is produced.

Complementarity among the basins? Although the climatic conditions are not too different, as all three are on the same eastern slope of the Andes, it is the social and political conditions that mark the differences and, certainly, the differentiated roles among the three countries.

Peru and Bolivia have many similarities in how coca leaf plantations expand. Colombia, however, shows periods of opposite behavior. Between 2000 and 2004, there was a slight increase in coca cultivation in Peru and Bolivia, and an extraordinary decrease in Colombia. At the beginning of this period, Colombia produced much more than the other countries combined, but, by 2006, it was approaching the same level of production. Colombia's production again was increasing as Peru and Bolivia continued their expansion until 2013. Colombia shows an inexplicable rise for one year (2007), with more than 20,000 additional hectares moving from one management to another (2006–2007). A sharp fall can be understood if cultivation is attacked with aerial spraying or a giant anti-narcotics campaign, but from one year to the next, 20,000 additional hectares cannot inexplicably appear. This situation suggests that there was coca that was not measured or that was hidden. The appearance is not easy to explain, since the maturation of coca for harvest requires more than a year for a good yield. This aspect is related to the reported differences in yields between Colombia and the other two countries, where the plantations are mature and do not recover randomly as they did in Colombia. In Peru and Bolivia, plantations continued to increase their production between 2006 and 2010. In 2010, both countries experienced slight decreases in production which continued until the present, but still maintaining the average production level of the period. On the other hand, in Colombia, the behavior remains erratic, falling below Peru's but turning up between 2013 and the present, with its production approaching 100,000 hectares.

This behavior cannot be explained as something preplanned. In the case of Colombia, one could think that the compensation was made through the exchange of base paste. In this way, the regional supply of the product, hydrochloride, is maintained. In addition, the higher yield in Peru and Bolivia, in terms of both shrub quality, more mature plants, and in the yield of leaf alkaloids, compensates quite well for the increase in global supply/demand.

For this to happen, a controlling hand is required, which in such a complex global system cannot be conceived as a single control, but a cartel system that "orders" the global market. Part of this complexity comes from the fact that three countries have the initial role of suppliers of the most basic materials, which are the leaf and the base paste.

The comparative microeconomics of Bolivia, Colombia, and Peru allows us to draw some lines that suggest the complementary role of the three countries

82 *Illegal Markets*

Figure 4.3 Production: Hectare/Price. Source: Campero (2014, 597).

with respect to the coca leaf, which introduces us to think about Bolivia's role in the circuit system. Focusing on coca leaf production, Bolivian expert José Carlos Campero (2014) compares the microeconomic characteristics of the coca leaf market in Bolivia, Peru, and Colombia and the behavior of coca leaf production values in the period 1986–2013.

Campero's study distinguishes three periods in Bolivia: (1) From 1986 to 1997, when there was a reduction in both the agricultural border (−27%) and the volumes of coca leaf produced (−24%) and a correlative increase in the price of the leaf (139%). (2) From 1998 to 2005, marked by the "zero coca" target in the Chapare in 2002, which caused a contraction of supply and demand of more than 60% between 1997 and 2000; in view of the shock of the reduction of coca supply, prices reacted upward as a speculative effect and remained until 2005, above $5 per kilogram. (3) From 2006 onward, there was an increase in the area cultivated and the volume of coca production; although it did not recover the levels of the past decades, it was constant until 2011, and then, it decreased again. At this stage, the price trend is upward, regardless of the area or volume of production, and there is a more oligopolistic type of behavior.

In terms of the value of coca leaf production, there was an increase of more than 250% in the period analyzed, equivalent to more than $5.5 billion between 1986 and 2013. In 2012, the value of coca production represented 1.2% of GDP and 13% of agricultural GDP.

Campero's thesis considers that prohibitionist policies create artificial conditions for legal markets and, on the contrary, sufficient incentives for the development of illegal markets. For example, in Peru, a coca market relatively controlled by the state-owned Empresa Nacional de Coca (National Coca Enterprise) (ENACO S.A.),[4] operates under a monopsonic regulatory framework, that is, as the sole buyer of legal coca leaf production, defining a price to the primary producer. This would have caused the narcos to increase the price a little above the price offered by ENACO, this being an incentive for illegal surplus coca production. In Colombia, on the other hand, the illegality of coca production added to the limited state control of the coca-growing areas, with a strong presence of drug traffickers and armed gangs, would generate the optimal conditions for these organizations to act as monopsony or oligopsony directly connected to the coca producers, so that they control not only their production but also the price of it.

Following Campero's reasoning, Bolivia would be a different case, since in this country the coca market behaves differently, as there is upward pressure on the price, determined by an oligopoly type of supply. This happens because almost all coca producers are members of very vertical union structures, which impose entry barriers to new producers. Regardless of the market in which the coca leaf is sold, the price is affected by the oligopolistic decisions of the unions.

Campero points out that, although there are several coca growers' organizations, they do not compete with each other, generating downward effects on the price of coca leaf, although they do not openly collude to determine prices as if they were a cartel. Each organization is aware of what the others are doing and makes rational decisions so as not to affect the whole, determining high prices that are very similar to each other. UNODC reports would corroborate that coca leaf prices in legal or illegal markets behave similarly. Thus, the effect of this structure, combined with the scale of production versus demand, would determine a final price substantially higher than the prices in the Peruvian and Colombian markets (Campero 2014, 604).

In any case, Campero warns that the capacity for organization and control over the production process, demonstrated by the coca trade union structure – and which in recent years has allowed for a 25% reduction in the agricultural border of coca crops – has not been transferred in a similar way to the link to the commercialization of coca leaf, where controls are rather weak, lax, or nonexistent, and, therefore, commercialization takes place as a highly deregulated process. This is also the reason for the high rates of evasion in the sale of coca leaves in the legal markets, reported in the annual coca crop monitoring reports made by the Bolivian government and the United Nations, and which, according to the author's own estimate, in the last ten years have always been above 50% of the amount registered as potential production. Disaggregated data show that, in the Yungas of La Paz, the evasion is around 30%, while in the Tropic of Cochabamba, it reaches more than 90% (Campero 2014, 608).

Campero's conclusion is that prohibitionist policies tend to generate incentives for the creation of illegal markets because "it implies monitoring, and monitoring generates additional costs to those in a situation without prohibition. Otherwise, the costs are normally greater than those in regulatory environments" (Campero 2014, 601). These incentives, added to the weak controls in the commercialization of coca leaf, would determine the practical impossibility of avoiding the vicious circle of surplus production-diversion of illegal coca-narcotics.

84 *Illegal Markets*

Bolivian legislation prohibits and sanctions the transformation of coca leaves into narcotic substances and the commercialization of these substances. In effect, Law 1008 on the Regime of Coca and Controlled Substances of July 19, 1988, defines as illicit

> all those uses destined for the manufacture of cocaine base, sulphate and hydrochloride and others that extract the alkaloid from the manufacture of some type of controlled substance, as well as the actions of smuggling and trafficking of coca, contrary to the provisions established in the present law.
>
> (Campero 2014)

Regarding cartels and emissaries, many Bolivian and foreign observers agree that drug trafficking in Bolivia has developed as a criminal activity linked to international markets and generally under the control of foreign criminal organizations.

According to the Bolivian Criminal Code, a criminal organization is an "association of three or four persons organized on a permanent basis, under rules of discipline or control, for the commission of illegal acts," including the illicit manufacture or trafficking of controlled substances. According to this definition, many persons engaged in this type of illegal activity fall into the legal category of criminal organization, and their conduct would be classified as both illicit and criminal. However, the opinion of the specialists is that the productive and commercial structure in Bolivia has edges of great diversity, complexity, flexibility, and opacity.

José Carlos Campero maintains that the international cartels have extended their radius of action to Bolivia:

> These organizations have extended their networks to legal sectors of the economy, taking advantage of the low presence and state control in the territory. They operate on a global scale with extensive transnational connections and have the capacity to challenge national and international sovereignty and authority.
>
> (Campero 2012, 18)

This author adds that the presence of Colombian criminal organizations (the North Valley Cartel and the FARC) and Brazilian (the Primeiro Comando da Capital and the Comando Vermelho [Red Command]), Mexican (the Zetas and the Sinaloa Cartel), Peruvian (Shining Path and the Túpac Amaru Revolutionary Movement), and Russian mafia has been evident in the country. It also notes that, in the shadow of these large criminal organizations, other smaller ones have been formed in Bolivia, but they have not yet consolidated themselves as hierarchical structures integrated into the global market. Their peculiarity would rather be to operate as local structures for the production and commercialization of drugs, associated and articulated with the transnational cartels.[5]

Illegal Markets 85

In police jargon, they speak of "illicit drug trafficking organizations (OTID),"[6] a generic term that alludes to criminal gangs with branches in Bolivia and made up of foreigners of different nationalities, many of them with the function of "emissaries," "technicians" in the laboratories, or simply hit men.[7] Other organizations specialized in crime,[8] as well as reports from foreign governments, also refer to the presence of international organized crime in Bolivian territory.[9]

From the Colombian Connection to a Network of Multiple Connections

The evidence of the presence of cartels on Bolivian territory is overwhelming, although the discussion about their true character and scope remains an open issue. However, there are certain issues that are beyond doubt: (i) Bolivia is a theater of operations for foreign cartels, either directly or through "emissaries," "intermediaries," "financiers," or other figures; (ii) these criminal gangs are connected to Bolivian drug traffickers (family clans or other mafia groups) through diverse and flexible forms of linkage and association. The national groups operate mainly as suppliers of base or refined cocaine, while the foreign cartels are the main vehicle for the internationalization of Bolivian production, but within a very broad and very dynamic network of relationships.

If in the past it was generally accepted that large drug traffickers retained control of a large part of the production process (coca collection, maceration, supply of precursors, preparation of base paste) and that they themselves negotiated the sale of cocaine to the Colombian cartels, today, this type of work would take place within a conglomerate (networks) of multiple actors (family clans, coca growers, peasants) and in very diverse areas (rural and urban), including refining work in smaller, mobile laboratories. This would be a more atomized and socially protected structure, and, therefore, more difficult to identify, repress, and eradicate.

To better understand the new reality of Bolivian drug trafficking, it must be remembered that between the 1970s and 1980s, the chief characteristic of drug trafficking in Bolivia was its connection with the Colombian cartels, first with Pablo Escobar's Medellín cartel, when practically 90% of Bolivian base paste, processed on the haciendas of the department of Beni, was sold to the Colombians to be converted into cocaine and then shipped to the United States.

The emblematic figure of the Bolivian narcos was then Roberto Suárez, known in Bolivia as the "Cocaine King"[10] and a direct associate of Pablo Escobar until his death and the dismantling of the Medellín Cartel.[11] That was also the end of the powerful Bolivian–Colombian connection, to be replaced by the new Colombian–Mexican connection, in which the Mexican cartels have control of the routes and of the North American market. The Bolivian–Colombian connection was also replaced by more diverse connections that the Bolivian narcos have been establishing with Brazilian, Colombian, Mexican, and other countries' criminal groups. These are the phenomena that have become more visible since the beginning of the twenty-first century and form part of the new regional geopolitics of drugs within the emerging global border system.

86   *Illegal Markets*

Table 4.4 The Global Geography of Cartels Latin American Presence in International and Global Organizations (2009–2014)

	Latin American International Organizations	Global Organizations	Illegal Groups		Total	Total News about Cartelization
		Latin American	Foreign			
Argentina	9	7	3	2	14	28
Bolivia	12	6	5	3	20	61
Colombia	40	16	6	5	51	267
Ecuador	15	10	5	3	23	273
Guatemala	32	14	0	0	32	248
Mexico	11	11	5	1	17	1,770
Perú	14	7	2	1	17	73

Source: Carrión and Alagna (2016, 10).

From the cartels to the global crime network, from the level of each national subsystem, a structure of relations between actors and functions that constitute the system of crime and illegality emerges and serves as the basis for the functioning of the global system. The study of Bolivia shows this type of linkage of the country with the global system, as well as the different forms of interrelation with other sectors, including, obviously, the legal ones, with the higher purpose of legalizing illegal money. The porosity of politics and the economy, the informality of justice and the economy, and the existence of a huge army of sectors that are auxiliary to crime are some of the conditions by which countries like Bolivia contribute to the global system within the framework of the cartelization of illegal markets.

In this context of drug trafficking and its new framework of international relations, Bolivia has a variety of connections with international criminal gangs, aimed at covering the global demand for drugs, including of course the demands of neighboring markets. Carrión and Alagna (2016, 4) introduce the changes in the process of internationalization of drug trafficking that have occurred in recent decades and summarizes them in the following form:

1. Colombian cartels until 2000. Process control.
   1.1.   Drug entry from Peru by air and sea through Florida.
   1.2.   Central Command: the Medellín cartel.
2. Mexican cartels until 2008. Routes control.
   2.1.   Peru, Colombia, and Mexico entry through land routes in the border with the United States.
   2.2.   Sinaloa, Golfo/Zetas cartels.
3. Cartels of globalization of consumption until 2015.
   3.1.   Global border system.
   3.2.   Plural Command: Global network.
4. Cartels of globalization of production until 2015.
   4.1.   Chemical

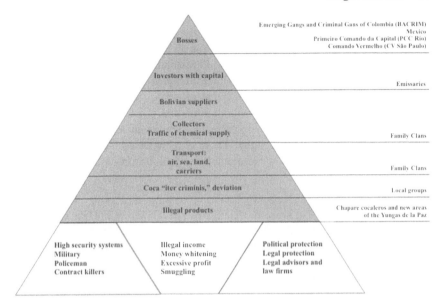

Figure 4.4 Cartelization and Articulation of Roles in Drug Trafficking. Source: Author's elaboration based on interviews.

The internal network of relationships developed with drug trafficking becomes more complex over time, especially as its volume increases, since they require more logistics at all levels and develop greater capacity to incorporate the contribution of more actors. In short, drug trafficking increasingly involves different sectors and national systems.

Outside the sphere of production, stockpiling, and transport, a very important range of auxiliary tasks necessary to the circuit are carried out, such as the different forms of protection: armed and legal/institutional and that of laundering (see Figure 4.4).

Money and asset laundering is articulated with the other three spaces: production, legal protection, and security. The sectors involved in laundering are very diversified, among which illicit profits, speculation and contraband, construction, and banking stand out.

This scenario shows a structure of actors that interact, assemble, and mobilize a grid of medium and small-volume activities. This scheme is very efficient in generating pores of infiltration of the illegal economy into the formal economy and shows how a system of criminal informality is constituted, which characterizes Bolivia's role in facilitating the efficient operation of crime in the border system, and which does not require major confrontations and violent conflicts in the dispute for resources and profits. In this case, there is no need to control territories; there is an internal control of "illegality."

On the new drug circuits, according to Jeremy McDermott, it is the phenomenon known as the "cockroach effect." As he explains:

88 *Illegal Markets*

> With the evolution of Latin American transnational organized crime, there have been events that now affect Bolivia directly. Although Colombians have been interested in Bolivia for four decades, the nature of this interest has changed in the last ten years. In Bolivia, using Peruvian (paste) base, Colombians can produce a kilo of high-quality cocaine for less than $2,000. That same kilo in São Paulo or Buenos Aires is worth up to $8,000. Thus, Colombians can earn more than $5,000 per kilo, but with minimal risk of interdiction and almost no risk of extradition; simply by moving drug shipments across the border with Bolivia into Brazil or Argentina. These two countries also act as transshipment points for the most lucrative markets of all: Europe and Asia.
>
> (McDermott 2014a, 7)

McDermott also says that since the Mexicans are taking the biggest slice of the U.S. market, Colombians are giving Bolivia more importance as an exit point for drugs to their neighbors and even to final destinations in Europe and Asia (2014a, 7). In the 1980s, the Colombian cartels established connections with Bolivian drug traffickers to serve as suppliers of base paste, so that the cartels would take over the crystallization and subsequent shipment to the United States. McDermott says:

> The so-called cockroach effect has also had a significant impact on Bolivia. When the lights are turned on in a room, the cockroaches run into the dark corners. Organized crime acts in much the same way. The lights are on in Colombia and the drug barons, once identified, have a short lifespan there, so they move abroad. Bolivia has not yet been able to find its electric switch.
>
> (2014a, 8)

An example of how flexible and dynamic the circuits of illicit trafficking have become is the information that shows the multiplication of points of shipment of drugs from Peru to Bolivia and the increasingly novel forms of transport. According to reports from the Fuerza Especial de Lucha contra el Narcotráfico (Special Force for the Fight Against Drug Trafficking) (FELCN), there are three areas considered "sensitive points" from which drugs are brought from Peru to Bolivia: (i) Alto Huallaga, department of San Martín; (ii) Puno; and (iii) the Valley of the Apurímac, Ene, and Mantaro rivers (VRAEM). The latter area would be one of the main suppliers of base paste, which is then refined in northern areas of Santa Cruz, Beni, and the North of the department of La Paz. Other reports attributed to the Dirección Antidrogas de Perú (Anti-Drugs Directorate of Peru) (Dirandro) refer to the use of *cargachos* (backpackers), who carry the drugs on foot for days to two new points of shipment (Alto Pichas and Pal-Cazú), where there are clandestine runways used by Bolivian airplanes, as a new procedure for introducing the base paste to Bolivia and then to Brazil.[12]

The same phenomenon of proliferation of points of shipment and transfer of drugs is repeated in the extensive Bolivian–Brazilian border, and the same in the other borders of Bolivia with Chile, Paraguay, and Argentina.

The Coca Leaf and Drug Trafficking: Trends

If this is the operating scheme, although it is much more agile and flexible, it is worth asking about the future role of the Bolivian subsystem in the larger framework of the cocaine market. Keeping the above-mentioned framework as a fixed variable, which is not necessarily the case, the variable that should be analyzed is the number of drugs produced, since apparently Bolivia's role is that of a producer in the first phase of drug trafficking. In this respect, the important variable and sine qua non is the production of coca leaf.

Reliable data exist, with the reservations of the case, since it is difficult to measure this product, which is produced in small proportions, dispersed, and mimicked with other crops. But the UNODC measurements can be perfectly reliable and serve our purpose, which does not lie in the extreme accuracy of the leaf production, but in terms of its proportions, to visualize the future of the subsystem from this corner of the illegal markets.

It should be taken into account that there will be more cocaine if:

- there is more coca leaf.
- productivity increases. The same hectares can produce more coca leaf, depending on the type of bush, its age, and the density of the crops.
- the procedure of extraction of the cocaine improves.
- a large quantity of coca leaves escapes from the legal market.
- the mechanisms for confiscating illegal coca leaf are not efficient.
- there is less confiscation of cocaine, in any of its forms.
- a lot of coca leaf comes in from Peru.
- there is a lot of coca paste coming in from Peru and in different states of processing.

But not everything that defines the role of the Bolivian border subsystem depends on the behavior of the above factors, which define internal productive capacity. It has been mentioned that Bolivia is a transit country and that a major part of the cocaine leaving Bolivia has entered from Peru. This is without considering that in certain areas of North La Paz, cocaine entering Bolivia is passing through to Brazil, without acknowledging Bolivia's role in the business, and above all the fact that there is a very important flow of coca leaf toward northern Argentina.

The role of demand is very important and defines many situations. We have an image, which cannot be verified due to the lack of sufficient and reliable information on the demand for cocaine, and many data point to the growth of drug trafficking activities in Bolivia. The incidence of demand operates as an important motor in production, which in turn generates the economic stimuli of a consumer market that has not ceased to grow in the world and that is acquiring more and more globalized characteristics, although it is decreasing in Europe and the United States.

Production/crop monitoring. Under the current legal regime, coca cultivation is an agricultural-cultural activity traditionally oriented toward licit, medicinal, and ritual consumption by Andean people. It is added that the licit consumption

90 *Illegal Markets*

and use of coca is understood as the social and cultural practices of the population such as *acullico* or chewing, medicinal uses, and ritual uses.[13] Unlike in Colombia, coca cultivation is licit, although always subject to various forms of control. Three coca production zones are defined and delimited in the national territory: (i) a zone of traditional production, in the department of La Paz; (ii) a zone of surplus production in transition, in the Tropic of Cochabamba (Chapare), subject to reduction and substitution plans; and (iii) an area of illicit production and where coca cultivation is prohibited, including protected areas.

The Executive Body has the power to determine periodically the amount of coca needed to cover the demand for legal consumption, establishing a maximum production equivalent to an area of 12,000 hectares of coca cultivation. In compliance with this provision, the Bolivian government implements annual plans for reduction, substitution, and development, starting with 5,000 hectares per year until the goal of 8,000 hectares per year is reached.

The processes of circulation and commercialization of coca leaf are also strictly regulated. In fact, the operation of two large urban markets has been regulated (the market in the Villa Fátima neighborhood in the city of La Paz and the market in the town of Sacaba in Cochabamba), which are the only ones authorized for the legal trade of coca leaf, and other control and monitoring measures have also been established for transport; all of them aimed at preventing and avoiding the diversion of coca to the illegal drug trafficking market.

Coca leaf production has started to decrease very slowly but steadily in recent years in the country, as mentioned in the UNODC[14] and Bolivian government monitoring reports. The monitoring of the 2014–2015 administration shows the same trend as the previous one: the country reduced 200 hectares of surplus coca, a figure that represents 1% compared to the previous period, according to the monitoring study. According to the 2015 report, 20,200 hectares of cultivation were identified, while in 2014 the area cultivated was on the order of 20,400 hectares. This figure was estimated to be 11% less than in 2013, when 23,000 hectares were estimated. "This confirms, for the fourth consecutive year, a net reduction in the area under coca cultivation and is considered the lowest amount recorded since UNODC started monitoring coca cultivation in the country, in collaboration with the Government of Bolivia"[15] (UNODC 2015). Obviously, there are variations from one area to another, with significant increases being observed in protected areas and on the outskirts of traditional areas (see Table 4.5).

Table 4.5 Coca Cultivation in Bolivia, 2000–2015 (per hectare)

2000	2001	2002	2003	2004	2005	2006	2007
14,600	19,900	21,600	23,600	27,700	25,400	27,500	28,900
2008	2009	2010	2011	2012	2013	2014	2015
30,500	30,900	31,000	27,200	25,300	23,000	20,400	20,200

Source: UNODC (2015, 7).

Table 4.6 Quantification of Coca Cultivation by Region, 2004–2014 (hectares)

Region	2004	2005	2006	2007	2008	2009	2010	2011	2012	2013	2014	2015	Change 2013–2014 (%)	Total 2014 (%)
Yungas	17,300	18,100	18,900	19,800	20,700	20,900	20,500	18,200	16,900	15,700	14,200	14,000	−10	70
Cochabamba	10,100	7,000	8,300	8.800	9,500	9,700	10,100	8,600	8,100	7,100	6,100	6,000	−14	30
North of La Paz	300	300	300	300	300	300	400	370	320	230	130	150	−43	1
Total	27,700	25,400	27.500	28,900	30,500	30,900	31,000	27,200	25,300	23,000	20,400	20,200	−11	100

Source: UNODC (2015, 10).

92 *Illegal Markets*

Table 4.7 Area of Coca Cultivation within Each Protected Area

Protected Area	2014 (ha)	2015 (ha)	Change 2014–2015
Isiboro Sécure	15	12	−20 %
Carrasco	127	104	−18 %
Cotapata	28	31	11 %
Amboró	17	27	58 %
Apolobamba	15	18	20 %
Madidi	13	12	−8 %

Source: UNODC (2015, 33).

Areas of coca cultivation in Polígono 7 and Línea Roja within Isiboro Sécure and Carrasco National Parks are not included.

The proportions in the distribution of crop areas by zones do not vary too much over time.

> In 2015, 69% of the area under coca cultivation was in the Yungas of La Paz, 30% in the Cochabamba Tropics and 1% in the northern provinces of La Paz. Compared to 2014, the first two regions showed a slight decrease of 200 and 100 hectares respectively, while in the northern provinces of La Paz an increase of 20 hectares of coca cultivation was observed compared to 2014.
>
> (UNODC 2015)

It is important to mention that approximately 94% of the leaf produced in the Tropic of Cochabamba is destined to cocaine manufacture. The Chapare produces a leaf with a higher alkaloid content, and the shrubs are higher yielding. This is a double comparative advantage in favor of drug trafficking. The coca fields in the protected areas are not included. This does not change this reasoning, although it is raising a lot of concern among organizations interested in the conservation of natural heritage. In 6 of the 22 protected areas defined by Bolivia, coca cultivation and possibly cocaine processing activities exist. "In the country's protected areas, where coca cultivation is not permitted, 204 hectares were quantified in 2015" (UNODC 2015). The current Political Constitution of the Plurinational State of Bolivia recognizes protected areas as a common good and natural and cultural heritage of the country; they fulfill environmental, cultural, social, and economic functions for sustainable development (see Table 4.7).

In this regard, Law 1178 on the Organization of the Executive Branch of September 16, 1997, approved the creation of the National Protected Areas Service (SERNAP), as a decentralized agency, which reports directly to the Ministry of the Environment and Water. Within this framework, 22 protected areas (PAs) have been defined in Bolivia, with a surface area of 170,700 square kilometers, representing approximately 16% of the national territory. The monitoring of coca cultivation in the process of quantification has identified six protected areas affected by coca cultivation. The National Institute of Agrarian Reform (INRA), through the process of remediation, has delimited Polígono 7 and the Línea Roja inside Isiboro Sécure and Carrasco National Parks, respectively, in order to avoid new settlements in these areas. Consequently, the area of coca cultivation within the cleared areas is not considered in these protected areas.

Regarding **crop yields**, important changes must be noted, which are reflected in prices, affected by the supply of the raw material. As an important crop in the peasant economy of the coca-growing areas, the increase in leaf production and the drop in prices is a permanent and sometimes dramatically oscillating game. The tendency in recent years has been for prices to rise.

The determinants of yield are many, such as the age of the plant, the age of the cultivation area, with greater or lesser erosion of the fertility of the type of land that defines the possibility of higher density, use of fertilizers and pesticides, among many others. This type of study is not being done, and satellite images only give approximations on images of homogeneous crops.

The monitoring study has contributed to this respect; after upper- and lower-limit studies, it was concluded that potential coca production ranges from 28 metric tons to 35 metric tons per hectare. The Cochabamba Tropics' cultivation area is thought to be about one-third less than that of La Paz, so it is closer to 18.6 metric tons (LP) than to 14.4 metric tons (Cbba). In total, it is estimated to be between 37,800 and 33,100 metric tons. What is interesting to note is that approximately 94% of coca for drug trafficking comes from the tropics.

The Commercialization and Prices of Coca Leaf

When we talk about commercialization, we are talking about the coca markets. The control of the markets has always been a reason for conflict and the consolidation of power structures within them. The markets of La Paz and Cochabamba are particularly strong, from where retail distribution is spilled throughout the country. Coca leaf is subject to legal provisions for its circulation in the country.[16] The exercise of these regulations has been at various times in trade union life a very important space for building power through the control of commercialization and in particular the evasion of the controls of legal markets.

According to information reported by DIGCOIN, the quantity of coca leaf traded on the Villa Fátima market increased from 18,459 metric tons in 2014 to 19,615 metric tons in 2015, an increase of 6%; the same phenomenon was observed on the Sacaba market, where the quantity of coca leaf traded increased from 1,338 metric tons in 2014 to 1,586 metric tons in 2015, an increase of 19%. Out of a total of 21,201 metric tons of coca leaves, 93% was traded at the Villa Fátima market in La Paz department, and the remaining 7% was traded at the Sacaba market in Cochabamba department (UNODC 2016).

These data show important aspects such as the fact that coca from the Chapare eludes commercialization in established markets, and that the illegal trade is as important a step in the functioning of drug trafficking as production. It is not the

Table 4.8 Estimation of the Potential Production of Sun-Dried Coca Leaf in the Monitored Regions (metric tons)

Monitored area	Upper Limit (UNODC)*		Lower Limit (EPMHCB)*		Estimated Potential Production*		Change 2013–2014
	2013	2014	2013	2014	2013	2014	
Yungas of La Paz	20,500	18,600	17,900	16,200	20,500	18,600	−9%
Cochabamba Tropics	19,600	16,900	14,500	12,500	17,000	14,400	−15%
North of La Paz	290	159	240	130	260	140	−46%
Rounded Total	40,400	35,700	32,600	28,800	37,800	33,100	−12%

Source: UNODC (2015, 37).

* The potential production of coca leaf was calculated based on the exact area data and then rounded to the nearest hundred.

Table 4.9 Average Prices of Coca Leaf 2013–2015

Market	2013		2014		2015		Exchange 2013–2014
	Bs./kg	USD/kg	Bs./kg	USD/kg	Bs./kg	USD/kg	
Average price at the market of Sacaba (Cochabamba)	54	7.8	67	9.6	61	8.8	13%
Average price in the market of Villa Fátima (La Paz)	54	7.8	48	6.9	57	8.3	5%
Weighted average national price according to quantity sold	54	7.8	65	9.4	58	8.3	6%

Source: UNODC (2015, 40).

Exchange rate according to the Central Bank of Bolivia (BCB): 6.96 Bs/USD. Date: 06/23/2015.

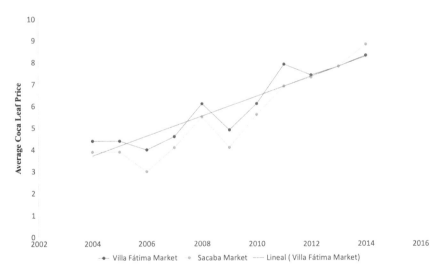

Figure 4.5 Evolution of Nominal Coca Prices 2004–2014. Source of statistics: UNODC 2015, 42.

producers who benefit from the best profits from coca cultivation, it is those with the control of both legal and clandestine trade. In many cases, the leaf reaches the confines of distant departments like Potosí and even northern Argentina.

At this stage of the process, due to the lack of information, it is no longer possible to compare production with commercialization, as we find that the

96 *Illegal Markets*

commercialization record is higher than the production estimates, which may be due to the lack of updated yield calculations.

> The largest commercial movement of coca leaf in the authorized markets of the country was generated by retailers who represented 62%, a lower percentage compared to last year (69%), followed by the retail producers (37%), which represented a higher percentage compared to last year (31%) and the other forms of commercialization of coca leaf, barter and industrialization have remained at 0.6 and 0.1%, respectively, the same percentage as last year.
>
> (UNODC 2016)

It would therefore appear that yields are higher and that estimates should be more accurate. Closely related to performance and marketing behavior is price behavior, either as a result or as a trigger. In 2014, the average nominal price of coca leaf traded on the authorized markets of Villa Fátima and Sacaba amounted to 8.3 $/kg and 8.8 $/kg, respectively, representing an increase of 6% in both cases. The weighted average nominal price of one kilogram of coca on both markets, for the year, was $8.3 (58 bolivianos), which is 6% more than in 2013 (UNODC 2016).

The prices of the leaf clearly show an increase in drug trafficking; leaves are being used for the manufacture of base paste, since there is no trend toward increased personal and domestic consumption, or other uses. Rather, everything seems to indicate that chewing is decreasing over time. In some cases, it has even been necessary to stop the price increase by importing base paste from Peru. There are not many indications that coca leaf is reaching Bolivia from Peru.

It was probably the coca leaf that managed to maintain its value, overcoming inflation. This has certainly had an impact on its sustained growth. During the period of 2005–2015, the statics recorded show the volume of coca leaf traded at the national level increased by 69%, from 12,536 to 21,201 metric tons. In the same period, the department of Santa Cruz continued to be the largest trader of coca leaves at the national level, except in 2008, when it was overtaken by the department of La Paz. According to DIGCOIN data, coca leaf trade in the country increased by 7%, from 19,797 metric tons in 2014 to 21,201 metric tons in 2015 (UNODC 2015).

On the global value of coca leaf production, UNODC estimates the total value of coca leaf production for 2014 at $282 million. This is under the assumption that all the coca leaf was traded in the authorized markets, which is certainly not the case. This amount represents 0.95 of Bolivia's GDP (estimated at $32.8 billion) and 8.8% of the agricultural sector's GDP (estimated at $3.2 billion).

As the GDP has been growing, the ratio of the value of the coca leaf to the GDP has been decreasing. For a comparative perspective, it should be noted that, in 2004, UNODC itself estimated the value of coca leaf production in the country at $240 million, which, at that time, was equivalent to 3% of the national GDP or 17% of the agricultural GDP of 2003.

Of the total value of GDP, which is currently around $32.76 billion, $282 million is estimated to represent 0.8% of the country's GDP and 8.1% of the agricultural sector's GDP, which is $3.3 billion. These data indicate that ten years later, coca leaf production has a much smaller impact on the Bolivian economy. To evaluate the real impact it has, we will have to view it through its relationship with the other sectors of the legal and illegal economy, and not compare it sector by sector as if they could exist without developing intertwined. But we will particularly look at its relationship with the other major sector of the illegal markets, which is smuggling.

Coca Eradication and Seizures

The impact of rationalization or eradication processes, i.e., the incineration of the coca leaf, must be subtracted from production, an indicator of the potential supply to drug trafficking, as supposedly occurs with drugs.

This is probably one of the most conflictive issues with producers at the beginning of the process. Especially in the case of the Cochabamba Tropic, where the grassroots union organization is very closed and strict, constituting a scenario of political power. In the first place, the union grants, although not formally, the right to own a chaco. Second, the amount of leaf allowed, one *cato* (40x40m) per associate. Third, the declaration of a surplus area, therefore subject to rationalization. At the same time these enclaves of power have served to have greater negotiating power with the government and cooperation, as well as the formation of leaderships, where this system of sociopolitical actors has worked best is in the Cochabamba Tropic, where it is very important at the national level to be the president of the six coca growers' federations. In the case of the Yungas of La Paz and the north of La Paz, the small farmers, although organized in unions, are more like communities than true vertical unions.

Probably because of the greater extension of the crops, it is in the Yungas of La Paz where the forces in charge of eradication have operated with greater intensity, thus achieving the programmed eradication goals. But the impact is very different, since almost all the crops in La Paz are within the legal category, while in the Cochabamba Tropic, where most of the coca destined for drug manufacture is produced, crops suffer eradication programs with greater intensity. This aspect has generated confrontations with the government.

The global data on the scope of rationalization show interesting advances, although it is never possible to end what is possibly the surplus that goes to drug trafficking. The results of the process of eradication and crop substitution reached 11,144 hectares in 2014, which translates to a decrease of 2% compared to 2013. In the Tropic of Cochabamba – the area of surplus crops – the area eradicated increased only slightly by 0.2%, from 7,406 hectares in 2013 to 7,423 hectares. Meanwhile, in the Yungas, the area eradicated decreased by 8%, from 3,470 hectares in 2013 to 3,194 hectares in 2014 (see Table 4.10).

It is important to note that the successes in rationalization/eradication have been announced, in the sense that the government must show the country and the international community that it is complying with the commitments to assuming responsibility for the issue of drugs. However, looking at the long-term series and taking the existing hectares as a reference, if we add up what has been eradicated, there would no longer be a single coca plant left. The key lies not only in the

Table 4.10 Summary of Coca Plantations Monitoring Results, 2015

Variables	2014	2015	Changes 2014–2015
Area Cultivated with Coca			
Area with coca plantations in Bolivia[a]	20,400 ha	20,200 ha	−1%
Area with coca plantations in the Yungasof La Paz	14,200 ha	14,000 ha	−1%
Area with coca plantations in the Cochabamba Tropics	6,100 ha	6,000 ha	−1%
Area with coca plantations in provinces north of La Paz	130 ha	150 ha	+15%
Area with coca plantations regulated by Law 1008[b]	12,000 ha	12,000 ha	–
Average Annual Yield of Coca Leaf Dried in the Sun			
Yungas of La Paz	1,305 kg/ha*	1,305 kg/ha	–
	1,137 kg/ha**	1,137 kg/ha	–
Cochabamba Tropic	2,764 kg/ha*	2,764 kg/ha	–
	2,047 kg/ha**	2,047 kg/ha	–
Northern Provinces of La Paz	1,250 kg/ha*	1,250 kg/ha	–
	1,037 kg/ha**	1,037 kg/ha	–
Total production of sun-dried coca leaf[c]	33,100 TM (28,800–35,700)	32,500 TM (28,400–35,100)	−2%
Rationalization/eradication of coca plantation[d]	11,144 ha	11,020 ha	−1%
Marketing and Seizures			
National nominal weighted average price of coca leaf in authorized markets	8.3 $/kg	9.4 $/kg	+13%

Estimation of the value of the coca leaf in Bolivia[e]	$282 million	$273 million	-3%
Value of coca leaf production as a percentage of the country's Gross Domestic Product (GDP)[f]	0.9%	0.8%	
Value of coca leaf production as a percentage of GDP in the agricultural sector[g]	8.8%	8.1%	
Coca leaf seizures[h]	582,186 kg	362,102 kg	-38%
Cocaine base seizures	18,258 kg	12,683 kg	-31%
Cocaine hydrochloride seizures	4,084 kg	8,602 kg	+111%

Source: UNODC (2016).

Note: The calculations of the annual coca leaf yield were based on studies carried out by the DEA in 1993, the UNODC in 2005 (*) and the "Study of Average Productivity of the Coca Leaf in Bolivia" carried out in 2010 (**).

[a] Quantification of coca plantations carried out based on the visual interpretation of high spatial resolution satellite images.

[b] Regulation of Law 1008 on the Regime of Coca and Controlled Substances, Supreme Decree 22099 of 1988.

[c] Potential sun-dried coca leaf production for the Cochabamba Tropic and provinces north of La Paz was calculated using a point estimate between the lower and upper limits of annual yield, and for the Yungas of La Paz production was estimated using the upper bound.

[d] Information from the Strategic Operational Command "Lt. Gironde" (CEO).

[e] This value was calculated using the nominal prices of the legal coca leaf markets in Bolivia.

[f] Value calculated from the country's GDP 2014 and 2015 (INE), which amounts to $32.75 and $32.76 billion, respectively.

[g] Value calculated from the GDP of the agricultural sector 2014 and 2015 (INE), which amounts to $3.2 and $3.3 billion, respectively.

[h] Information from the Special Force to Fight Drug Trafficking (FELCN).

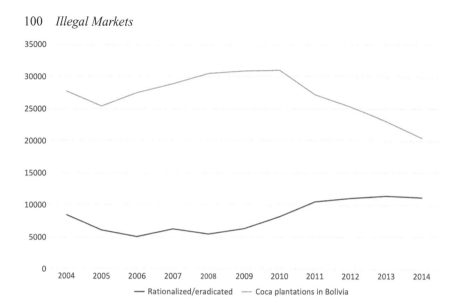

Figure 4.6 Rationalization/Eradication of Coca and Area under Cultivation. Statistical source: UNODC 2015, 44.

solidity of the monitoring figures, but above all in the process of rethinking. The eradication of seedlings is still significant, which indicates that the existence of coca leaf is far from endangered. It means that there are many new plants, which are the most productive, even though they need at least one year to produce well.

With all this, the annual announcements are important insofar as they communicate the will and the official position regarding the origin of drug trafficking. Notwithstanding the last few years, the U.S. government continues to place Bolivia among the countries that are not complying.[17]

In perspective, the results of crop eradication in the Cochabamba Tropics, in the period 2008–2012, had an increase of 60.7%, from 5,118 to 8,223 hectares; between 2012 and 2014, there has been a moderate decrease from 8,223 to 7,423 hectares, a decrease of 9.7%. In the Yungas, the area eradicated during the period 2007–2013 showed a sustained increase from 300 to 3,470 hectares and then, a slight decrease. The figures show an image of stability over time in the supply of this basic raw material. This balance is probably quite close to the natural replacement cycle. The plant has a maximum life cycle of 13 years and needs to be pruned or eradicated. It is possible that the intervention of the programs' effect is a coincidence. In any case, everything seems to suggest that the supply of leaves remains static with respect to the needs of the population and the drug trade.

Seizures of illegal coca. In 2014, the anti-narcotics force seized 582 metric tons of coca leaf, representing an increase of 22% compared to 2013, when the value reached 476 tons. Seizures of coca leaves followed an upward trend since 2004, reaching a peak in 2008 of 2,065 metric tons. However, this trend has been reversed since 2009 and has even dropped abruptly (see Table 4.11).

Table 4.11 Coca Seizures by Department, 2004–2014 (in kilograms)

Department	2004	2005	2006	2007	2008	2009	2010	2011	2012	2013	2014	Changes 2013–2014
La Paz	66,396	172,331	197,854	315,463	196,829	290,394	322,013	172,134	204,585	221,330	353,671	60%
Cochabamba	37,748	591,803	1,030,834	1,203,767	1,628,706	1,031,999	540,816	347,538	291,431	192,460	165,156	−14%
Santa Cruz	30,441	68,508	52,018	130,703	155,464	161,244	78,027	48,896	219,573	26,170	18,008	−31%
Tarija	10,183	16,499	19,604	11,843	21,030	20,081	37,457	7,077	1,422	4,750	2,794	−41%
Oruro	6,120	24,814	21,913	24,393	34,075	45,674	7,076	21,746	17,877	29,120	39,752	36%
Potosí	1,942	1,509	4,010	4,999	7,149	5,764	2,655	1,034	232	1,810	702	−61%
Chuquisaca	1,448	3,229	11,780	7,013	8,444	3,924	20,875	1,053	1,148	20	0	−100%
Beni	904	7,525	4,778	6,768	13,076	14,959	6,058	3,843	3,536	240	1,078	349%
Pando	0	50	271	686	50	0	58	0	79	70	1,025	1,364%
Total	155,182	886,268	1,343,062	1,705,636	2,064,823	1,574,041	1,015,035	603,319	739,884	475,970	582,186	22%

Source: UNODC (2015, 51).

102 *Illegal Markets*

Cocaine Production

One of the main critiques of the annual monitoring report is that it only monitors coca leaf and not drug trafficking. If these estimates could be made, the country would be in a better position to evaluate the contribution it makes to the illegal drug markets. Supported by the UNODC study and other documents, we try to show a picture through indirect calculations on this issue.

With respect to cocaine seizures, they are usually taken as an indicator of the volume of production and flow, and it is even said that seizures are equivalent to approximately 10–15% of the volume. Such an unreliable number can offer limited insight. It is possible to know how much potential cocaine Bolivia produces by indirect methods, based on the conversion of leaf to hydrochloride. However, this is limited, as we do not know how much of the cocaine that circulates in Bolivia comes from Peru and how much is produced in Bolivia.

Nor can we make projections of the country's potential because the conversion factors could not be put into practice. In the case of Bolivia, although it has not been explicitly discussed, the official message from the state is that it would be illegal and unconstitutional to make this kind of projection. Coca could be exported to be processed outside the country, but such export would be prohibited by the Vienna Convention itself.

Taking examples from neighboring countries, who are also not very fond of this projection exercise, we have some approximate figures that can help us to get a little closer to the potential volume. In this investigation, this was not the objective, but rather it was to try to understand how the Bolivian subsystem is anchored in the regional and global system of borders through its participation in the drug market. Only the volume in terms of *proportions* is of interest as the main data.

The European Union is willing to contribute to the performance calculations. Following the presentation of the last report (2016) of monitoring carried out by the UNODC, the European Union (EU), which supports Bolivia in this area, now without the presence of the U.S. aid of previous years, offers to finance a study on cocaine's potential production in Bolivia.[18] The European official Timothy Torlot added that for this particular study it would be necessary to export coca leaves from Bolivia, which is prohibited by the 1961 UN drug convention. Torlot spoke about the issue after the UNODC representative, Antonino Di Leo, presented the Bolivian authorities with the recommendation to carry out the study of "coca-cocaine conversion" (El Diario 2015). According to Antonino Di Leo, this study can estimate "the potential for cocaine production in the country. Although the Bolivian government has stated that its legal system does not allow it to carry out this study, the UNODC considers it necessary to find mechanisms that will allow it to be carried out," said the UN agency representative (El Diario 2015).

The study also established that Bolivia has a potential for coca leaf production of 32,500 metric tons, of which only 65% is traded on legal markets. The coca leaf is protected in Bolivia by the Constitution propagated by President Evo Morales in 2009 "for its cultural, religious, and medicinal uses, although the plant is also destined for drug trafficking as it contains alkaloids which are the basis of cocaine production" (UNDP 2016).

Illegal Markets 103

Some background. UNODC studies of Peru share important data with the account of several attempts.

> Based on the information on conversion factors established by the Operation Breakthrough, carried out by the United States between 2003 and 2004, it is established that 375 kilograms of sun-dried leaf are necessary to produce 1 kilogram of cocaine hydrochloride.
>
> (UNODC 2013, 14)

According to this study, in September 2012, DEVIDA and UNODC, financially supported by the French Embassy and other State entities, started a work to determine the conversion factor of coca leaf to cocaine hydrochloride. In the first stage of this work, 40 chemists – also known as cooks in the drug trafficking market – of five of the most important coca-growing areas were interviewed. In its second stage there should have been conducted field process simulation, to carry out, in the third stage, a laboratory analysis that would determine the purity of the cocaine obtained (UNODC 2013, 58).

According to Peru's Dirandro, 1,100 tons of cocaine are globally produced and 200 tons of that are produced in the Peruvian jungle, of which 95% leaves for Bolivia. Each year, 90 tons of cocaine paste travels to Bolivia (El Deber 2015b). In Bolivia,

> phenacetin is mixed with the paste and the weight of the substance triples. If that kilo costed $900, when it leaves Bolivia, it would be worth $9,000 because it was stretched, and the quality of the drug was improved.
>
> (El Deber 2015c)

National Congressman Luis Felipe Dorado of Convergencia Nacional (CN) refers to the 2012 UNODC report and says that

> another aspect that UNODC must consider is that currently much more cocaine is manufactured with less coca using the so-called "Colombian Method." In the past, Bolivian narcos manufactured one kilo of cocaine in 12 hours from 350 pounds of coca. Now, with the same amount of leaf, two kilos are produced in two hours. In other words, the technological modernization of drug trafficking allows them to dispense with some crops.
>
> (Opinión 2012)

But what does the Colombian Method consist of?

> Using a water-pit, leaf-stomping technique, both the Peruvian and Bolivian "chemists" were capable of extracting some 45% of the cocaine alkaloid from the leaf … Colombian cocaine base processors use and entirely different production method … it is reasonable that Colombian "chemists" may be capable of extracting as much as 70% of the cocaine alkaloid from the leaf.
>
> (DCI 2000)

104   *Illegal Markets*

Minister Cáceres stated that

> the gangs have incorporated the Colombian method to achieve greater drug production. Until two years ago, the *pisacocas* used 350 pounds of coca to process a kilo of cocaine in 12 hours. Now with 350 pounds of coca, two kilos of cocaine can be produced in two hours, but chemical precursors, fuel, and cement are used.
>
> > (Página Siete 2012)

Cáceres explained that the Colombian Method consists of using homemade mills to grind coca, while also using plenty of fuel. In addition, washing machines and microwave ovens are used to make drugs in small spaces in the suburbs of the cities, without the necessity of creating cartels. (Página Siete 2012). Finally, it can be estimated that Bolivia has a production capacity of approximately 350 tons of hydrochloride.

Additionally, the process enriches an important amount coming from Peru.[19] According to a report from the Anti-Drug Directorate of Peru (Dirandro), Bolivia refines 95% of its base paste production and manages to increase the volume up to three times with the use of phenacetin (El Deber 2015c).

Drug Trafficking in the Economy

What is the participation of drug trafficking in the national product? Of course, there are no official estimates to answer this question, and the known estimates differ from one another because the methods of calculation are different. The main problem is to reduce drug trafficking to the coca leaf or to the coca leaf with its derivative products such as coca paste and hydrochloride. As there are no isolated-reliable figures for these three factors, we refer to various estimates that are usually circulated.

In 2010, for example, Bolivian Vice President Álvaro García Linera stated that drug trafficking represented about 3% of GDP. If this were true and applying this 3% to the GDP for 2012 (estimated at $27 billion), the flow of drug trafficking would be in the order of $800 million. Many think, however, that this figure underestimates the real size of this activity, especially considering the growing value of exports.

Painter (1994) reported a share of up to 12% of GDP for the coca-cocaine chain in 1990, a ratio that could have decreased, however, because at that time the hydrocarbons sector was not as large as it is today.

The *Wall Street Journal*, for the year 2003, estimates income generated by drug trafficking at $500 million, equivalent to 6% of that year's GDP (Lifsher 2013). Meanwhile, Campero (014) estimated that by 2012, coca leaf production alone would be worth close to $300 million; these numbers do not consider the value added in the process of refining coca to obtain derivatives such as cocaine base paste and cocaine hydrochloride. For our part and using the method of uses and sources of the balance of payments, equating them in our hypothesis with

Illegal Markets 105

smuggling, the flow of drug trafficking is estimated at approximately 6.7% of GDP; that is, $1,809 million, for the same year of 2012 (Ferrufino 2015, 23).

The differences stem from the problem of wanting to isolate it as a measurable sector of the economy. Given that it interacts and intertwines with the other illegal sectors – drug trafficking, smuggling, illegal mining, and human trafficking – it is not possible, and to get lost in this task could be dangerous. Regardless of these estimates, it is important to take these numbers as a reference, which will show the great structuring power of drug trafficking in the illegal markets. This does not include Bolivian cocaine or Peruvian cocaine.

> In the Bolivian context, two important flows of cross-border economic activity are identified. On the one hand there is smuggling and on the other drug trafficking. Both activities have been growing over decades and have gradually been inserted into other legal spaces of commercial and even productive activity.... Bolivia has one of the most informal economies in South America. From the perspective of occupation and employment, 61.7% of the work force is concentrated in informality... From the perspective of contribution to the economy, informality represents a value equivalent to 22.7% of urban productive activity. Considering the total (rural and urban), the contribution would be comparable to 17% of total GDP. The sectors with the largest informal presence are transport, construction, trade, and, to a lesser extent, manufacturing. (Ferrufino 2015, 28)

In terms of volume, contraband is very close to drug trafficking, but, above all, it is important because of its impact on the economy, in which imported goods compete with national ones. An equally serious situation occurs with agriculture, given the large amount of food imported from neighboring countries thanks to increased competitiveness, determined by technology and exchange rate policies. Nonetheless, even countries as far away as the United States and Malaysia are exporting food to Bolivia.

In many of these imports, legal and illegal imports are confused, either because many are smuggled in or because of the under-invoicing methods used to carry out customs procedures. Below is an overview of the different informal/illegal sectors.

Trade and Imports, Volume, and Performance

Without a doubt, the central activity in the country's border areas is the import trade that has been booming for the past ten years. There are many factors contributing to this, such as price differences between Bolivia, neighboring countries, and more distant countries such as China, and differences in competitiveness, the extractive economy, and exchange rate policies.

In the case of Bolivia, and due to its conditions of access to ports, massive legal trade is mainly by land, including the one that arrives by sea and enters through Chile. In this activity, the legal and the illegal are intermingled, or it ends up in a "legal in half." There are press data showing how the legal market itself operates based on under-invoicing of goods in the place of origin and double invoicing according to customs and their tariffs.

During the last years, the Bolivian economy growth has been due to the purchases of goods and services from abroad with the increase of the commercial deficit with practically all the countries. Imports have risen from $2,020 million at the beginning of the past decade to $9,353 million at the close of 2013. This is an accumulated growth of 363% for the period 2000–2013. The work contracted for this calculation reports this series and presents the participation of this nominal value of imports in the GDP at current prices of each period (Ferrufino 2015, 8).

At the end of 2000, imports represented nearly 24% of GDP, while at the end of 2013 they rose to 30%, reflecting the greater importance of imports in the national economy. Figure 4.7 shows the evolution of the composition of these imports, where a classification is presented that tries to isolate relevant components that are not visible in the aggregate.

The individual component with the greatest weight corresponds to industrial supplies ($2,735 million as of December 2013), mainly motor vehicles for industrial use; other motorized vehicles for the transport of people occupy the second place, and then there are the other capital goods which are particularly industrial machinery and equipment. An important segment of external purchases corresponds to fuels ($1,237 million), and finally food and beverage imports are reflected, along with durable consumer goods such as electrical and electronic appliances and other less durable devices that could be included in a broader consumption aggregate.

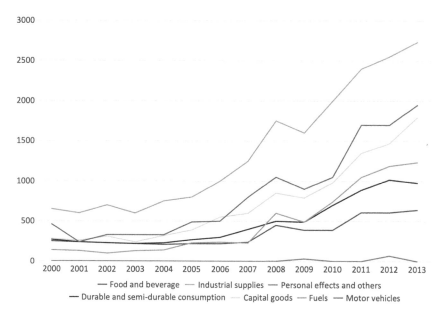

Figure 4.7 Imports by Sector Evolution of CIF Imports in USD MM. Source: Own elaboration, based on data from the INE.

Illegal Markets 107

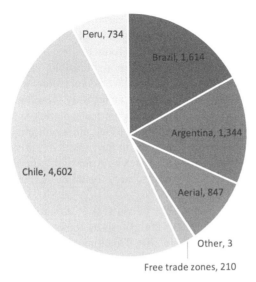

Figure 4.8 Imports by Country of Origin. Source: Own elaboration, based on INE data.

The numbers highlight the relevance of Chile as a border country through which goods of Chilean origin enter in a smaller proportion (12%); most of them are from overseas that have disembarked in Chilean ports in the Pacific and have entered directly to customs in Bolivia or have been for a time in the free zones (ZOFRI-Iquique) to then enter the country (Ferrufino 2015, 10). Brazil is the second most important point of entry, where most of the products imported from that country have a manufacturing origin. The third relevant border country is Argentina; and, finally, there is the entry of goods by air and Peru.

The importance of the Pacific ports stands out, due to the existence of free trade zones in the north of Chile (Arica and Iquique) and in the south of Peru (Tacna) that represent a very great potential of commercial flow and access to tens of thousands of overseas products, an aspect that is not repeated in the border areas with other countries. Income from Arica is the most important and represents mainly goods shipped from Iquique (42.7%), but direct income from Iquique, arriving at Pisiga, is also reported (4.6%). Corumbá, with 17.1%, is in the second place and Pocitos, with 12.4%, in the third place.

In the case of northern Chile, sales from the Iquique Free Zone (ZOFRI) represented 26% of total sales in 2002. This structure changed significantly by 2013 and, in particular, the share of sales to the Tarapacá, Arica, and Parinacota regions.

Approach to Smuggling

ZOFRI's sales for export are subject to a set of records and procedures that guarantee legality, from the moment of invoicing to the delivery of goods in Bolivian

108   *Illegal Markets*

customs. However, this has not been always the case, and variations can occur: a mechanism by which it is decided which merchandise shipped will not reach the control of Bolivian authorities and will be disembarked en route to illegally enter the country at various points along the border. Another, more plausible, way is that the merchandise is sold in these regions and captured by organizations with the aim of entering it irregularly into Bolivian or Paraguayan territory. Thus, one could understand the strong growth of ZOFRI's sales to the local market as a mechanism to avoid the formal process of export, registration, and monitoring. The tariff and tax costs in the free zone area are zero, but in the so-called "extension" zone, which includes large territories and cities such as Arica and Iquique, the tax burdens are relatively low, so even paying these charges could be lucrative to take nationalized merchandise to the borders.[20]

By the end of 2013, smuggling was close to $2.1 billion (6.9% of that year's GDP), equivalent to 23% of total imports that year. In the analysis by border country, Chile is the most important; if we add the estimate for illegal internments of Chilean products plus those from overseas that enter through Chile, we can infer that just over 70% of contraband enters through this border. In order of importance, the illegal internments from Brazil follow, which are produced and commercialized in that country, rather than internments from overseas and reembarked to Bolivia illegally.

Considering the calculated volumes, the borders with Chile and Brazil, and to a lesser extent Peru and Argentina, are the entry doors for illegal goods into the country, with differentiated participation.

Journalists' reports state that the Chilean government's so-called "Northern Border Plan" has identified around 114 illegal routes to Bolivia, particularly to

Table 4.12 Estimate of Smuggling 2000–2008 and Extrapolation 2009–2013

Year	Argentina	Brazil	Chile	Paraguay	Peru	ZOFRI	Total
2000	16	114	23	6	7	165	331
2001	12	80	14	6	5	203	321
2002	52	64	23	3	6	192	340
2003	17	51	26	6	6	198	303
2004	40	84	35	5	11	179	354
2005	39	102	58	4	18	270	492
2006	38	157	87	8	11	416	716
2007	23	171	50	8	12	538	802
2008	22	273	116	12	33	592	1,048
2009	25	233	82	7	31	514	892
2010	27	299	94	9	37	692	1,157
2011	34	413	103	15	45	1,039	1,649
2012	37	451	128	23	53	1,198	1,889
2013	40	473	191	21	57	1,331	2,114
Total	422	2,966	1,029	133	331	7,529	12,409

Source: Ferrufino (2009).

the department of Oruro (Mendoza 2014). These routes are said to be used to smuggle some products into Bolivia (vehicles and other items) and to smuggle out Bolivian and Peruvian cocaine. According to these reports, the Chilean authorities are exercising greater control in the interest of curbing the flow of narcotics from Bolivia to Chile, which could also eventually help to mitigate the problem of smuggling (Mendoza 2014).

In the case of Argentina, it should be mentioned that the devaluation of the currency and the strong difference between the official market and the parallel market were factors that encouraged greater activity in both legal and illegal imports. In contrast, Brazil has experienced a process of nominal appreciation that only began to reverse toward the end of 2011, an aspect that made Brazilian products less competitive during most of the analysis period.

Main Smuggled Products

The ten main chapters of the Common Tariff Nomenclature (NAN- DINA), corresponding to the smuggling estimates made for the period 2006–2008, express the respective accumulated values.

Argentina

The data show that the main group of smuggled products is wheat flour and its derivatives. This result is consistent with the productive leadership that the country has in the area. Machines and mechanical devices are another group of smuggled products along with vehicles, a category that includes tractors and agricultural machinery. In the category of iron or steel casting manufactures are included all those inputs required for construction (corrugated and others) that are not produced in Bolivia.

Brazil

In this case, leather products such as shoes, sandals, and other similar items within the saddlery sector predominate. The category of boilers, machines, and appliances appears in the second, and, in the third, we have, as in the previous case, steel and iron products. Plastics and their manufactures form another important category, in addition to cotton, rubber (possibly vehicle tires), and aluminum, which is used in window frames and other construction requirements.

Chile

In the case of Chile, the category of boilers and machinery, which includes a variety of products, takes the first place, followed by vehicles and iron and steel products. Electrical appliances continue to be important, and alcoholic beverages can include products such as wine that are mass-produced in that country. It is worth noting the significant amount of agricultural machinery that resides

110 *Illegal Markets*

in the country without any kind of registration and is not nationalized. Within this great item there is also another type of machinery: items such as photocopiers, machinery used in construction, and others. Many of these enter through the borders closer to the Pacific but are distributed in different regions of the country.

Paraguay

In the case of Paraguay, there are tobacco, chemical industry products, and machinery that can include many varieties. There are also animal and vegetable fats and oils, where the latter may be linked to the chain of soya, sunflower, and other similar products in which the country has some competitiveness.

Peru

In this case, mineral fuels, oils, and others are in the first place followed by products such as machines, cereals, pharmaceuticals, clothing, and iron and steel castings. It is interesting to note that it is not possible to capture the information on the entry of a variety of foods such as potatoes, fruits, and others, since the method of differentiation is unable to detect which has not been declared as export at origin; a situation that prevails with this type of nonindustrial food.

ZOFRI

In the case of products from the Free Zone of Iquique, the main unreported entry item is vehicles; then there are machines and electrical sound devices, televisions, and similar. Machines and other various items take the lead again, in addition to shoes, toys, clothing, and other textiles.

Illegal Exports: Drug Trafficking and Smuggling

The work of Ferrufino (2015) provides the main traces of informality with respect to drug trafficking and smuggling, which make up one sector of the clandestine and illegal economy, with large criminal passages linked to them. Two other sectors with clearly delinquent characteristics are not included here: trafficking and arms smuggling. To acknowledge the importance of these two sectors, one can estimate the amounts of money they move with what approximates the dimensions and the places of origin. In this section an effort is made to isolate the smuggling sector, to see its characteristics and dimensions.

Quantitative Approach to Illegal Exports

The method of sources and uses in the balance of payments allows the estimation of those foreign currency income flows associated with undeclared exports. A basic principle is the balance that must exist between the sources and uses of foreign currency, expressed in balance of accounting payments. When the uses of foreign exchange are greater than the sources, then it can be deduced that there is some source of undeclared foreign exchange and this can be linked to undeclared exports and to a lesser extent to foreign exchange income in the hands of travelers, remittances that are not recorded, and other amounts of money that could physically enter through the borders.

In summary, the methodology consists of finding by difference the foreign exchange that enters the country and whose origin cannot be linked to legal activities. The legal sources include unilateral current transfers (TUC), capital transfers (TDK), foreign direct investment (FDI), portfolio investment (CI), other capital, and, of course, legal exports, which are the main source of foreign currency. By 2012, illegal exports exceeded $1.806 billion, a significant part of which was accounted by drug trafficking. Note that the estimate of the value of smuggling, for the same year of 2012, is $1,889 million, which is almost similar to the value of illegal exports, suggesting a correlation between the two items: a significant part of smuggled imports would be financed with foreign exchange generated by illegal exports.

How Much Does Smuggling Amount To?

In concluding this brief, very quantitative, description of import and export smuggling activity, the same question can be asked to apply to the case of drug trafficking. If this sector of the economy could not be separated and isolated, it is because of the overlap with drug trafficking and the other illegal sectors, though in this case the overlap is with the formal and legal sector of the economy.

According to Ferrufino (2015, 28), considering the smuggling projections previously estimated by other sources up to 2008 and extrapolating data to have figures up to 2013, it is estimated that a total of $2,114 million in smuggling occurs. Considering the method of differentiation that contrasts the export declarations (abroad) to Bolivia, with the import declarations in National Customs for the year 2012, the respective data shows $1,889 million. This data allows, as an approximation, to hypothesize that this amount exists as capital that is not available in the local banking system, and that it is used as the financial cushion for illegal markets. If the impacts on the related sectors were considered, it could be a very high amount, since not all medium and small smugglers necessarily use the resources of drug trafficking or large smugglers, data that is very difficult to guess at. This assumption may be consistent with the difference between the formal sector of registered businesses and the large informal sector.

Illegal Mining and Gold Smuggling

In Bolivia, there have been reports of significant tax fraud in gold exports in 2012, registered under the tariff items of waste and amalgamation.[21] The value exported then was $1.1 billion, for a volume, according to official data, of 20.5 tons. Unusually, the volume exported was almost three times the entire volume

112   *Illegal Markets*

of gold produced that year, in various forms (no more than seven tons). "One area where significant cross-border flows have been detected in recent years is linked to gold smuggling. The estimates presented in this document show a flow that could be in the range of $700 to $1 billion" (Ferrufino 2015, 29).

A report by the Minister of Mining, Mario Virreira, confirmed that this millionaire export was made without the corresponding payment of mining royalties (quoted in Navarro 2014). According to some unofficial estimates, tax evasion on unpaid royalties could reach $77 million, applying the 7% rate to the $1.1 billion of gold exported.

Since then, the suspicion of massive gold smuggling into Bolivia has been present in national public opinion. How else could one explain the sudden and dramatic growth of national gold exports? This is the question that several experts have asked, arguing that the country's installed capacity for gold production is modest, partly because of the very productive limitations of the mining cooperatives responsible for the largest gold exploitations, and partly because of the lack of investment in gold mining.[22] It has also been pointed out that once important gold mining operations, such as those in the Suches and Araras areas, bordering Peru and Brazil, would be practically exhausted.

In this way, it is assumed that the increase in official gold export figures does not correspond to a real and verifiable growth in gold production in Bolivian territory, at least not in correlative quantities, but, in any case, to the smuggling of gold originating in neighboring countries, and mainly in Peru, the main gold producer in Latin America. From its gold deposits, between 2011 and 2013, an annual average of 184 fine metric tons (TMF) was extracted, with a significant portion corresponding to illegal and informal gold mining in the Peruvian region of Madre de Dios. It is also a fact that, over the past five years, Peru has stepped up the fight against illegal mining, especially in the southern region bordering Bolivia.

In fact, journalistic investigations in that country support the hypothesis of massive gold smuggling between Peru and Bolivia. Thus, a report in the digital newspaper *Ojo Público* states that the Peruvian authorities managed to seize a shipment of 35 tons of gold of suspicious origin at the Jorge Chávez airport in Lima, on commercial flights arriving from Bolivia between February and October 2014 (Castilla 2014). According to Torres Cuzcano, there is, for the period 2012–2014,

> a close negative correlation between the lower production of illegal and informal mining in Madre de Dios in Peru and the higher export of gold in Bolivia, a country in which the production of this metal was not significant until 2011, despite the strong incentive represented by the sustained rise in its international price since late 2002. Thus, until 2011, the figures for gold production and exports were quite modest in Bolivia: they did not even exceed the levels shown by informal mining in Madre de Dios.
>
> (Torres Cuzcano 2015, 36)

Illegal Markets 113

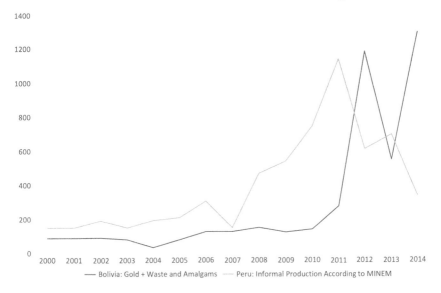

Figure 4.9 Gold Exports, Peru and Bolivia, in Millions of Dollars. Source: Own elaboration.

Taking the year 2011 as a reference point to evaluate the evolution of gold production and exports in both countries during 2012 and 2014, Torres Cuzcano finds that, in the case of Bolivia,

> its exports multiplied by a little more than four times during 2012, reaching $909 million above the level registered in 2011. In contrast, informal mining in Madre de Dios reduced its production value by $527 million during 2012 (−46.2%). During 2014, while Bolivian exports increased by $1.084 billion (+390.7%), Madre de Dios' informal production decreased by $820 million (−71.9%), compared to 2011. In terms of volumes produced, informal mining in Madre de Dios reduced its gold production by 11.1 metric tons during 2012 (−49.3%), while Bolivia increased it by 16.5 metric tons (+149.5%). By 2014, while the informal miners' production in Madre de Dios decreased by 14.6 metric tons (−65.0%), Bolivia's total production increased by 23.2 metric tons (+210.0%), in both cases compared to 2011.
>
> (Torres Cuzcano 2015, 36–37)

Torres also adds that "[i]f we assume that the 11 tons of gold Bolivia produced during 2011 is its 'normal' production level, then its excess production amounted to 47 tons during 2012-2014" (Torres Cuzcano 2015, 37). What Peru loses in informal gold production, Bolivia gains in legal exports of the same mineral.

114   *Illegal Markets*

How did Peruvian gold manage to infiltrate the Bolivian export chain? Torres notes that the high increase recorded in gold exports from Bolivia during 2012 (over 327.7%) is mostly explained by the item "gold waste and amalgamation," which represented 92.4% of gold exports that year, while "metallic gold" represented only 7.6% of the total. He adds that the same item – "waste and amalgams" – showed an unprecedented increase in the record of gold production in Bolivia during 2012–2014, explaining – on an annual average – 77.8% of the total; the difference was contributed by the production of "gold" (Torres Cuzcano 2015, 38).

Torres' findings and explanations coincide with the results of studies and journalistic reports in Bolivia, which, since 2013, have warned that the phenomenon of illegal mining, which other countries are fighting, is being legitimized in the country. This traffic is attributed to the controls and repression of illegal gold exploitation in neighboring countries, especially in Peru. This production arrives in Bolivia via smuggling and is re-exported as "waste," without paying taxes, taking advantage of the lack of controls in export operations and perhaps also because this type of illegal activity has managed to insert itself into a system of cover-up, complicity, and corruption, which makes it possible. This places this activity within the scope of the illegal economy.

Based on several interviews, the interlocutors are not declared, it is suspected that money laundering operations could be involved in uncontrolled gold exports, similar to the one documented from Mexico.[23] It can also be suspected that there may be some connection between gold trafficking on that side of the Peruvian–Bolivian border and the movement of gold. A veritable army of bearers has been formed on that side of the border who can carry either of them on their backs, since high skill is required to know the roads through the jungle.

In Summary

From this brief account of data, several conclusions can be drawn which make our study possible.

- Regardless of whether Bolivia is a clandestine gold producer (more than 70% of the companies are small) or whether it serves as a "legalizing" bridge for this activity, supposedly controlled in Peru, gold smuggling is one of the most important activities that swell the army of illegal markets in Bolivia. In terms of value, for example, the 35 tons of gold exported via Lima would represent more than $1 billion to date.
- Million more-million less, it represents a sector that requires a significant amount of money to do business and that can get it out of the bank. Interviewees reported people carrying briefcases with $5 million and protected by bodyguards, who granted loans to small cooperatives operating dredge barges in one of Beni's rivers.
- This sector, apparently legal in Bolivia, introduces dirty money in significant amounts, increasing the demand for goods in population strata, which generates multiplier effects in the rest of the market, an aspect that can

Illegal Markets   115

be seen in recent years in a series of luxury consumer items, in the middle of the real estate bubble. This includes a major spill from corruption payments.

- Obviously, an important part is directed to the tax havens, but we suppose that with the presence of such important plaintiffs as contraband, a good part of that money is "legalized" in the Bolivian economy.
- Interviewees estimate that in Bolivia approximately 40 tons of mercury alone is dumped into the river. This amount is introduced almost entirely from Peru, a traditional producer of mercury since the colonial period.
- Finally, although not as much as in the case of drug trafficking, a more complex activity, a stratified and numerous labor market, is developed.
- It is easy to imagine why this powerful sector is connected to corruption and human trafficking and smuggling, since they have links with public officials, lawyers, prosecutors, hired assassins, among others.

In this scenario, it is highlighted how compact the so-called illegal market can be in Bolivia, causing the informalization of all actors and regulatory mechanisms.

Trafficking and Human Smuggling

Due to the characteristics of this fragment of the illegal market, which contains many edges, we will only consider in this section some general and purely descriptive traces of the dimensions, the routes, and their relations.

The topic covers two different sub-sectors: trafficking and smuggling for the purpose of the sex trade, and trafficking in persons more closely related to the use of persons for labor exploitation outside their usual place of residence, usually outside the country. We present both topics together to show the characteristics of this market; often, both situations are operated by the same agents.

According to Fundación La Paz,

> Bolivia is a country of origin, transit and destination of human trafficking, giving rise to internal and international trafficking that takes as its main victims children, adolescents, and women, making up 73% of the cases opened before the judicial body by 2014.
>
> (2015, 7)

From 2012 to 2015, only 12 of the 2,119 cases of human trafficking and smuggling reported in Bolivia were given a sentence, which would represent the 99.5% of impunity (Fundación La Paz 2015, 7). The progressive growth of this crime is visible and perceived by the general public, who witness the numerous cases of missing persons on a daily basis. Fundación La Paz also reports that, by 2015, 1,552 girls and adolescent women and 825 boys and adolescent men were reported missing (Fundación La Paz 2015, 8). It cannot be said how many of their families had the resources to initiate or continue legal proceedings against their perpetrators.

116　*Illegal Markets*

Table 4.13 Bolivia: Complaints of Trafficking and Smuggling in Persons According to Management and Type of Related Crimes

Year	TOTAL	Human Trafficking	Migrant Trafficking	Trafficking of Minors	Related Crimes
2012	345	279	28	0	38
2013	469	423	9	3	34
2014(p)	485	440	1	0	44

Source: Own elaboration.

(*) Related crimes include pimping, pornography and obscene shows involving children and adolescents, commercial sexual violence, aggravated corruption, and labor exploitation.

(p): preliminary.

Trafficking is a sector that feeds and grows in the shadow of the high-income sectors of illegal origin. Trafficking in persons – who most of the time happen to be migrants – is a response to aspirations for a better life, and in many cases to the narrowness of the global market. Regarding the first issue, people relate violence with drug trafficking and other illegal activities that have driven criminality with theft, extortion, assaults, and others that have increased with the increase of an aggregate demand that grew not because of the increase in productive activity but because of speculation, fiscal crime, and other illegal activities. This violence has spread in a generalized way from the violence at the borders, of which the statistics give almost no information, to the cities where the news cameras do focus. We call this border violence, in the sense that it is linked to the illegal markets of the global era. In the second case, human trafficking refers to migrants who are exploited by traffickers in transit to their destination and at that destination by labor contractors, who, in many cases, reduce them to explicit slavery.

Both crimes, which yield significant amounts of profit, are related to, or fed by, the neglect of governments, which is also reflected in the extraordinary weakness of official information on crime, even more so on the border. In both cases, violence occurs, part of which occurs in border areas, in relation to the logic of both types of business, or away from them, generally in cities or in mining and drug production sites. Information systems in this regard are deficient. Three years and nine months after the enactment of the Comprehensive Law against Trafficking and Smuggling of Persons (Law 263), and three years and two months after the approval of its regulations, Bolivia has still not implemented the Integrated Information and Statistics System.

In Bolivia, the press makes these crimes visible and shows them as news, therefore in a sporadic, and sometimes anecdotal way, typical of the red press. State institutions, both the judicial bodies and those responsible for monitoring public security, lack complete information that would allow them to identify appropriate operational policies. The justice system only provides the cases that are dealt with in its administrative sphere; thus, it is not possible to gain a clear idea of what the real dimension is. People do not trust information from the police or the justice system, given the precariousness of these bodies in terms of information. Also included is information from the INE, which only reports cases declared by the justice system and the police, based on complaints administered in their fields and rather partial records.

This market is present in all border areas, facilitating, due to its precarious functioning and lack of attention to security, the action of human trafficking networks. The project, as stated in Chapter 1 of this book, provides a very good picture of the last few years, in which the most frequent issues, such as human trafficking and the disappearance of persons, are highlighted.

By differentiating trafficking and smuggling, the proportions reflect the closeness of one crime to another. Both are on an upward trend. However, it should be considered that this increase as of 2012 may have been due to the approval of Law 263. From the point of view of complaints registered with the justice system and the police, the picture is similar and the growing trend in the case of human trafficking is clearer (Vásquez 2016).

According to data from the Special Force to Fight Crime (FELCC) between 2011 and 2013, cases of human trafficking and smuggling increased by 40%. This figure includes related crimes such as child pornography, trafficking in migrants, corruption of minors, pimping, kidnapping of minors, and other crimes (El Día 2013).

Bolivia Is Not Just a Transit Country

This problem not only flows from Bolivia to the outside, but there is also a domestic market. Using the same data from the International Organization for Migration (IOM), it is estimated that around 2,300 women are victims of "commercial sexual exploitation," many of them from neighboring countries or rural populations. Bolivia is one of the five countries in South America with the most cases of human trafficking and smuggling, according to the Organization of American States (OAS), which demonstrates the urgency of a frontal and effective fight against these crimes that can affect any child or young person (Mendoza 2013).

Bolivia is a country of origin, destination, and transit of children, adolescents, women, and men traded for labor or sexual exploitation. It is mainly concentrated in the main cities and reaches all economic strata. News coverage of this subject is very frequent when it is related to acts of violence. In some cases, the networks that were infiltrated by the police are more visible.

The main destination countries for Bolivian victims of trafficking are Argentina, Brazil, Peru, Chile, and Spain, where they are exploited in factories, agriculture, and the sex trade. It is also common for girls and adolescents to be trafficked within the country, between rural and urban areas, for the purpose of commercial sexual exploitation. Adolescent girls and women of indigenous origin are at constant risk of labor exploitation in domestic service, the sugarcane harvest, and work in the chestnut fields.

The data collected from the press leads to the conclusion that this is a growing market and that it is closely related to the increase in the flow of money to

118 *Illegal Markets*

luxury consumer sectors. The statistical data issued by the Bolivian Police and the National Institute of Statistics reveal that about three to four persons between 13 and 17 years of age disappear every day, victims of trafficking and smuggling, and that this crime increased by 40% (Erbol 2015). The increase in reports could be indicating a continued increase in trafficking and smuggling, particularly in the departments of La Paz, Oruro, Potosí, Santa Cruz, and Tarija. The most vulnerable group is children aged 0 to 6, followed by those aged 7 and 11, and adolescents between the ages of 12 and 17, particularly females (Erbol 2015).

Bolivia is currently a major transit country, with people of African and Asian origin being trafficked to neighboring countries such as Peru, Brazil, Mexico, Paraguay, and Argentina. Bolivia is also a country where trafficking has become a common crime, and there are indications that several networks are operating, probably as part of transnational businesses. Above these, there is a veil of shadow and silence, until a scandal erupts that exposes them. This happened with the Katanas case, which revealed a prolific high-level network. The lower-level businesses are known in a massive way, especially in La Paz, El Alto, and the cities of Cochabamba and Santa Cruz.

The Katanas case, which produced a scandal in the city of La Paz, affected the whole country. After a short time, news coverage was redirected to the story of the internal family issues of the owners, due to the supposed complicity of some authorities. This behavior is accompanied by the low value given to research and the production of statistical information, which makes it easier for the supposedly large business to operate peacefully in the shadows.

The Katanas case has revealed the tip of a much more worrying iceberg for society: the existence of trafficking and smuggling networks legitimized in nightclubs with the complicity of local and/or national authorities. According to the OAS, Bolivia is among the five countries in South America with the highest rates of human trafficking and sexual exploitation; trafficking and smuggling networks use 12 routes at the national and international levels to capture their Bolivian victims (La Patria 2014).

Traffic and Trafficking according to Border

The Argentine border is the most used by land migrants, and it is through this border that the trafficking of children, who are the main victims, is most easily executed. "There are about 900 minors who cross the border between the cities of La Quiaca and Villazón every day in an irregular manner" (El Comercio 2016). This problem was revealed thanks to an investigation by *La Nación*, a paper from Argentina. According to Argentine NGO Esclavitud Cero (Zero Slavery),

> there are cases of Bolivian girls between the ages of 12 and 13 who are offered 'for all services' in Argentina, at a price of $2,500 per year, where they are paid $1,250 upon delivery and the rest upon completion of the year's work. The girls work without timetables, are not allowed to go out, live in terrible conditions and are also sexually abused.
>
> (El Comercio 2016)

Bolivia–Peru Border

This border, in smaller volume, is used for the entry and exit of people, mimicking trade flows in the density of flows in both directions, due to the cultural homogeneity of the population on both sides. Cases of trafficking and smuggling of persons are increasing, and up to 25% of border crimes are due to trafficking and smuggling between the illegal crossing of the Bolivia–Peru border, the recurrent destination being the mining center "La Rinconada," in Puno, Peru (CHS 2010).

From the review of the news about the Bolivia–Peru border for the years 2010–2014, we identified that the most recurrent types of crime are: trafficking of persons for sexual and commercial exploitation, mainly adolescents and young people between 13 and 17 years old, and trafficking of migrants for the purpose of labor exploitation and sex work. The greatest number of cases of trafficking and smuggling are recorded in La Paz, with the municipality of Desaguadero being the main border crossing point for trafficking and smuggling involving mainly children and adolescents.

Economic Dimensions

At the international level, studies qualify human trafficking as the third largest business among illegal markets. Despite the risk of calculating this type of market, about which they do not give information as a matter of principle, it is worth to point out their quantitative appreciation that the business of trafficking and smuggling is among the largest in the world. According to Pontón, the flow is approximately $31 billion (Pontón 2015, 138).

In Bolivia, there is no estimate of the economic spin-offs from these activities in the market: they generate dirty money and, at the same time, are an opportunity to launder money from any of the sectors of the illegal market. Analyzing some key news items, one can suspect that this is big business: the casinos and houses that manage trafficking have shown us the existence of networks that are not easily visible, given the protection of the police and the judicial system with which they operate. There is no argument for assuming that these are not similar dimensions to those shown by the business at a global level. "This problem would mobilize an estimated $6.6 billion a year in Latin America, out of a total of $32 billion in the world" (Mendoza 2013).

The Insertion of Illegal Flows into the Legal Economy (Money Laundering)

There is no doubt that a robust informal economy, where tens of thousands of small traders, producers and others operate, is fertile ground for the insertion of illegal flows into the money circuits of the legal economy. In an economy such as Bolivia's, which is highly informal, a veritable army of small operators uses a complex logistical and operational system of insertion. Certainly, most of these

120   *Illegal Markets*

informal workers have no direct link to the wholesale operators who are eventually more directly linked to the large producers of black money, large drug traffickers, and smugglers. But these small players receive resources and convert them into legal money in thousands of ways, including eventually the banking system (Ferrufino 2015, 26).

The spaces that informality uses run through successive phases of capital legalization. The placement phase occurs with the entry into the financial system of small amounts of capital of dubious or spurious origin. For example, a few wholesale importers who enter merchandise – one part legal, the other illegal – are handed over to dozens of intermediaries, who, in turn, redistribute them to thousands of micro-traders. The product reaches the consumer in informal markets, fairs, etc., and issuance of invoices or presentation of policies or other documents is required. The merchants place the product and the income from the sales is deposited in tens of thousands of small accounts in the financial system. Money from sales is transferred from small accounts to larger wholesale accounts and so on. Wholesaler accounts report payments for goods delivered, in installments, and through legal and dispersed channels. Because of laws regulating special systems, they do not need to bill. Considering that over 70% operate in this way, we are faced with a huge army of laundering merchants. These are loose in the streets or organized in an enormous quantity of deregulated markets in all the cities of the country and parallel fairs that pass through the cities (Ferrufino 2015, 26).

This is the opposite of a regulated economy in other countries, where this situation would be impossible. Absolutely everything is sold in legally established businesses (shops, supermarkets, shopping malls, etc.). Everything is sold with an invoice; the distribution companies also require invoices from the wholesalers, and the State controls the import policies and other documentation such as the invoice of origin, official registers, etc. as a wholesale operator.

In formal economies, most transactions, including consumer transactions, are completed through the financial system, with the use of credit and/or debit cards, which is not usually the case in informal economies where cash predominates. In a system with 70% or more being informal, almost nothing is paid in value added tax (VAT). A second level is related to activities that involve complex operations, in which the initial trail of this capital can be eliminated; money transactions that are unrelated to their origin due to the lack or extent of control. Among the options available is economic diversification toward real assets, such as the purchase, sale, construction, and financing of real estate, which is usually one of the modalities used, origin of the so-called real estate bubbles; automotive transactions, purchases of bonds that do not require showing the origin of the money: consumption of luxury. In this way a wide space is created. No one can question a resource that is "registered in licit activities," that can play in the stock market, justify its origin with goods, etc., or the capital stock has already been formed (Ferrufino 2015, 26).

Because of the phase in the drug trafficking circuit in which Bolivia finds itself, extraction and production of goods, including hydrochloride – in which approximately 20–25% of the total product is managed – little is required to migrate to tax havens outside the country. There is an enviable "paradise" in the informal economy and a sufficiently flexible regulatory framework.

Figure 4.4 traces the imaginable flows among the multitude of actors both between triangles and within each stage. If we imagine a graph in which the whole of the illegal market can be dissected and the flows that operate within each triangle can be dissected, we will have an image of the extraordinary complexity and magnitude of the porosity that facilitates laundering. We can hypothesize the similarity in size and complexity of the illegal market as well as the ease with which such a powerful and globalized sector can be constituted in the structuring sector of the border relations of the Bolivian system.

Sectors of the Economy Most Used in Money Laundering

According to Ramírez (1996, 15), it is impossible to prevent the intermingling of resources from illicit activities with trade and the banking sector, but, according to authorities, there are some sectors that are easier to penetrate. The more so when, in Bolivia, many economic activities are carried out without the intervention of banks or other financial mechanisms.

> The Public Ministry identified at least five areas in which people linked to drug trafficking in Bolivia engage in money laundering, among them the automobile industry, real estate buying and selling, construction, investment in company shares, and the purchase of bonds.
>
> (Los Tiempos 2016)

In an interview with *Los Tiempos*, Freddy Larrea, National Director of Controlled Substances of the Attorney General's Office, explained about money laundering and other crimes that are related to the world of illicit trafficking of controlled substances. He explained that in Bolivia there are currently 115 cases under investigation for the crime of legitimization of illicit profits from drug trafficking, of which eight were sentenced in 2015.

> We have the automobile industry with the purchase and sale of vehicles, it's a way of laundering money. We have real estate cases, with the purchase and sale of land, apartments, or condominiums; investment in company shares and the purchase of bonds. In construction we also have many cases.
>
> (Los Tiempos 2016)

Larrea explained that these items are used because this type of transaction can be generally carried out between private individuals, without any intermediary such as banks. "Maybe that's where we're failing as an institution to exercise better control. A mechanism that can, in due time, alert us so that we can activate the operation" (Los Tiempos 2016).

Regarding the overlap between smuggling and the rest of the illegal sectors, the Vice Minister of Tax Policy, Susana Ríos, assured that the illicit activity of

122 *Illegal Markets*

smuggling in Bolivia is used to launder money of dubious origin. She mentions that

> It is necessary to differentiate between two specific issues. Unfortunately, smuggling is closely associated with money laundering, the latter is covered up by the former. That is why many times one finds merchandise that is much cheaper than in the factory and that is not normal because nobody sells at a loss.
>
> (Los Tiempos 2016)

According to Ríos, the costs of smuggling are higher than in a legal import. She also clarified that the price involved in an illicit smuggling action can be equivalent to a legal import, and in some cases smuggling is more expensive, despite being produced in a larger-scale. (Los Tiempos 2016).

The hypothesis that we are dealing with in the Bolivian situation is that it is not required for tax havens, but rather for very few cases of the high domes of drug trafficking, and the clans of smuggling of gold imports or exports. The enormous porosity of the informal economy and, given the predominance of medium and small-sized businesses, the large number of businesses that operate outside the banking system define a situation in which the country is an easy space for the infiltration of black money into the economy, facilitating the laundering or legalization of the money.

The final question, under these conditions, is to what extent money laundering can be called an illegal market sector or rather the same sectors that are involved in this stage of legality. It is understood that it is an international actor when it has an institutionality and a headquarters of operations, like those of tax havens, but in the case of Bolivia, 70% of the economy is a haven for laundering.

Notes

1. One *cato* is equal to 1,600 square meters or about a third of an acre in the Chapare and 2,500 square meters in the Yungas (where farmers contend that the coca bush yields less than in the Chapare).
2. The 2015 report of the U.S. Department of State on the fight against drugs, based on reports from Peruvian police authorities, states that 95% of the cocaine paste that leaves Peru does so through Bolivian territory (United States Department of State 2015).
3. In addition to this, the price of the coca leaf in the legal markets of Bolivia would be higher than in Peru. "More than double and even triple," says the Bolivian researcher José Carlos Campero (Campero and Barrancos 2013, 75).
4. ENACO produces 92% of pure cocaine and exports 300 kilograms a year to international pharmaceutical companies; the annual demand of these organizations would exceed one ton per year. See http://www.enaco.com.pe/.
5. For his part, the North American journalist and researcher Jeremy MacDermott points out that "organized crime in the country is mainly limited to criminal clans, which participate in a wide variety of criminal activities, mainly smuggling. Sometimes these

Illegal Markets 123

clans involved in drug trafficking are also involved in the production of coca base" (2014a, 3). Quoting a high-level source in the Bolivian Police, McDermott says that "the most sophisticated of these clans can gather up to 1,000 kilos of coca base and send it to Brazilian organized crime groups. This coca base, or cocaine base, will later feed the *bazuco* market" (2014a, 4).

6 Interview for this report with Gonzalo Quezada, former national director of the Fuerza Especial de Lucha contra el Narcotráfico (Special Force to Fight Drug Trafficking) (FELCN), June 2015.

7 In another interview with the newspaper El Día, and when he was still holding that high position, Gonzalo Quezada stated: "The illicit traffic of cocaine is monopolized by Colombian citizens. They have been in charge of looking for markets in Europe, the United States United States, and other emerging markets. In South America, they have joined with criminal gangs in Brazil such as the PCC, the Comando Vermelho, to whom they supply cocaine" (2012).

8 "Colombians run most of the crystallization laboratories in Bolivia. They know how to produce very high purity cocaine. They prefer the base from Peru, which costs around $1,400 per kilo. It tends to be of better quality and is cheaper than the Bolivian one, where it normally costs $1,800. There are three types of Colombians in Bolivia: first, there is the high-level narco, who appears to be a businessman or rancher, then the sicario, the murderer, and, finally, by far the most common type of Colombian, is the low-level thief or criminal. The latter is practically the only one who is actually arrested" (McDermott 2014b, 1).

9 The 2014 report on the International Narcotics Control Strategy (INCSR) of the U.S. Department of State observes that Colombian, Brazilian, Peruvian, and other foreigners are engaged in the financing, production, and export of drugs, as well as money laundering (United States Department of State 2014).

10 The book *Cocaine King* contextualizes the period between the 1980s and 1990s, where the market with the United States worked in a personalized form and was shared by the Bolivian Roberto Suárez (Levy 2013).

11 At the height of their power, Suárez and Escobar would have financed the so-called "cocaine coup" in Bolivia, which installed the military "narco-dictatorship" of General García Mesa (1980–1981). These events are described by the journalist Boris Miranda in "El Carnicero y el Patrón: la conexión oculta entre Pablo Escobar y Klaus Barbie," which also recounts the important role of the ex-Nazi Altmann, known as the "Butcher of Lyon," and based in Bolivia (see Miranda 2015). From here, he organized and directed a sinister paramilitary group, the Novios de la muerte (boyfriends of death), to support the 1980 military coup. He later put himself at the service of Suárez's drug businesses and Escobar. See also Bill Conroy 2012.

12 According to reports mentioned in the report "Narcos del Perú cambian vías para entrar a Bolivia," the Bolivian Vice Minister of Social Defense, Felipe Cáceres, corroborated such versions, assuring that Peruvian drug traffickers "change embarkation points constantly" (El Deber 2015a).

13 Coca and Controlled Substances Regime Law, enacted on July 19, 1988.

14 The volume of crops is an old topic, although with changing facets, of which today there are two versions. On the one hand, the government supported by the UNODC report, prepared with official sources and figures (monitoring of coca crops) and, on the other, the U.S. government with its Control Strategy Report (CSR). In its 2016 version, it contains data that question the study carried out by the UNODC. The report insists on the current existence of 35,000 hectares of coca leaf in Bolivia, instead of 20,200 (Martínez 2016).

15 This report, the 13th, has been published since 2003 by the UNODC in coordination with the government of the Plurinational State of Bolivia and provides information on the extent of coca cultivation in the Yungas of La Paz, Cochabamba Tropics, and the northern provinces of La Paz, as well as the potential production of coca leaf. Likewise,

124 *Illegal Markets*

it presents complementary information, from Bolivian state institutions, on coca leaf prices, its commercialization, rationalization/eradication, and other related topics. The methodology combines the technique of visual interpretation of satellite images and the validation of the interpretation through ground and airfield verification missions.

16 In the Vice Ministry of Coca and Integral Development (VCDI), the General Directorate of the Coca Leaf and Industrialization (DIGCOIN) fulfills the functions established by the regulation of circulation and commercialization of the coca leaf in its natural state.

17 "The US Department of State released its 2016 report on anti-narcotics control, where it reiterates Bolivia's 'manifest failure' in the fight against drugs, indicating that between 2013 and 2014 there was a 30% increase in coca plantations, which according to the report would reach 35,000 hectares" (United States Department of State 2016).

18 The European Union financed a study published in Bolivia and established that the legal and traditional use of the plant only requires a production of around 14,700 hectares. Bolivian legislation admits a maximum of 12,000 hectares of coca leaves for legal use, but the Executive is discussing a bill, in consultation with the peasant sectors, that could raise that limit to 20,000 hectares.

19 "'In Bolivia, drug traffickers take advantage of an even greater lack of control than occurs in Peruvian territory,' the Dirandro report ends explaining that in the country it is 'easier' to crystallize and put chemicals into the cocaine base paste that comes out of the Valley of the Apurimac, Ene, and Mantaro Rivers in Peru. This area has no police control and, according to official sources, the Shining Path operates there" (El Deber 2015b).

20 Tariff=0% in extension zone; import tax=0.6% on CIF value; VAT=0% on the first sale and 19% from the second (Ferrufino 2015, 11).

21 "They estimate evasion of up to $500 million Bs for gold exports ... According to official data, last year the country exported gold for $1,215 million and 90.4% ($1,099 million) of that production was sold under the figure of waste and amalgam waste, which allowed paying less royalties, in favor of the regions. In this sense, the governmental National Service for Registration and Marketing of Minerals (SENARECOM) calculates a tax evasion that ranges between $21.4 and $71 million (between $150 million and $500 million Bs, approximately)" (Belmonte and Mamani 2013). It adds that the amount defrauded in taxes could approach $400 million.

22 See also Garzón (2013) and Fundación Milenio (2013).

23 See Excelsior (2016).

References

Belmonte, M., and L. Mamani. 2013. "Estiman evasión de hasta bs 500 millones por exportación de oro." *Página Siete*, August 11, 2013. https://www.cedib.org/noticias/estiman-evasion-de-hasta-bs-500-millones-por-exportacion-de-oro-pagina7-11-8-13/.

Blanes, José. 1990. "La cocaína, la informalidad y la economía urbana en La Paz, Bolivia." In *La Economía informal. Estudios en países avanzados y menos desarrollados*, edited by Alejandro Portes. Buenos Aires: Planeta.

Campero, José Carlos. 2012. "Estudio exploratorio sobre Problemáticas de seguridad en ciudades frontera. Caso: Ciudad de Cobija." *Policy Papers*, No. 3.

———. 2014. "Los retos para Bolivia ante un nuevo marco mundial de política de drogas." In *Bolivia: Encrucijadas en el siglo XXI. Ideas y visiones para una agenda de país*, edited by Henry Oporto, 583–633. La Paz: Fundación Pazos Kanki.

Campero, José Carlos, and Horacio Barrancos. 2013. "Alternativas a la política actual de drogas desde el eslabón de la producción." In *De la represión a la regulación: Propuestas para reformar las políticas contra las drogas*, edited by Hans Mathieu and Catalina Niño, 65–115. Bogotá: FES.

Carrión, Fernando. 2015. *La Red Global del Narcotráfico. Perspectivas de una corte penal regional en el marco de la UNASUR.* Ecuador: Friedrich Ebert Stiftung/ILDIS - Fiscalía General del Estado, Ecuador.

Carrión, Fernando, and Federico Alagna. 2016. *La cartelización de América Latina y sus vínculos con Europa.* Unpublished PowerPoint Presentation. Quito.

Castilla, Oscar. 2014. "Los vuelos secretos del oro ilegal." *Ojo Público*, December 15, 2014. https://ojo-publico.com/12/los-vuelos-secretos-del-oro-ilegal.

CHS. 2010. *La trata de personas en el Perú. Manual para conocer el problema.* Lima: CHS alternativo.

Conroy, Bill. 2012. "Asesinato de la "Reina de la Cocaína" de Miami revela momento aleccionador." *The Narco News Bulletin*, October 7, 2012. http://www.narconews.com/Issue67/articulo4629.html.

DCI Crime and Narcotics Center and the Drug Enforcment Administration. 2000. *Colombia: Coca Cultivation and Preliminary Results From Operation Breakthrough*, May 8, 2000. http://www.drugpolicy.org/docUploads/bigwood_coca_op_breakthrough.pdf.

El Comercio. 2016. "El horror de la trata de personas en Bolivia y Argentina." September 7, 2016. https://elcomercio.pe/mundo/latinoamerica/horror-trata-personas-bolivia-argentina-256233-noticia/on-mas-casos-de-trata-y-trafico-en-sudamerica.

El Deber. 2015a. "Narcos del Perú cambian vías para entrar a Bolivia." November 22, 2015. https://eju.tv/2015/11/narcos-del-peru-cambian-vias-para-entrar-a-bolivia/.

———. 2015b. "Bolivia adultera la droga de Perú para aumentarla de peso." June 7, 2015. https://eldeber.com.bo/bolivia/bolivia-adultera-la-droga-de-peru-para-aumentarla-de-peso_32467.

———. 2015c. "La hoja de coca boliviana cuesta más del doble que la peruana." August 28, 2015. https://eju.tv/2015/08/la-hoja-de-coca-boliviana-cuesta-mas-del-doble-que-la-peruana/.

El Día. 2013. "Entre 2011 y 2013 los casos de trata y tráfico de personas se incrementaron en 40%." September 24, 2013. https://www.eldia.com.bo/noticia.php?id=127939&id_cat=1.

El Diario. 2015. "Antonino De Leo: "Falta estudio sobre conversión de coca en cocaína"." September 1, 2015. https://eju.tv/2015/09/antonino-de-leo-falta-estudio-sobre-conversion-de-coca-en-cocaina/.

Erbol. 2015. "Trata y tráfico: Hubo 439 casos el 2013 y 515 el 2014." August 28, 2015. https://anteriorportal.erbol.com.bo/noticia/seguridad/28082015/trata_y_trafico_registraron_439_casos_el_2013_y_515_el_2014.

Excelsior. 2016. "Cártel usa oro para lavar dinero en EU; investigación en Chicago." May 6, 2016. https://www.excelsior.com.mx/nacional/2016/05/06/1090979.

Ferrufino, Rubén. 2009. *Comercio exterior ilegal en Bolivia: Estimaciones 2000–2008. Confederación de Empresarios Privados de Bolivia.* Unpublished Document. La Paz.

———. 2015. "La economía transfronteriza de Bolivia: Aproximación a los flujos económicos ilegales." *Unpublished Document for the Centro Boliviano de Estudios Multidisciplinarios CEBEM*, La Paz.

Fundación Milenio. 2013. *Informe de Milenio sobre la economía. Gestión 2012.* July 2013, No. 34.

Garzón, Dionisio. 2013. "The Magic of Numbers." *La Razón*, June 14, 2013. Printed.

INE. 2007. "Plan Nacional de Desarrollo Bolivia Digna, Soberana, Productiva y Democrática Para Vivir Bien." In *Lineamientos Estratégicos 2006–2011.* La Paz: Estado Plurinacional de Bolivia.

126   *Illegal Markets*

La Patria. 2014. "OEA: Bolivia entre los 5 países con más casos de trata y tráfico en Sudamérica." May 26, 2014. https://impresa.lapatria.bo/noticia/183700/oea-bolivia-entre-los-5-paises-c.

Levy, Ayda. 2013. *El rey de la cocaína. Mi vida con Roberto* Suárez *y el Nacimiento del primer Narcoestado.* Mexico: Random House.

Lifsher, Marc. 2003. "In U.S. Drug War, Ally Bolivia Loses Ground to Coca Farmers." *The Wall Street Journal.* May 13, 2003. https://www.wsj.com/articles/SB105277602959745000.

Los Tiempos. 2016. "En Bolivia los narcos lavan dinero en 5 rubros legales." January 18, 2016. https://www.lostiempos.com/actualidad/nacional/20160117/narcos-lavan-dinero-5-rubros-legales?page=1.

Mallette, J., Casale, J., and Jordan, J. 2016. "Geographically Sourcing Cocaine's Origin – Delineation of the Nineteen Major Coca Growing Regions in South America." *Science Report*, No. 6. https://doi.org/10.1038/srep23520.

Martínez, Cué F., Daniel, Mauricio Chumacero V., and Labor. "VII. La contribucion del sector informal urbano al pib nacional urbano y al pib sectorial, 1995–2005." In *El sector informal urbano en Bolivia, 1995–2005. Empleo, ingreso, productividad y contribución al Producto Interno Bruto urbano.* La Paz: Labor.

Martínez, Emilio. 2016. "EEUU vs MAS, informe sobre coca/cocaína." *El Deber*, March 14, 2016. https://eju.tv/2016/03/eeuu-vs-mas-informe-cocacocaina/.

McDermott, Jeremy. 2014a. "El desafío de Evo: Bolivia, el epicentro de la droga." *InSight Crime*, October 2014. https://insightcrime.org/wp-content/uploads/2019/10/Desafio_Evo_Bolivia_epicentro_droga.pdf.

———. 2014b. "Las voces del hampa de Bolivia." *InSight Crime*, October 16, 2014. http://es.insightcrime.org/investigaciones/voces-hampa-bolivia.

Mendoza, Luz. 2013. "El 2013 marca un incremento en los casos de trata y tráfico de personas en Bolivia." *ANF*, December 23, 2013. https://eju.tv/2013/12/el-2013-marca-un-incremento-en-los-casos-de-trata-y-trfico-de-personas-en-bolivia/.

———. 2014. "Identifican más de 100 vías ilegales en fronteras de Bolivia-Chile." *El Deber*, July 13, 2014. https://eju.tv/2014/07/identifican-ms-de-100-vas-ilegales-en-fronteras-de-bolivia-chile/.

Miranda, Boris. 2015. "El Carnicero y el Patrón. La conexión oculta entre Pablo Escobar y Klaus Barbie Boris." *Nueva Sociedad*, No. 257 (May–June). https://nuso.org/articulo/el-carnicero-y-el-patron-la-conexion-oculta-entre-pablo-escobar-y-klaus-barbie/.

Navarro, Jaime. 2014. *La verdad sobre la evasión de impuestos en las exportaciones de oro.* La Paz: Unidad Nacional.

Opinión. 2012. "Oposición duda del informe sobre monitoreo de la coca." September 17, 2012. https://www.opinion.com.bo/articulo/el-pais/oposicion-duda-informe-monitoreo-coca/20120917210900432047.html.

Pacheco, Napoleón, and José Luis Evia. 2010. "Bolivia." In *Sector informal y políticas públicas en América Latina*, 22–33. Santiago: SOPLA and Konrad Adenauer Stiftung. https://www2.congreso.gob.pe/sicr/cendocbib/con4_uibd.nsf/B8F5C7E52A6A425D05257D5800787207/$FILE/SectorInformal_y_Pol%C3%ADticasP%C3%BAblicasEnAm%C3%A9ricaLatina.pdf.

Página Siete. 2012. "Gobierno dice que en Bolivia operan narcos itinerantes." June 20, 2012. https://eju.tv/2012/06/gobierno-dice-que-en-bolivia-operan-narcos-itinerantes/.

Painter, James. 1994. *Bolivia and Cocal: A study in Dependency.* USA: Lynne Rienner Publishers.

Pontón, Daniel. 2015. "La economía del narcotráfico y su dinámica en América Latina." *ICONOS*, Vol. 47, 135–143. Quito: Flacso.

Quezada, Gonzalo. 2012. "Interview by Lubomir Endara Sánchez." May 2012. https://www.eldia.com.bo/noticia.php?id=92230&id_cat=1.

Ramírez Romero, Juan Ramón. 1996. "El lavado de dinero y la economia en Bolivia." *Revista de Analisis Económico*, Vol. 16. http://www.udape.gob.bo/portales_html/AnalisisEconomico/analisis/vol16/art07.pdf.

Torres Cuzcano, Víctor. 2015. "Minería Ilegal e Informal en el Perú: Impacto Socio-Económico." *Cuadernos de CooperAcción*, No. 2 (August).

UNDP. 2016. *Reflections on Drug Policy and its Impact on Human Development: Innovative Approaches*. New York: UNDP.

United States Department of State. 2014. "Bolivia." In *2014 International Narcotics Control Strategy Report*.

———. 2015. "Bolivia." In *International Narcotics Control Strategy Report*. March 2015. Bureau for International Narcotics and Law, Enforcement Affairs.

———. 2016. *International Narcotics Control Strategy Report Volume 1*. Bureau for International Narcotics and Law, Enforcement Affairs.

UNODC. 2013. *World Drug Report 2013*. New York: UNODC.

———. 2014. *Perú. Monitoreo de Cultivos de Coca 2013*. Lima: UNODC

———. 2015. *Estado Plurinacional de Bolivia. Monitoreo de Cultivos de Coca 2014*. La Paz: UNODC.

———. 2016. *Global Report on Trafficking in Persons 2016*. Vienna: UNODC, 97–102.

Vásquez, Katiuska. 2016. "Pese a denuncias, falta saber estado real de trata." *Los Tiempos*, July 27, 2016. https://www.lostiempos.com/actualidad/local/20160727/pese-denuncias-falta-saber-estado-real-trata.

Part 3

Policies

5 Public Policies and the Border Subsystem

This chapter on state actors in charge of public policy considers two issues that affect policy implementation. Firstly, we refer to the level of definition and the conditions of implementation, highlighting their centralist nature, which is not very appropriate if it refers to very specific local issues such as border issues. Secondly, a very brief account will be given of some of the policies most related to illegal markets.

In recent years, border policies have focused on several issues directed from the central level, and, since the 1930s, some regions have begun to put forward their own plans and programs, especially Santa Cruz and Tarija. However, until very recently, these regions concentrated their demands around the problems of income and investment in the capital cities. Only since the mid-1990s has importance been given to the provinces and border areas whose municipalities were consolidated in 1995.

With respect to the issues that we consider to be structuring factors of the border system, centralism has dominated sectoral polities, policies have been national, and customs, its police, and collection mechanisms have taken charge. Regarding smuggling and drug trafficking, the problem has become police-led and punitive, with the involvement of international cooperation. However, in contrast to this reduction in policy and its simplicity are the complexity and diversity of actors that emerged in the forces that generated the illegal markets. Policies not only do not appear to correspond to the issue and its evolution but are increasingly lagging.

Legality versus legitimacy was one of the main fields that was defined, under the impulse of the illegal markets. A confrontation – nothing theoretical but very practical – was established between the content of the legal, of the institutionality implicit in the policies, and the deepening of the contempt for these same policies. The application of laws was politicized and "pragmatized," following the subordination of the definition of their contents and general inability to remember legal contents. Although smuggling and drug trafficking are illegal, it has been accepted as, simply, another job, since so many people make a living from these businesses that provide employment.

The power of the narcos and smugglers is very great, and police force is inadequately armed before them; they surpass the media. This is another narrative that legitimizes the "inefficiency of the Police."

DOI: 10.4324/9781003203117-9

132   *Policies*

The main adversity the policies face has been their implementation, among other factors, because of the recognition of the legality, that the crime is there and must be fought, but it is very difficult to implement the policies for a number of reasons; the argument being that "we must be practical" and "we cannot afford" policy implementation. There is a lot of corruption in the justice system and the State is weak. Everything is a structural problem, and the change that is beginning has a long way to go.

The system of laws in several of the policy fields is very well defined. The adhesion of successive governments to international conventions, in which they have been involved and from which many of the laws have been nourished, has been decisive in this aspect.

Under an Environment of Legality and Adaptation of Policies to the Domain of Illegality

In this book, policies are understood as the set of rules that should regulate the practices and overall performance of society and the economy. Policies have their own actors, not only those charged by law to implement them, but also those interested in their enforcement. But it is here that informality is in charge of generating the steps that allow rules to be broken and can be imposed as a more or less deep and generalized system, until becoming special cases. In this field of forces there are actors who have imposed a general situation of impunity.

The Triangle of Informality, Drug Trafficking, and Smuggling versus Institutionality

Illegal markets push the conditions to the maximum to adapt the rules to their impulses and pressures. Conditions where the rules are very flexible and the authorities are not adequately prepared, equipped, updated, etc. facilitate the adaptation of the illegal markets. In a country with rigid and prepared rules and authorities, it would be difficult to imagine letting thousands of cars illegally pass through borders, especially years after their explicit prohibition. The same happens for used clothes, "ant" smuggling, etc. It is not the police's fault that such looseness occurs under their authority, but it is the system as a whole that grants permissiveness of illegality.

Social practices put more emphasis on legitimacy, on actions that are "not so legal," but which are justified by the people's necessity. These issues are fundamental, since in a country, depending on how the institutions behave, conditions of ease to illegality can be generated.

This type of widespread informality is an important source of income and generates an economy of illegality. The institutions are not prepared; narcos are very powerful. People have to find something to live from; the lack of jobs generates other types of businesses. And, since it is crudely true, the illegal manages to achieve such legitimacy that sometimes it becomes almost the norm.

Public Policies and the Border Subsystem 133

In Bolivia, a triangle of informality has been established, configuring a complex and motley network of socioeconomic relations, around which a wide range of informal and illegal businesses and activities take place, especially around popular economy, mostly informal, but with ramifications to other areas and sectors of the national economy. This triangle constitutes a system of interactions between the informal sector, smuggling, and drug trafficking, where informality is nourished by activities that can be openly criminal, and these, in turn, are subsumed and protected by the informal behavior of the economy and other areas of social and political life. Its capacity is high, to the point of becoming a real attraction for many of the legal activities by definition: construction, banking, import/ export trade, and many other "industries."

On the other hand, drug trafficking is influenced by criminal groups (national and foreign), but with a dynamic that is spread over a wide population and diverse economic agents, many of them acting in the border areas, but not exclusively. This also explains the enormous complexity of the criminal world operating in Bolivia, which is immersed in a dense social fabric and has a dislocated territorial presence with connections in other countries, mainly neighboring ones.

It is common for the press and media to be in favor of a law or against it, and, at the same time, to recognize pragmatism in its application. For pragmatic reasons, coca producers, peasant and indigenous organizations, mining cooperatives, unionized transporters, traders' guilds, labor unions, and used clothing and car dealers are presented as legitimate situations justified by their means; no matter how illegal they could be.

Despite the fact that Bolivia is a model in the recognition of rights and their legal connection with laws, it is not among the countries where legality and the strength of institutions prevail.

Drug trafficking and smuggling – the two most important pivots of our illegal markets – exert great power toward the consolidation of these types of sociopolitical practices.

Following are considerations of some of the institutional features in the field of policy implementation.

A Collapsed Justice System

The erosion of legality and the rule of law are most noticeable is in the collapse of the administration of justice, which is surrounded by an environment of very high disrepute, not only because of its inefficiency, but because of corruption. The worst thing that can happen to the justice system is to lose the trust of the population.

The judicial arrears are growing. According to official data, the cases resolved in all judicial matters barely reach 31%, while the pending cases reach 69%. Of every three cases filed in the courts, at least two are pending. In certain matters (pretrial investigation, criminal enforcement, and administrative-prosecution), the backlog of cases is between 85 and 90% (Oporto 2014, 3–5).

134   *Policies*

Procedural overload in the courts: The gap between the increase in cases and the reduced number of courts is growing. As a result, the average number of cases per judge has continued to grow, reaching extraordinary and unprecedented proportions. The national average in terms of preventive criminal investigations is 2,470 cases per judge. In the cities of Cochabamba and Santa Cruz this average even exceeds 3,000 cases per judge in a single year (Oporto 2014, 5).

Overcrowded judges and prosecutors: The lack of judges is reproduced in the Public Prosecutor's Office. Between 2008 and 2011, the number of prosecutors throughout the country grew by only 2%, compared to the growth in cases which, over the same period, increased by 13.5%. Thus, between 2008 and 2012, the number of cases per prosecutor (as a national average) in the nine departmental capitals had risen from 165 to 179 cases (Oporto 2014, 7). However, in the last two years, this figure may even have increased.

Overcrowded prisons: With the lack of court sentences, the number of prisoners without enforceable sentences is also increasing. According to Molina Céspedes (2013), the prison population in Bolivia as of 2011 reached 13,500 prisoners, 84% of whom had no sentence. This enormous mass of prisoners, without enforceable sentences, who should not be in prison and yet are condemned to subhuman prison conditions, is one of the main causes of prison overcrowding, estimated at 233%. Bolivia is the second country in the hemisphere with the greatest prison overcrowding (Wickberg 2012).

Lower budget for justice: In 2005, investment in the justice sector (the Judicial Branch, the Public Prosecutor's Office, and the Public Prosecutor's Office) was just under 2% of total public sector spending. Over the next nine years that percentage has fallen. In 2013, the programmed budget for the justice sector ($826,727,362 Bs) was just 0.36% of the nation's general budget ($228,285,224,092 Bs or $31,928,400,000) (Oporto 2014, 10).[1] This situation especially affects the regulation of drug trafficking and smuggling, which are the main causes of the presence of pretrial detainees in prisons.

Another disturbing fact in this situation, which generates distrust in the justice system, is that there are more and more Bolivians who approve the practice of vigilante justice. This is a sign, par excellence, of informality as an empire of direct practice.

Criminal Prosecution on Principle

The excessive use of the Penal Code often shows many flaws in the justice system. In recent years, it is around the crime of drug trafficking that it is most often applied; thus, the prisons are full of people accused of this crime. The situation is more serious because these charges are not resolved and the delay in justice affects an exaggeratedly large number of small offenders. The crimes covered by Law 1008 of the Coca and Controlled Substances Regime are the main cause of imprisonment in the country's prisons (PIEB 2012, 2–7).[2]

The prevalence of drug trafficking cases in the procedural situation of the prison population has much to do with the extremely rigorous nature of the

Table 5.1 Prison Population per Criminal Act

Variable	2008		2009		2010	
	N^o	%	N^o	%	N^o	%
Crimes against national security	79	1	32	0	22	1
Drug trafficking	2.796	38	2.522	31	2.741	28
Rape	917	12	1.420	18	1.717	18
Assassination	782	11	822	10	916	10
Homicide	373	5	407	5	511	5
Robbery	1.210	16	1.538	19	1.934	21
Other crimes	1.276	17	1.355	17	1.565	17

Source: Fundacion Construir (2012).

anti-drug legislation in force, which does not differentiate between large drug traffickers and criminal organizations and small producers or occasional suppliers of base paste or other inputs, so that the penalties applied are usually hugely disproportionate and discretionary[3] and almost always inclined toward the criminalization of minor crimes and poor people.[4] Women represent one of the most critical populations. Out of a total of 1,157 women deprived of their liberty in Bolivia, 448 were held for crimes related to the Law on Regime of Coca and Controlled Substances (Law 1008). This figure represents twice the proportion of men deprived of liberty in Bolivia for similar crimes (UNODC 2016). According to UNODC's point of view, the authors of minor and nonviolent drug-related crimes should be able to benefit from alternatives to the deprivation of liberty, including fines, community service, or house arrest (UNODC 2016).

Corruption and Illegal Funding Networks

The formation of corruption networks involving leaders of social organizations, public officials, politicians, police officers, and judicial officers has brought to the fore actors who are entrenched in the public apparatus. The most notable case has been the unveiling of an extortion, fraud, and possibly illegal political financing network around the commercialization of coca leaves. The network of corruption discovered in the commercialization of coca exemplifies the emergence within the state apparatus of a type of criminal articulation involving authorities, officials, political operators, prosecutors, judges, and lawyers, who act with impunity and exercise discretionary powers that allow them to use this power to pressure and harass people and obtain from them enormous sums of money, which are then distributed within the corrupt circle. Other examples refer to different forms of corruption through extortion networks involving police, prosecutors, and judges.

It is typical of drug traffickers and criminal organizations to penetrate state institutions – such as the police and other intelligence and interdiction agencies

136   *Policies*

– to coopt their bosses and officials or to bribe politicians, judges, and prosecutors. This infiltration has been happening since some years ago and has turned the state apparatus into a more fragile and unprotected one. This situation is exacerbated by the concentration of power, the lack of a legal tradition, a nonfunctioning justice system, uncontrolled prisons, unguarded or permissive borders, territorial areas without law and order,[5] poor security policies, and the fight against crime.

The public force, police, and armed forces (FFAA) are burdened by a deep institutional crisis and with serious deficiencies in professionalism and technical capacity, human resources, equipment, and budget, as well as with appropriate social and labor conditions; thus, they lack the confidence of the citizens. All this is a breeding ground for corruption as an endemic evil,[6] making it common for the Police to be shaken by recurrent scandals with great political and media repercussions. One very significant case is the capture in Panamá City, in February 2011, of General René Sanabria, former director of the FELCN and of the main intelligence agency, the Center for Intelligence and Information Generation (CIGEIN). He got caught attempting to ship more than 140 kilos of cocaine to the United States. Prosecuted in Miami Federal Court, Sanabria was sentenced to 14 years in prison in that country. Another example is the arrest of General Oscar Nina, former commander of the Bolivian Police, in March 2015, in the city of Santa Cruz, for the crimes of legitimization of illicit earnings and illicit enrichment. In this case, the same government accuses him of having collaborated with drug traffickers who arrived from Mexico and Colombia in 2011, when he was Director of the Special Force for the Fight against Drug Trafficking. Other episodes show police chiefs involved in drug trafficking, who have been found in possession of significant amounts of cocaine (ANF 2015).

Gap between Crimes and Laws

Applicable to all crimes related to illegal markets, there is a gap between the characteristics of these markets and the legal regimes that regulate and punish them. Organized crime and its local ramifications are developing and changing in character faster than our regulatory systems. That is why justice is not functional in containing crime.

It is not a question of international regulations, but of local ones. Border crossings are not suited to the current forms of trafficking and smuggling that have become complex, changing, and quick to find ways and means. For example, changes in criminal codes often take quite a long time; during that period, forms of crime might have already changed. This issue is observed in a differentiated way according to each of the sectors of the illegal markets. Smuggling has changed forms to circumvent the old customs regimes; drug trafficking migrates from one point to another, as well as forms of human trafficking and smuggling. There is a marked difference in the timing of the crimes and the temporality of an anachronistic legislation that must pass through long routes, such as international mechanisms, binational agreements, national parliaments – which translate them into laws and regulations and to which in turn must be provided with budgets, training, and the necessary resources

Public Policies and the Border Subsystem 137

for their implementation. These routes do not coincide in their temporalities with the agility with which the various forms of crime change. Laws and their implementation always come late and behind the phenomenology of crime.

Sectoral Policies

What has been broadly discussed applies to each of the particular sectors that make up illegal markets. Although each of the sectors is involved in the same general problems, they have their own particularities, depending on the type of practices to be regulated and the actors they encounter.

Two areas of regulation have received greater attention with respect to illegal markets: smuggling and drug trafficking. Within each of these areas, there is no complete and comprehensive picture of regulation and implementation of conditions for the operation of policies, so efforts have been partial and in general need to update and complement regulatory mechanisms, budgets, and equipment.

In this chapter, the illegal markets which are most related to the role that Bolivia plays in the border system are referred to. In this case of policies and regulatory frameworks, we refer to smuggling, drug trafficking, money laundering, arms trafficking, and human trafficking. All of these are related to the management of border crossings.

Anti-smuggling Policies

At the legislative level, given the increase in the smuggling sector to levels never seen before, policies have been improved and so have been the regulations and operational mechanisms, the equipment and training of specialized police forces, and the incorporation of the Armed Forces in the repression of smuggling.

Never before has there been as much regulation as now nor has ever been so much smuggling activity, both in volume and in value, as well as in the variety and number of actors involved. Without approaching to a detailed description of the aforementioned regulatory depth on the subject, some aspects related to guidance and operational mechanisms are referred to.

Although until two decades ago there were instruments regulating the customs issue of border trade and the prosecution of smuggling, in recent years, this has been the most recurrent news in the press; although, at the same time, never has the flow of smuggled goods through all the crossings increased as it does now. These increased in number, and control mechanisms were formalized in most cases.

Recent Standards without Any New Developments

The rules being used are the classic ones used to guard an airport customs office or a border point where the bearer presents himself to the police. However, much of the large contraband has a different form of operation, challenging control mechanisms.

138 *Policies*

For example, the General Law on Customs (Law 1990 of 28 July 1999) is being applied mainly and almost exclusively in customs areas, for example land, river, or air border crossings, while massive smuggling occurs outside these areas, often beyond the means of the limited police. In almost all border crossings there is a physical flow parallel to the official crossings. It is not necessarily large transport but ant smuggling that passes through parallel and clandestine roads. For example, on the border with Chile, there are three large, controlled border crossings and approximately 114 clandestine ones. All of them lead through desert areas, though there is also the lush tropical route along the Argentine and Peruvian borders.

It is not worth going into detail in describing the legal and administrative mechanisms and the actual resources available, apart from the fact that in the last three years the police force – which operated on all the borders with few personnel – has been strengthened, with the participation of the Armed Forces. Even so, the problems have not been solved and the capacity to circumvent these control mechanisms is enormous. The power of corruption over the forces of law and order has not been resolved under these conditions. The weakness of law enforcement is expressed in the recurrent threat of helicopters and other means at borders, such as the Chilean one, through which hundreds of high-tonnage trucks – supposedly controlled at the Pisiga and Tambo Quemado – pass from the free zones of Iquique and Arica.

Guidance on Collection

Most of the successes reported by the National Customs are presented more as a fight against fraud and not as protection of national businesses by strengthening legality. It is a mean to raise resources for the treasury, as shown by the citizen campaigns to award prizes for unsuccessful complaints.

This happens despite the generalized pressure from small and medium enterprises against smuggling that is "drowning" national industry, especially due to noncompliance with the prohibition on the import of used clothing. Added to this are protests against the import of Chinese clothes, among other products, which, in addition to low prices due to low quality and influx of contraband, have effectively dealt a significant blow to textiles.

Centralism

The fact that customs policy is concentrated on national mechanisms and that the centralist persistence of their main activities gives advantages to smugglers implies that they can negotiate large consignments with important prerogatives for macro-corruption.

Training and profound changes in control and collection mechanisms are required at border crossings but mainly the strengthening of border municipalities, since, at that level, corruption is a mechanism more related to micro smuggling – the "ant" smuggling – which is, above all, a socioeconomic problem.

Public Policies and the Border Subsystem 139

More streamlined procedures could be established than those emanating from the national level.

The State's behavior in the regulation of smuggling is not really one of the main problems of the sector, which is more related to the informal, elusive, and corrupting nature of the Police.

Sterile Protectionism

Bolivia does not have a strong, preponderant domestic productive sector to protect, although many small sectors of the primary industrial and agricultural sector are affected by smuggling. It is mainly a country with an extractive primary economy, and its customs service is more of a collection mechanism than a protectionist apparatus. Neighboring countries are light-years ahead of the country's production and marketing capacity in terms of productivity and market management. It is the effort of giants with similar bilateral synchronies, from agricultural products to the industry of internal consumption, as is the case of drinks, the fruits, etc.

Border populations, generally considered among the poorest in the country, cannot be expected to forgo income from smuggling, which complements their traditional survival economies. This phenomenon has become widespread at all border posts, to the extent that in cases where smuggling is reversed due to Bolivian competition, Brazilians, Peruvians, and Argentines enter Bolivia, building real border economies, which provide significant income to families. The main problem lies in the capacity to coordinate national policies with local policies in order to define the most appropriate instruments.

Coca Policies

At the beginning it was emphasized that this sector of regulation, protected by Law 1008, is concentrated on coca, the predominant object of the current legislation. A proposal to change the regulations has been under discussion and negotiation with coca producers for more than three years. A division of the future law is proposed that would establish two regimes: a law on the coca leaf regime and another on controlled substances or drug trafficking itself. This is an important situation since the coca leaf is also used for legal purposes. Due to its licit nature, the protection of the latter covers drug trafficking under a veil of confusion, pushing it to the darkness of police persecution. When the coca growers who produce 90% for drug trafficking are accused, the sacred character and cultural use of the leaf are alluded to.

But the lack of definition around the first case is preventing progress in the approval of the new law. Defining the line between legal and illegal coca leaves is a serious political problem that involves relations of force, first between coca growers and second between coca growers and the president (Evo Morales).

The legal regulations and the system for their implementation go through a panorama of appearances of legality in the control of the coca leaf. Although the

140 *Policies*

real actions appear to be in pursuit of drug trafficking, in practice, it is a case of exercising informality expressed in laws that are not enforced for reasons beyond the law; this is social behavior of high political significance, since it is usually through blackmail. Both sides, the illegal coca growers and the State, present a "respect" for the law limited by uses and customs that are above the norm. In terms of controlling drug trafficking, this is a policy that criminalizes and harms the most vulnerable sectors and is carried out by the Police.

"Coca yes, cocaine no." This the slogan of the anti-drug policy of the last 20 years and could be mentioned as one of the most important loopholes for maintaining ambiguity in favor of the illegal coca leaf. What is usually considered as the new policy of control of coca crops – founded on the idea of revaluing the coca leaf as a heritage protected by the state – has a fundamental basis in the change of the Bolivian Constitution in 2009. The constitutional text states:

> The state protects the original and ancestral coca as a cultural heritage, a renewable natural resource of Bolivia's biodiversity, and as a factor of social cohesion; in its natural state, it is not a drug. The revaluation, production, commercialization, and industrialization shall be governed by law.
>
> (Article 384)

Although, conceptually, this constitutional definition basically reflects the treatment already established in the 1988 Law on the Regime of Coca and Controlled Substances – better known as Law 1008 – the fact that this treatment has been elevated to constitutional status has been interpreted by many popular and left-wing sectors, represented mainly by the peasants and cocaleros, as a political victory, but also as one of the emblems of the process of change and of the peasant and cocalero movement.

That same year, the government requested an amendment to Article 49 of the 1961 United Nations Convention on Narcotic Drugs – better known as the Vienna Convention – to eliminate the prohibition of coca leaf chewing, which led to the beginning of a period of consultation among the signatory countries, with the result of a majority rejection of the amendment requested by Bolivia. The response of the Bolivian government, formally notified to the UN Secretary General on June 29, 2011, was the withdrawal of the Bolivian State from the 1961 Single Convention on Narcotic Drugs. In December of the same year, the Bolivian Foreign Ministry requested the multilateral organization the readmission of Bolivia, with its reservation to the penalization of coca-chewing. Finally, in January 2013, and after only 15 of 183 countries objected to Bolivia's request – that is, without reaching the necessary third of votes to veto the request – the UN General Secretariat decided to admit Bolivia's reincorporation into the 1961 Convention with an exception for coca leaf chewing.[7]

The agreement was celebrated in Bolivia as a diplomatic victory for the country,[8] maintaining this space of unquestionable legitimacy for many, but also a space to defend the ambiguity in which the policy of permissiveness of leaf destined for drug trafficking is hidden. Thus, these events have had a special symbolic value in legitimizing the defense of the coca leaf in the face of pressure from the international community for the Bolivian state to continue developing coca crop eradication programs. This has given the government a margin of action to make the eradication policy more flexible and, in fact, consolidate the goal of stabilizing coca crops over an area of around 20,000 hectares, through a gradual and concerted eradication process with the coca growers' unions, also known as the rationalization of coca crops.

The message of "coca yes, cocaine no" summarizes the content of the new Bolivian strategy to fight drug trafficking, which the government of Evo Morales defined for the period 2007–2010, with two differentiated lines of action: on the one hand, the aforementioned rationalization of the crops and, on the other hand, the interdiction of drug trafficking; the same policy that has important difficulties to be approved.

Plan Colombia and Dignity Plan in Bolivia (1998) have been considered by many as twin policies, which represent the effect of imitating Bolivia to obtain important resources similar to those of Colombia. In this chapter, Plan Colombia represents a moment of pressure that impacted on the region and Bolivia.

There has been no lack of attempts to assimilate Dignity Plan – Bolivia's anti-drug trafficking strategy – with Plan Colombia. A comparison that sought to highlight certain common or convergent elements in both national programs, such as the participation of the Armed Forces in counter-narcotics operations and the forced eradication of coca plantations, but above all the enormous influence of the United States in the design and implementation of both plans, an influence that, according to some observers, accounts for "an intervention model" in Latin America and especially in the Andean region (Ledebur 2002).

The dimensions and consequences of one program and the other are not comparable. In one case, what became known as Plan Colombia was an integrated strategy to address Colombia's most pressing challenges in the late 1990s, including combating the powerful drug cartels and, at the same time, stopping guerrilla violence in order to restore internal peace and revitalize the country's economy and democracy. That huge effort involved a budget of $7.5 billion, with an extraordinary external contribution, estimated at $3.5 billion, which came mostly from the United States. In the case of Bolivia, the Dignity Plan has been much more modest and restricted to the fight against drug trafficking, with more limited external participation.

The Dignity Plan was the most genuine Bolivian expression of the paradigm of the war on drugs, which is shared with Plan Colombia and promoted by the United States. However, its implementation had to consider and adjust to the peculiar situation of a predominantly coca leaf–producing country and around whose production has developed a broad-based economic sector and a social movement with unusual strength of pressure and resistance to the State, capable of questioning the political stability and governance of the country. The fact that Bolivia was not a field of action for revolutionary armed groups – as Colombia and Peru have been – is another circumstance that differentiates the situation generated by Plan Colombia, which would also contribute to lowering the profile of the

142   *Policies*

warring components in the interdiction of drug trafficking. Nonetheless, this does not mean that the connections and reciprocal influences between Plan Colombia, designed and negotiated by the Colombian government in 1999, and Dignity Plan, conceived and implemented in Bolivia by the government of Hugo Banzer since 1998, are not known. It is very significant, for example, that the financing of Plan Colombia, approved by the U.S. Congress in 2000 for an overall amount of $1,319 million, also included assistance to Bolivia of more than $100 million, of which $85 million was for the alternative economic development component, and the rest for interdiction activities. In other words, Plan Colombia became, in a way, a window that allowed Bolivia, as well as Ecuador, to access U.S. funds for its own anti-drug strategy.

However, Plan Colombia has not been the only instrument that has channeled U.S. financial assistance to Andean countries in the fight against drugs. Complementary to Plan Colombia, it is the trade preference program that eliminated tariffs in the U.S. market for a wide range of exports from Bolivia, Colombia, Ecuador, and Peru, through the Andean Trade Preferences Act (ATPA), enacted in 1991 under the administration of George H. W. Bush, with the aim of strengthening legal industries in those countries, as alternatives to drug production and trafficking.

The program was renewed in October 2002 by the Bush administration as the Andean Trade Preferences and Drug Eradication Act (ATPDEA), a unilateral system of preferences granted by the United States and assumed as economic compensation for the fight against drug trafficking and, above all, the eradication of coca crops.

In this regard, two aspects are worth noting: first, the assumption by the United States that one way to encourage alternative production in the Andean region to the coca-cocaine economy and, with it, the commitment of countries involved was to facilitate access for their exports to the U.S. market, duty free. This recognition, consistent with the principle of co-responsibility, was not contemplated within the assistance measures for Plan Colombia approved by the U.S. Congress; in that sense, it can be said that the Andean tariff preferences complement and make up for an absence in the Plan Colombia and other counternarcotic programs. This is often overlooked in criticisms that emphasize the predominantly repressive nature of the war on drugs. Secondly, the ATPDEA law was the product of a block negotiation of the four Andean countries, thus marking a stellar moment in the process of the convergence of their national interests, paradoxically, because of Plan Colombia and the other national plans promoted by the great power. The political importance of this issue is out of the question.

But not all assessments agree on the merits of the ATPDEA. Thus, a report by the United States International Trade Commission (2009) attributes to the program a very modest effect on the economy and on American consumers, which highlights its equally minimal positive impacts on the reduction of and job creation in the Andean countries.[9]

Clearly, the significance of the tariff preference arrangement has been, and will continue to be, a controversial issue. But it is not without prominence that the ATPDEA has been subject to successive renewals and extensions, all at the request of the Andean governments, until it finally expired in early 2011. This, in exchange for a free trade agreement (FTA) negotiated by the United States with Colombia and Peru and in force since 2013. In this sense, it could be said that the greatest achievement of the ATPDEA is precisely to have paved the way for the germination of a permanent trade agreement, such as the FTA, which consolidates preferential access to the U.S. market for Colombian and Peruvian products.

The same has not happened with the other two Andean countries: Bolivia and Ecuador. Bolivia lost the benefits of the ATPDEA in November 2008. According to the then President George W. Bush, this happened "due to its lack of cooperation in the anti-narcotics efforts" (Morales Luján 2008). However, it can be said that Bolivia's exclusion from the Andean trade program was a political decision by the United States, certainly unilateral, but also completely predictable, in the context of the strained diplomatic relations between the two countries. Thus, it became evident that the ATPDEA also served as an instrument to put pressure and sanction governments that deviated from the political-diplomatic agreement that gave it life.

The Dignity Plan embodies the most aggressive effort made by the Bolivian state to carry out the process of reduction and substitution of coca crops to its maximum term and to take Bolivia out of the drug trafficking circuit, through the complete eradication of surplus crops, an impetuous and voluntary effort as it would later be seen.[10] According to Washington Office on Latin America's (WOLA) researcher Kathryn Ledebur,

> Bolivian government officials generally met the minimum eradication targets for U.S. certification to cooperate with anti-drug efforts and thus retain funding and access to international loans, but eradicated coca was quickly replaced. Three successive governments (of Víctor Paz Estenssoro, Jaime Paz Zamora, and Gonzalo Sánchez de Lozada) were reluctant to push too hard for fear of generating confrontations with the coca growers, who retained some degree of popular support. The Paz Zamora government (1989-1993) eradicated the required 7,000 hectares, but the net cultivated area increased by 312 hectares. (Ledebur 2002, 2)

Between 1994 and 1995, Bolivia received $69.8 million in aid from the United States, more than any other Andean country at that time. Ledebur notes that although President Bill Clinton certified Bolivia in 1995, his administration would demand approval of an extradition treaty with the United States, a complete eradication plan, and the eradication of 1,750 hectares of coca, posing a delicate challenge to his Bolivian counterpart, the government headed by Gen. Hugo Banzer Suarez (Ledebur 2002, 5).

This intensified U.S. pressure may explain the turnaround produced by Dignity Plan in 1998,[11] when the restraint and caution that had characterized Bolivian policy until then – more inclined to negotiate with the coca growers' unions than to use force – was unexpectedly abandoned, to impose hard-lining in the process of

144 *Policies*

eradication, with the objective of finishing off in five years all the surplus crops, located mainly in the Tropic of Cochabamba, in the region known as Chapare, which has become the main headquarters of the coca farmers' movement.

The "zero coca" strategy in the Chapare meant, above all, privileging forced eradication over voluntary substitution, involving greater military intervention and even the direct participation of the army in eradication tasks through the Fuerza de Tarea Conjunta (Joint Task Force), a combined police and military force, and the use of military service conscripts of peasant origin in the manual eradication of coca plants. This "militarization" of the crop reduction and substitution program, which involved strengthening logistics and military equipment in the area, would eventually become one of the most irritating elements for the local population, exacerbating to the limit the susceptibility to a possible U.S. military presence.

In previous years, coca producers had received financial compensation of $2,000–2,500 for each hectare eradicated. The five-year strategy tended to replace individual compensation with "community compensation" – not only in cash, but also in kind – which would also decrease over time.

Despite the harsher conditions, what is surprising is that the plan almost achieved its goal of eradicating around 28,000 hectares, to the point that government authorities, in an excess of enthusiasm, anticipated that this goal would be achieved even before the planned five years. During the years of Dignity Plan, what later opinions would show is that the eradication process achieved considerable and unprecedented advances but without being able to reach the total elimination of coca crops, due to the active resistance of the Chapare farmers and their response of successive re-plantings of coca plants. In short, the goal of zero coca in the Chapare proved to be illusory.

In the opinion of independent observers, the underlying problem would have been the failure of alternative development, a key component of the Dignity Plan. Indeed, for the plan to gain credibility and for crop substitution to become viable, it was crucial that alternative development programs generate income capable of replacing, at least partially, the income that producers lost when they stopped planting coca. However, this is what did not happen, according to all evidence.

In this regard, Ledebur notes that aggressive eradication efforts have always exceeded the income-generating capacity of alternative development and that the international community failed to provide the more than $700 million budgeted for the plan (2002, 6). This criticism is not alone in calling into question the effectiveness of alternative development programs in providing livelihoods to the affected population and, consequently, in accompanying and sustaining the rapid achievements of coca leaf eradication. The Dignity Plan achieved successes in the eradication of coca crops, as had not been possible before, but at an extremely high price and without consolidating its achievements. The country had to live for several years in a spiral of intense and sustained violence with conflicts that left many dead, many injured, hundreds of detained, roadblocks, exacerbated social tensions, a context of growing instability, and political powers besieged by protests.

The repeated violations against human rights recorded in or following the successive clashes between the police and military forces and the coca growers organized

Public Policies and the Border Subsystem   145

in trade unions and "self-defense committees," with increasingly violent positions, brought victims from both sides, including savage killings of civilians and uniformed persons by irregular groups, and which were the subject of international denunciations. The Bolivian economy would also be seriously affected. According to the official agency UDAPE, the eradication carried out in the Chapare, in the framework of the Dignity Plan, meant a loss of net added value of $656 million, between 1997 and 2000, with an accumulated impact of 8% on the GDP, in addition to the decrease of 59,000 direct and indirect jobs (Pacheco 2014, 16). But the consequences were probably more political than merely circumstantial. The conflict that broke out in the Chapare, added to other events such as the economic crisis and political corruption, had the effect of wearing down the political leadership and the parties, by exacerbating anti-American sentiment in broad sectors of the country.

Self-regulation and control as "rationalization of coca crops" has been a euphemism for continuing to apply crop eradication programs in the two major coca-producing areas of the country: the Yungas of La Paz and the Tropic of Cochabamba, commonly known as the Chapare. Such programs are not new in Bolivia, but the basic difference is that the government has gained the acceptance and adhesion of coca producers' organizations, and, above all, of the six federations of the Chapare,[12] which understand that it is not politically possible for the government to mitigate the free cultivation, planting, and production of coca leaf in national territory, and that they must remain regulated and restricted.

The government has agreed to involve the coca growers' unions and federations in the tasks of monitoring and controlling the coca plantations, within a series of agreements and commitments negotiated with them. The negotiation parameter has been one *cato* of coca per family, as the maximum extension permitted in the Chapare, the most conflictive zone. In fact, this has implied the legalization of coca crops in this region, which is no small thing.[13]

This is, therefore, a genuine policy of self-regulation and social control in coca eradication[14] and, at the same time, a reciprocal pact, by which the coca growers ensure a stable and secure production margin, respected by the government, while it prevents the indiscriminate growth of crops and preserves a climate of tranquility and social peace, as well as the political and electoral support of the coca growers' population.[15]

Above and beyond the figures, what is important to highlight is that the government has established a field of political negotiation that is skillfully used by both sides, including in front of international bodies, defending the concept of sovereignty, even if this is not an accomplished goal.[16]

The government has carried out, with the financial support of the European Union, the "Integral Study of the Legal Demand for the Coca Leaf," aimed at

> generating information on production, commercialization, and demand for the coca leaf, for legal use and consumption in households, economic establishments, and commerce in border areas; in order to establish a baseline for the implementation of an integral information system for the coca leaf.
>
> (UNODC 2013)

146 *Policies*

A review of this study, prepared by UNODC, indicates that in the period 2008–2011, the first approximations were made to determine the legal demand for coca leaf (2014, 40). Additionally, complementary studies were conducted in 2013, which were financed with resources from the National Treasury, allowing to complete, strengthen, and give more consistency to the baseline (2008–2011). The results, presented in November 2013, show that, in 2012, the estimated population of coca leaf consumers was of 3,082,464 inhabitants. Thirty-three percent of this population lives in rural areas and 67% in urban areas. The results of the survey also determined that the demand for coca leaf to cover the legal consumption in *pijcheo*,[17] medicine, rituals, social events, and transformation requires an amount of 20,690 metric tons, which represents a coca cultivation area of approximately 14,705 hectares. Observers believe that the results of this study have not corresponded to the expectations of the government, which expected to justify an area of 20,000 hectares, that is, similar or close to the area cultivated in recent years and which, according to official management figures for 2015, were 20,200 hectares (UNODC n.d.).

This situation is probably delaying the approval of the new law, in addition to the lack of agreement between the two production areas on how to distribute the eventual 20,000 ha legally. However, in anticipation of a conflict scenario, on July 13, 2016, President Evo Morales decided that the limit would be 20,000 hectares, making this figure official, which corresponds approximately to the one mentioned in the UNODC (2016) monitoring document.

Law 1008 of the Coca and Controlled Substances Regime (1988) implied the implementation of alternative development programs in search of integral development. The law provides for actions to change agricultural production patterns, credit assistance, the development of agro-industry, and the strengthening of marketing systems and territorial articulation of the affected regions. This process should be conducted by the Executive Branch, in coordination with coca producers.

By law, the National Fund for Alternative Development (FONADAL) manages the financing of alternative development and coca crop substitution plans and programs with funds from the national budget and from bilateral and multilateral financial cooperation. It establishes that the State should provide coca producers with economic compensation for the reduction and substitution of their crops. Throughout two decades of eradication of surplus crops, what became known as "alternative development" was implemented. A diverse range of productive, infrastructure, and social investment projects were implemented in the coca-growing regions, and also, to some extent, in other areas that expelled the rural population. The excluded actor was the United States Agency for International Development (USAID), both in funding and in the provision of technical assistance, supported by the cooperation programs of the European Union and other developed countries.

USAID's exit from Bolivia, as determined by the government, implied a cut in U.S. aid, the main source of project funding. There is no evaluation of the impact of the suspension of this funding on economic and social programs and projects

Public Policies and the Border Subsystem   147

in the areas affected by crop eradication; nor are there any known independent studies that could have assessed its consequences. The political decision to expel USAID has been, at the time, a very welcome decision by the coca growers' unions as a step in the recovery of a sovereign policy in defense of the coca leaf.

Although the government has publicly reneged on alternative development, in practice, care has been taken to give continuity to the process of substitution of coca crops, providing support to alternative crops such as pineapple, palm heart, bananas, coffee, and others, as well as to fishing, beekeeping, processing plants, training, and other projects. Infrastructure projects (such as roads, irrigation, commercialization) and social investment (school and health units, housing, basic sanitation, training) have also received attention. This process, now called "integral development," maintains similar objectives to alternative development; the main executor of the program continues to be FONADAL, and the projects are financed, in part, with resources from the European Union and public resources from the national government and from municipal and departmental governments.

Little is known about the results of the projects and their socioeconomic impacts, and it is not possible to know whether the focus of the projects has been changed or whether efficiency and transparency in resource management have been gained. Nor is it possible to know to what extent it has been possible to replace the levels of funding, or the technical assistance previously provided by USAID, not even what the effective capacity of the State is now to assume such responsibilities. Nevertheless, certain changes are evident. The national cocalero movement has acquired enormous weight in the definition and execution of integral development programs. The highest levels of decision-makers, such as the National Council for the Fight against Illicit Drug Trafficking (CONALTI-D),[18] the National Council for the Revaluation, Production, Commercialization, and Industrialization of the Coca Leaf (CONCOCA) and its technical and operational bodies have direct representatives of the coca producers' federations and unions in their ranks. In other words, it may be the most important thing. There is a negotiation table of interests and government control where everything is decided and, in general, how the law is interpreted and applied, as opposed to international cooperation that also justifies a space for cooperation in the fight against drug trafficking.

Without a doubt, a key element for this new social situation, especially in the region of the Tropic of Cochabamba, is the agreement of the "one coca *cato* per family," which fulfills a double function: on the one hand, it gives security to the producers that they can preserve their coca crops within a certain extension (the *cato*), and, on the other hand, it acts as a sort of barrier to the expansion of the coca border. This reciprocity pact with a government that is also recognized as "its" government would explain why the mandate of Law 1008 to compensate those affected by the reduction and substitution of their coca crops is no longer fulfilled. The new form of economic compensation now has a collective character and is given only through works and projects in the communities and rural localities, and within a logic of community self-management, which also results in the strengthening of the decision-making and control role of the coca growers' union

148   *Policies*

network. The municipal governments, for their part, seem to have strengthened their participation in projects financed with integral development resources, to which they themselves must contribute a share of around 40%, while the remaining percentage must come from FONADAL resources.

On the other hand, if in 20 years of alternative development the coca-growing regions –especially the Chapare – were the recipients of important investments in road infrastructure, energy, and other basic services, carried out with combined resources from the State and international cooperation, in an extraordinary effort to lay the foundations for the economic take-off of these areas, it is even more true that the current administration has focused on prioritizing public investment in the coca-growing regions.[19] Furthermore, it has incorporated a new component of "integral development": the installation of state factories (paper, dairy, and the urea and ammonia plant), which the government is demanding as part of its policy of industrializing natural resources and strengthening the presence of State companies, this time, in the heart of the coca-growing region par excellence.

In the task of interdiction and repression of drug trafficking, in the situation of a country conditioned by its subsidiary insertion as a primary producer, the government of Evo Morales is the protagonist of the most audacious, risky, and difficult attempt: to break with U.S. tutelage and redefine the anti-drug strategy from a nationalist and anti-American perspective; something that very few governments in the region have attempted. Predictably, the different positions of the two governments on this issue have been at the center of a rarefied and strained bilateral relationship, which has led to the withdrawal of the ambassadors of both countries. But that is not all. In the struggle that Evo Morales has maintained with the White House, and as if to leave no doubt about his temperament and his decision to confront the "empire," he expelled the Drug Enforcement Administration (DEA) in 2009 and, later, USAID. Previously, in September 2008, U.S. Ambassador Philip Golberg was persona non grata to President Morales, accused of political interference in the internal affairs of the country, which led the White House to respond in the same way, so there are no diplomatic relations at the ambassadorial level (Laserna 2011a, 252–260). The U.S. response has been the closure of the U.S. Embassy's Anti-Narcotics Division (NAS) and the progressive cessation of anti-drug cooperation programs (Youngers and Ledebur 2015, 14–16).

Nearly 40 years of increasing technical and financial assistance from U.S. agencies to Bolivia have been broken, in which the United States has borne the brunt of the good or bad done in drug interdiction and repression. Since then, not only have the two governments ceased to cooperate with each other, but they have occasionally been involved in verbal and political skirmishes. Bolivia is "blacklisted" as one of the countries with little or no progress in combating drugs and failing in its international responsibility to prevent the diversion of coca leaf to cocaine processing, to achieve net reductions in coca cultivation, and to enforce the law and investigate and prosecute drug traffickers.[20]

Thus, following the withdrawal of U.S. assistance, repressive action against drug trafficking in Bolivia has come to depend mainly on the national budget

Public Policies and the Border Subsystem 149

itself, with subsidiary support from the European Union. National authorities themselves admitted that these resources are generally considered insufficient.

Regarding the seizure of controlled substances, UNODC reports show an increasing trend in the quantities of cocaine base seized in the period 2004–2012, rising from 8 meters to 32 meters in 2012, and then, in 2013 and 2014, dramatic drops in the volumes seized (2015, 53).

Trafficking in Persons Act

The Deputy Minister for Equal Opportunities of the Ministry of Justice expressed, on July 13, 2016, his concern about the poor results in the implementation of policies on trafficking and smuggling of persons: "Governors and mayors know that these resources cannot be reallocated to other purposes and must be invested in the fight against violence, but they do not have the political will to make the planned investments concrete" (ANF 2016).

Indeed, much progress has been made in the institutional design for the implementation of policies, in which Bolivia can be considered at the level of the most advanced countries. However, even though the State has been very active in recent years in combating gender-based violence, it has not yet managed to bring this legislation to the border cities, with very few examples.

At the national level, centers have been established where people who are suffering violence can be taken care of, especially in the main cities. Progress has been made in the design of the legal, institutional, and regulatory system promoted by international agencies to which the State automatically pays attention.

It is necessary to highlight a recent assessment, carried out by Fundación La Paz, that shows the extraordinary panorama of what has been done, of which we highlight important aspects (Fundación La Paz 2016).

- In 2000, the United Nations adopted the "Protocol to Prevent, Suppress, and Punish Trafficking in Persons, Especially Women and Children," supplementing the United Nations Convention against Transnational Organized Crime, also known as the "Palermo Protocol." Subsequently, the "Protocol against the Smuggling of Migrants by Land, Sea and Air."
- In 2006, Act No. 3325 on trafficking in persons and other related offenses was adopted, amending, and extending the Criminal Code, which defined the offense of human trafficking.
- In 2009, the Political Constitution of the State (CPE) was approved, and in 2011 the Plurinational Legislative Assembly resumed the drafting of the law on trafficking in persons and constituted the technical committee on migration.

But it is on July 31, 2012, that the fight against the crime of trafficking takes shape with the enactment of Law 263, the Comprehensive Law against Trafficking in Persons and Related Offences. This Act defines the crime of trafficking in persons and amends Article 281bis of the Criminal Code by establishing that

150   *Policies*

> anyone who, by any means of deception, intimidation, abuse of power, use of force or any form of coercion, or threats, shall be punished by deprivation of liberty for ten (10) to fifteen (15) years, abuse of the victim's situation of dependence or vulnerability, the granting or receipt of payments by himself or by a third party, to carry out, induce or favor the recruitment, transfer, transport, deprivation of freedom, reception or shelter of persons within or outside the national territory, even if the consent of the victim is involved.
>
> (Fundación La Paz 2016, 10)

The law incorporates, among other aspects,

> the reduction to slavery or a similar state; labor exploitation, forced labor or any form of servitude; customary servitude; commercial sexual exploitation; forced pregnancy; sex tourism; guardianship or adoption; forced begging; servile marriage, free union or servile de facto; the recruitment of persons for participation in armed conflict or religious sects; employment in criminal activities; and the illegal conduct of biomedical research.
>
> (Fundación La Paz 2016, 11)

In August 2012, the Plurinational Council against Trafficking and Smuggling of Persons (CPCTTP) was established "as the highest body of coordination and representation, to formulate, approve, and implement the Plurinational Policy on Combating Trafficking and Smuggling of Persons and Related Crimes" (Fundación La Paz 2016, 12). It is made up of representatives of nine ministries of the Executive Branch, the Public Prosecutor's Office, the Office of the Ombudsman, and organized civil society.

The plurinational policy to combat trafficking and smuggling of persons was designed and approved in 2014. It has five strategic lines: prevention; protection, care, and comprehensive reintegration, prosecution and criminal sanctions, international cooperation, and national cooperation.

These guidelines are to be implemented in the autonomous territorial entities and in all public and private institutions involved in the fight against trafficking and smuggling of persons. The following actors are responsible for the implementation of the multinational policy:

- Plurinational Council against Trafficking in Persons.
- Departmental Councils against Trafficking and Smuggling of Persons.
- State institutions within the framework of their competencies.
- Private institutions combating trafficking and smuggling of persons.

Supreme Decree No. 1486 of February 6, 2013, regulates the mechanisms and procedures for the implementation of Act No. 263, establishing that organized civil society shall elect its representatives to the CPCTTP, in accordance with its own procedures, within the framework of the principles of participation, equity, interculturality, and equal opportunities. In December 2013, the Pastoral de

Movilidad Humana and Visión Mundial Bolivia were elected to the Plurinational Council, and it was until January 2015 that their incorporation was recognized.

The National Plan to Combat Trafficking in Persons 2015–2019 was adopted on April 23, 2015, by Resolution No. 003/2015 of the Plurinational Council against Trafficking in Persons. This National Plan is "an instrument that guides the implementation of public policies committed by the various institutions that make up the Plurinational Council against Trafficking and Smuggling in Persons" (Fundación La Paz 2016, 13).

The Fundación La Paz study mentions the number of services provided over the past ten years and, after collecting and systematizing information, lists the sectoral policies that have been developed (protection, care and reintegration of victims, prosecution and criminal sanctions) and describes a leafy institutional architecture that is based on the principle of inclusion of the State's main mechanisms. This commendable inclusion contrasts with the meager results and heavy structure that will make it difficult to operate.

The Main Operational Institutions at the State Level

- Dirección General de Lucha contra la Trata y Tráfico de Personas (Directorate General for the Fight against Trafficking in Persons (DGLCTTP)
- Dirección General de Migración (Directorate General for Migration) (DIGEMIG)
- Observatorio Nacional de Seguridad Ciudadana (National Observatory for Citizen Security) (ONSC)
- Ministry of Justice: Directorate General of Justice and Fundamental Rights/ Area of Trafficking and Smuggling of Persons. Other actors under the Ministry of Justice related to the area of protection and assistance to victims, these entities are detailed below. Servicio Plurinacional de Asistencia a la Víctima (Plurinational Victim Assistance Service) (SEPDAVI), Servicio Integral de Justicia Plurinacional (Comprehensive Plurinational Justice Service) (SIJPLU)
- Ministry of Health: General Directorate of Health Promotion
- Ministry of Labor, Employment, and Social Security: Directorate General for Employment
- Public Prosecutor's Office: Directorate for the Protection of Victims, Witnesses and Members of the Public Prosecutor's Office
- Judicial Branch
- Ministry of Foreign Affairs: Directorate General of Consular Affairs
- Bolivian Police: Trafficking in Persons Division; General Directorate for the Protection of Victims
- Ministry of Economy and Public Finance: General Directorate of Fiscal Accounting
- Ministry of Defense: Directorate General for Human Rights and Interculturalism in the Armed Forces
- Instituto Nacional de Estadística (National Institute of Statistics) (INE)

152   *Policies*

- Red Nacional de Servicio de Gestión Social (National Network of Social Management Services) (REDNAGES)
- Media monitoring as a secondary source of information

There is a complex structure that is difficult to mobilize, although at the same time this large structure shows a willingness of the government in all its organs (Fundación La Paz 2016, 63).

In contrast to all the above, it stresses that the small number of police officers assigned to the nine divisions of human trafficking and smuggling and the small number of prosecutors in the Specialized Prosecutor's Office for Victims of Priority Attention (FEVAP) – which is responsible for investigating the cases – explains the enormous procedural burden in the Public Prosecutor's Office, reflected in the 421 cases of trafficking in persons in the preliminary stage over the eight cases in the accusatory stage (Fundación La Paz 2016, 60). Similarly, "the four sentences for human trafficking (three convictions and one acquittal) and three other sentences for related crimes (two for pimping and one for pornography) express a 98.3% rate of impunity for these crimes" (Fundación La Paz 2016, 60). In other words, these efforts necessarily suffer because of the operating conditions of the State sectors mentioned, for example, the delay of justice.

With respect to access to public information on human trafficking, state institutional weaknesses and strengths were identified regarding the availability and systematization of information on the actions and results achieved in the fight against human trafficking. It refers, above all, to the reluctance of several institutions to provide information for the study, similar to the difficulties in providing for public bodies that centralize information and make it available for use by the population.

Other weaknesses of this structure are related to:

- Difficult access to anti-trafficking budget information.
- Problems of inter-institutional articulation in the implementation of public policy.
- Weak information and statistical system on trafficking and smuggling of persons and related crimes.
- The lack of specialized and sustained training on human trafficking.
- Public access to information.
- Anti-trafficking budget.

It is necessary to highlight the creation of the **Consejo Plurinacional contra la Trata y el Tráfico de Personas** (Plurinational Council against Trafficking and Smuggling of Persons) (CPCTTP) as the highest coordination and representation body to formulate, approve, and implement the plurinational policy to combat trafficking and smuggling of persons and related crimes. It is an indicator of what Fundación La Paz mentions as "compliance with the regulations in force" (2016, 16). However, after analyzing the weak relationship and coherence of the approach of some of its actions planned for the year 2015, with regard to their contribution to the National Plan, "it is recommended that the technical approach to planning be strengthened, in order to improve the design and use of the tools for planning, monitoring, monitoring and evaluation of what has been implemented" (Fundación La Paz 2016, 16).

Despite Institutional Progress, Bolivia Has a Huge Challenge

A statement from the Attorney General's Office reports that of the 1,340 cases handled, 32 sentences were handed down, which contradicts the information provided by the Ministry of Justice. According to the Deputy Minister of Justice and Fundamental Rights, Diego Ernesto Jiménez Guachalla,

> the most frequent victims in trafficking and smuggling are minors, especially women ... Of 1,340 cases that reached the Office of the Prosecutor, 786 were for girls or female adolescents, 518 to male minors, 283 to female adults and 137 to males.
>
> (Página Siete 2015)

The Deputy Minister explained that most of the cases (38%) correspond to crimes of illegal adoption or retention of persons, 24% to sale of persons or organs, 19% to labor exploitation, and 10% to exploitation commercial sex. The rest of the percentage are less frequent types. The report is more encouraging; from 2012 to 2014 the FELCC received 8,606 reports of missing persons. Of these, 5,562 were found; the rest, who didn't show up until now, are presumed to have been victims of trafficking and smuggling (Página Siete 2015). During this management, with the assistance of different state and civil society institutions, the proposal was drawn up of a plan for the implementation of the shelters and model for care and reintegration of victims of trafficking and smuggling with related crimes. In addition, courses were held to take action when it comes to combating these crimes.

The Critical Scenarios

Border populations are among the most important critical scenarios, as populations entering the labor market, faced with the narrowness of the market, find the doors that open often cross over into informality. Among them, the populations of the border municipalities, especially the rural ones, offer little or no attention to the future of young people. The situation is often like the one that occurs in certain municipality on the border with Chile – whose name better not be revealed – where all the high school graduates from 2015 are migrants in Chile or in cities like Oruro. It is obvious that the borders provide the best offer of informality; this involves smuggling of various types, drug carrying, or migration to seek work abroad. It is in these conditions that human trafficking and smuggling have their deepest roots.

Policies should pay more attention to this type of especially critical scenario, where the most vulnerable groups are found, such as young people of both sexes,

154   *Policies*

indigenous populations, and the elderly. **Human trafficking and smuggling in the country are increasingly an "uppercase" problem**, as children, adolescents, and women continue to be reported missing every day. People with scarce economic resources are mainly transferred to Argentina, Brazil, Peru, Chile, and Spain for the purpose of labor and sexual exploitation. As of 2013, the number of people who have disappeared has increased, according to official information from the Bolivian Police. "In 2011 there were 289 cases of trafficking and smuggling. Later, in 2012, there were 421 cases, and from January to July this year [2013] there were 267 cases" (ANF 2013). Within the 2013 management statistics, 288 cases of disappearances have been recorded, 127 of them involving women between the ages of 13 and 18. Abandonment of the home, sexual and labor exploitation, child pornography, illegal adoptions, pimping, and the illegal sale of organs are some of the factors that lead to the disappearance of persons, facts that are analyzed during the process of investigation by the police (ANF 2013).

> This industry moves an estimated of $6.6 billion per year in Latin America, out of a total of $32 billion in the world. Two million people are victims of trafficking each year and 1.2 million children are victims of trafficking in the world; 80% of the victims of this crime are women.
>
> (ANF 2013)

Gun Control Act

The Law on the Control of Arms, Ammunition, Explosives, and Other Related Materials – promulgated by President Evo Morales on September 18, 2013 – states that the fight against drug trafficking, terrorism, and other crimes against the security and defense of the State and citizen security are part of the State's policies. The purpose of this law is to regulate and control the manufacture, import, export, temporary admission, commercialization, disposal, donation, transport, transit, deposit, storage, possession, handling, employment, carrying or carrying, destruction, deactivation, rehabilitation, registration, control, monitoring, kidnapping, seizure, confiscation, and other activities related to weapons, ammunition, explosives, and other materials. The importance of this law lies in bringing together and articulating in a single legal body a dispersed set of previous and lesser legal norms, including the creation of new criminal offences linked to illicit arms trafficking and the punishment of such offenses.

The law seeks to strengthen the capacity of the Bolivian State to prevent and combat such crimes, establishing institutional coordination mechanisms and others of a technical-operational nature. The National Committee against Illicit Firearms Trafficking (CONCTAFI) was established, composed of the Ministers of Defense and Government and the General Attorney. The main function of this high-level body is to design policies, strategies, and programs against the manufacture of and trafficking in arms and other related crimes and to monitor and

Public Policies and the Border Subsystem 155

evaluate compliance with them; it also develops plans and programs for border control and information exchange with other countries on arms trafficking.

The Act also establishes a general register of arms, ammunition and military, and police and civilian use of explosives and defines standards and procedures for the manufacture, acquisition, storage, transport, internment, and donation of arms and the granting of licenses for the use of civilian use weapons, as well as establishing express prohibitions on the import, transport, and disposal of such weapons without the corresponding official authorization. Among the new criminal offenses, the illegal manufacture and trafficking of arms is punished, with penalties of between 10 and 15 years, and which can be extended to 25 years for members of criminal organizations. Finally, the law defines an amnesty for persons who take advantage of the regularization of possession of weapons for civilian use, within the following 180 days, under penalty of incurring the crime of illegal possession. Once this period has elapsed, and within 30 days, the Ministry of Defense, on the one hand, and the Bolivian Police, on the other, are empowered to proceed with the active disarmament of weapons for military, police, and civilian use, as well as the seizure of weapons, ammunition, and explosives that are not duly authorized and registered.

By acquiring this legal instrument, Bolivia is undoubtedly bringing itself up to date with the international conventions that oblige States to adopt regulations to control illicit arms trafficking and is joining those countries that already have such regulations. However, two years after the entry into force of the Bolivian arms control law, the pending issue is the effective application of the new law and its regulations, on which progress has been very slow. This is especially true in terms of the effective capacity of the Police, as well as of the Armed Forces, the Public Prosecutor's Office, and the justice agencies to fulfill their duties of controlling arms trafficking, as well as of the disarming and kidnapping as provided for in the law, and to bring violators to court and sanction them accordingly, notwithstanding the expiration of the amnesty period.

There is also no credible evidence that the registers of arms, ammunition, and explosives established in the law function effectively, and that the State currently has more and better information and inventories of the arms existing in the country than it did before the law came into force. All of which demonstrates, once again, that the law and plans alone are not enough if their implementation is not sustained by a strong political will and if the necessary changes have not been made in key institutions such as the Police, the Prosecutor's Office, and the Judiciary, to eradicate corruption, to qualify and professionalize them, and to strengthen their independence from political power.

The most important news on this subject has to do with Bolivia's role as a transit point for armed groups operating in other countries. Apparently, the news dedicated to the implementation of firearms control and registration in Bolivia do not scare anyone, anymore. What does call attention is the silence on the trafficking that, although not part of Bolivia, is apparently important, but about which there is very little information.

Fight against Money Laundering and Other Assets

Since the 1990s, the fight against money laundering has also been a component of anti-drug policies in Bolivia. Since then, the country has been aligned with international efforts in this field and has progressively adjusted its regulations and institutional mechanisms for regulation, control, and monitoring. This process has led to the creation of the Financial Investigations Unit (FIU), as a technical body specialized in combating money laundering and the legitimization of illicit profits, through financial analysis of assets, investigation of suspicious cases or operations, and the prevention and detection of crimes.

At the international level, Bolivia is a member of the Financial Action Task Force (FATF), which sets standards and promotes the implementation of legal, regulatory, and operational measures to combat money laundering, the financing of terrorism and the financing of proliferation, and other threats to the integrity of the international financial system. It also participates in the Inter-American Drug Abuse Control Commission (CICAD) and its Anti-Money Laundering Section, which provides technical assistance and training to the member states, within the framework of the OAS.

Notwithstanding its well-known differences and critical positions on the work and development of international organizations and multilateral agencies involved in the fight against drugs, the government of Evo Morales has continued the policy of previous governments of honoring the commitments of the Bolivian State in the area of money laundering and financing of terrorism, which includes assuming internationally accepted standards and submitting to monitoring and evaluation by intergovernmental agencies and missions. In fact, Bolivia is off the FATF lists of countries with deficiencies in their anti-money laundering and anti-terrorist financing systems.

However, the controversial step taken by Evo Morales' administration has to do with the decision to transfer the FIU to the direction of the Ministry of Economy and Public Finance. Until April 2014 – and for 20 years – the unit in charge of investigating and supervising operations in the financial system was within the scope of the Superintendence of Banks and Financial Institutions, currently the Autoridad de Supervisión del Sistema Financiero (Financial System Supervisory Authority) (ASFI), with a very wide margin of functional autonomy. Precisely, the question that is made is to the loss of independence in the work of FIU, as well as a possible impairment of its technical character, and the political submission of the entity to the government of the moment.[21] But, in reality, political interference in the FIU is something that had already been occurring in previous years, since the body that was supposed to protect its functions (the ASFI) was far from being an independent entity, as it was the mandate that the previous law of the financial system (of 2003) conferred on the then Superintendence of Banks and Financial Entities. The new Financial Services Act 393 of August 2013 consolidates the integration of both IFSA and the FIU into the Ministry of Economy and Public Finance.

For FIU officials, the important thing is that institutional changes do not affect the permanence and commitment with the objectives of the entity, including the

Table 5.2 Related Cases Referred, Answered, Closed, and in Process

Origin /	Financial and Equity Analysis Cases and Links as of December 31, 2015											
	Addressed Cases		Referred Cases		Pending Cases				In Process		Total	
					With Analysis		With Initial Legal Report					
	N^o	Linked	N^o	Linked	N^o	Linked	N^o	Linked	N^o	Linked	N^o	Linked
Suspicious transaction report	29	24	0	0	48	44	511	587	489	487	1077	1.142
Tax injunction	41	147	0	0	15	42	9	16	243	860	308	1.065
Written request	12	37	0	0	1	5	4	17	41	190	58	249
Application for International Cooperation	0	0	47	394	0	0	1	22	28	137	76	553
By trade	0	0	0	0	1	13	0	0	6	25	7	38
Total	82	208	47	394	65	104	525	642	807	1.699	1.526	3.047
Total by state%	5.38	6.83	3.08	12.93	4.26	3.41	34.40	21.07	52.88	55.76	100	100

Source: Own elaboration.

158 *Policies*

commitment to gradually comply with FATF recommendations, that is, the international standard on money laundering and financing of terrorism, translated into the "40 Recomendaciones" that indicate essential measures for all countries, among which the definition of the crime of money laundering, regulation and supervision of financial institutions, regulation on bank secrecy, control of money transfer services, reporting of suspicious transactions, financial intelligence capacity, etc. stand out. In this regard, and as far as it can be seen, Bolivia has taken important steps to establish norms and mechanisms of control and supervision in the financial system and to adjust its functioning to international standards in prevention measures, risk identification, transparency, and availability of the information generated in the system. There are also more controls on foreign exchange transfer and transportation services. The same cannot be said in many other areas, which are critical for detecting, curbing, and dismantling the multiple operations of money laundering and legitimization of illicit profits. This is recognized by the FIU staff themselves, who are otherwise aware of the limitations surrounding their work, as well as the vast and complex task ahead.

What is noticeable is that the cases on which the FIU has worked in the last seven years have a growth trend, probably in correlation with the progressive increase of money laundering and legitimation of criminal profits.

However, the weaknesses that mark the performance of the FIU are notorious, among other things, the lack of risk maps, reports on border areas, and other studies that enable it to enhance its capabilities for identification and timely detection of criminal acts and suspicious transactions. Available statistics are extremely scarce and leave more questions than answers. There are no estimates of the resources involved in money laundering operations; nor are there any data that could serve as reference points to assess the results of the investigative work and appreciate their impact. In the absence of a national strategy to combat money laundering and other assets, the scope of its interventions is necessarily restricted. Nor does the lack of professionalism and human resources for highly specialized work, such as financial intelligence, go unnoticed.

For the time being, there are many more institutional deficiencies and fragilities which, of course, contrast with the magnitude of the challenges, especially if one considers the reality of a country like Bolivia, with a predominance of the informal economy and in which the fields of legality and illegality often appear to be mixed up and confused, and, for that very reason, plagued by interstices for money laundering and other concomitant crimes.[22]

"Anti-laundering Efforts Are Unsuccessful"

The analysis of Los Tiempos (2011) mentions the main issues that make it difficult to apply universal standard rules in the country that is predominantly informal and where the bancarization of the economy has grown, but it is still not universal. It will become increasingly difficult to open a bank account because of the number of requirements being made for the purpose of "reliably" guaranteeing a customer's data. Banks are required to report any "rare or suspicious" financial movement by a customer to the FIU. In Bolivia this task is much more difficult than in a developed country because of the enormous economic informality that exists. Here is the problem: there are many people who should be working with the banks, who have nothing to do with illicit drug activities, but who operate informally, which is the same as saying that they do not comply fully with the payment of taxes. This can already be described as "illegal earnings."

Therefore, to the extent that banks are hard on clients when demanding information on everything they do, making it difficult for them to use their deposited resources, they will discourage people's integration into the banking system.

The Politicization of Illicit Profits

Another not insignificant problem is the politicization of enforcement, since a complaint about allegedly illegal profits can lead to penalties before the accusation is proven. The accused must prove that his or her earnings were not illegally obtained, not by presuming innocence. This leads to the fact that, in practice, this offense becomes the subject of an administrative decision and not of the judicial system.

In a country where corruption is recognized by the State itself, the result of this regulatory system is an informal, concerted application that serves to generalize and legitimize the regime of informality. This is an important weapon in the exercise of the judicialization of politics, applied in most cases of trials against opposition politicians.

Following are the laws that regulate the fight against the crime of legitimization of illicit profits:

- Law on Amendments to the Criminal Code No. 1768
  - Article 185 (bis) establishes the offence of legitimization of illicit gains.
  - Article 185 (ter) creates the Financial Investigations Unit.
- Supreme Decree 24771. Approves the regulation of the Financial Investigations Unit.
- Act No. 004 Marcelo Quiroga Santa Cruz (10/03/2010)
- Act No. 170 Financing of Terrorism Separatism (09/09/2010)
- Act No. 262 Regime for the Freezing of Funds and other Assets of Persons Associated with Terrorism and Terrorist Financing (30/07/2012)

But the enormous number of small and medium-sized penetration pores into the legal economy remains to be analyzed. It is enough to consider the network of sectors of the illegal market that are interrelated and multiply the flows until control is really impossible. Control through the banking system is inefficient, and the justification of the possession of goods can be one of the greatest sources of corruption in the country.

Under these conditions, in the case of Bolivia, the existence of external tax havens is not a defining issue.

160   *Policies*

Notes

1 For broader analysis of the problems of Bolivian justice system, see Oporto (2014); Herrera (2013); Fundación Construir (2012).
2 "Until the end of 2011, 45% of the country's pre-trial detainees were in jail for crimes related to the Coca and Controlled Substances Regime, making Law 1008 the major cause for the determination of pre-trial detention in Bolivia" (PIEB 2012, 3).
3 This is, precisely, a concern that appears in most reports of national and international organizations, such as the Defensoría del Pueblo and the TNI Drugs & Democracy (TNI 2010).
4 Regarding the deplorable prison conditions in Bolivia, the State allocates less than $1 a day per capita for inmates. Access to a cell is not free; inmates must pay an amount to the inner mafias who exercise control and internal government of the prisons (TNI 2010).
5 The 2014 international transparency corruption index places Bolivia in the 102nd place, among 175 countries evaluated, with a score of 35 out of a maximum of 100. According to this ranking, in the Americas, Bolivia is the country with the highest percentage (36%) of the population that perceives a high degree of payment of bribes in public administration. Similar evaluations are offered by the international measurement of the Natural Resource Governance Institute (NRGI) that relate corruption with governance and the validity of the rule of law (Wickberg 2012).
6 According to the Barómetro Global de Corrupción de Transparencia Internacional (2013), Bolivia's most corrupt institution is the Police, followed by political parties, and the judicial system.
7 José Carlos Campero interprets that, with this decision, "in the eyes of the world, especially in the region [surrounding Bolivia], the possibility of a more flexible interpretation of the conventions has become evident, especially when dealing with sovereign aspects that do not generally affect the rest of the countries" (2014, 591).
8 As a result of the United Nations decision, the government instituted March 12 as "National Acullico Day," which is celebrated with festive events and demonstrations.
9 Without pretending to evaluate the economic impacts of the Andean trade preference program, the Andean products exempted from tariffs totaled more than 6,300, which translated into a rapid growth of trade between the United States and the four beneficiary countries. Exports from the North to the region increased from $6,463.8 million in 2002 to $11,636.5 million in 2006, while their imports increased from $9,611.5 million to $22,510.6 million in the same period. Among the Andean exports favored by the ATPDEA are products such as oil, clothing, copper cathodes, flowers, gold jewelry, asparagus, and sugar. Of total U.S. imports, Ecuador accounted for 60%, Colombia for 36%, Peru for 24%, and Bolivia for 1%, the latter being the country that has been able to obtain the least advantage due to its limited export supply.
10 The government's obligation to eradicate surplus coca crops stems from the Coca and Controlled Substances Regime Law (1988), better known as Law 1008. Eradication, according to the law, must be carried out through annual reduction, substitution, and development plans. And, in fact, this is how it had been happening for ten years, although the established goals were not met.
11 The Bolivian government's new policy was never conceived solely as a strategy of forced eradication with militarization. The Dignity Plan had four pillars: (i) alternative development; (ii) eradication of surplus coca; (iii) interdiction based on shared responsibility with the international community; and (iv) prevention and rehabilitation.
12 On the other hand, the adhesion of the unions of the Yungas, the traditional coca-producing region, has not been free of tensions since Law 1008 protects them in this condition.
13 The agreement of one coca *cato* per family comes from a previous agreement of the Chapare unions with the government of Carlos Mesa, in 2004, which at that time was

Public Policies and the Border Subsystem 161

of a temporary nature. With Evo Morales as president, the agreement was revalidated and without time limit. The idea of legalizing a minimum extension of cultivation per family had already been raised in 1997, within the framework of a National Dialogue convened by President Hugo Banzer (Laserna 2011a, 240). It was also considered in the following government of Sánchez de Lozada but was unable to prosper due to the reluctance of Bolivian anti-drug agencies, the United States, and the rejection of the coca growers' unions.

14 Union sanctions can range from the prohibition of planting coca for certain periods of time to prohibiting the right to plant and, in extreme cases of serious recidivism, to expropriate their plots of land.

15 Everything seems to indicate that this strategy of self-regulation has reduced – not eliminated – the social conflicts and abuses in the coca-growing areas that were previously attributed to the police forces, but it does not imply that the human rights violations have ended. Many times, it is the now union leaders – protected by political power – who perpetrate such violations against other producers and residents, and especially against those who do not submit to their designs and arbitrariness.

16 The government of Evo Morales has not been able to design or implement a clear and sustainable strategy for its defense of coca. In fact, it "has adhered to the prohibitionist logic, reiterating the idea that cocaine is a Western problem and alien to Bolivians and claiming shared responsibility in drug control. In that order, the Bolivian commitment would be to prevent the expansion of crops and cooperate in the repression of drug trafficking, in exchange for being allowed to authorize a larger area of coca leaf cultivation" (Laserna 2011b, 268).

17 Pijcheo alludes to the act of chewing coca leaves in order to extract its juice, which produces a stimulating effect.

18 The CONALTI-D is the highest body for defining and executing policies to combat illicit trafficking in drugs and controlled substances, chaired by the President of the State and made up of the Ministers of Foreign Affairs, the Presidency, the Government, Defense, and Health and Sports; the Technical and Coordination secretariats of CONALTID depend on the Ministry of Government. The CONCOCA Coordination Secretariat depends on the Ministry of Rural Development and Lands. FONADAL is an organic dependency of the Ministry of Rural Development and Lands and of the Vice Ministry of Coca and Integral Development.

19 The work that perhaps most symbolizes the dimension of the state commitment is the construction of the Soberanía de Chimoré International Airport, in the very heart of the coca-growing region of the Cochabamba Tropics, recently inaugurated, with an investment of close to $35 million. This airport is considered a mega-project due to its large dimensions, with a runway length of 4,000 meters, similar to that of the El Alto International Airport in La Paz. President Evo Morales has justified this work by the need to promote exports of alternative tropical products and tourism (El Deber 2015).

20 The States Department's 2014 International Narcotics Control Strategy Report (INCSR) highlights that Bolivia remains one of the three largest cocaine-producing countries in the world and an important transit zone for Peruvian cocaine (2014). It is noted that considerable amounts of cocaine of Peruvian origin were intercepted in Bolivia in 2013. Most of the Bolivian cocaine flows to other countries in Latin America, especially Brazil, for internal consumption or to continue its transit to West Africa and Europe. In September 2013, President Barack Obama determined that Bolivia has "manifestly failed" to make sufficient efforts to comply with its obligations under international anti-narcotics agreements (United States Department of State 2014). He also claims that Bolivia's ability to identify, investigate, and dismantle drug trafficking organizations remains greatly diminished after the expulsion of the U.S. DEA and that the Bolivian FELCN does not even have the ability to pay informants.

162 *Policies*

21 Precisely, Armando Méndez, former president of the Central Bank of Bolivia, said: "It is not appropriate for the FIU to depend on the Ministry of Economy because money laundering is carried out through financial institutions, so its previous dependence was the most appropriate … I do not know why the transfer was made, what is the purpose? Could it be that the ASFI did not do a good job?" (Campos Vélez 2014).
22 See also Erbol (2017).

References

ANF. 2013. "El 2013 marca un incremento en los casos de trata y tráfico de personas en Bolivia." December 23, 2013. https://eju.tv/2013/12/el-2013-marca-un-incremento-en -los-casos-de-trata-y-trfico-de-personas-en-bolivia/.

———. 2015. "Detienen al jefe de CACIP de El Alto con más de 42 kilos de cocaína en su casa." December 11, 2015. https://www.noticiasfides.com/nacional/sociedad/detienen -en-santa-cruz-al-jefe-del-gacip-de-el-alto-con-mas-de-42-kilos-de-cocaina-en-su-casa -360418-360354.

———. 2016. "Gobierno admite que no existe voluntad política para invertir en la lucha contra la violencia de género." July 13, 2016. https://www.noticiasfides.com/nacional /sociedad/gobierno-admite-que-no-existe-voluntad-politica-para-invertir-en-la-lucha -contra-la-violencia-de-genero-367957-367859.

Campero, José Carlos. 2014. "Los retos para Bolivia ante un nuevo marco mundial de política de drogas." In *Bolivia: Encrucijadas en el siglo XXI. Ideas y visiones para una agenda de país*, edited by Henry Oporto, 583–633. La Paz: Fundación Pazos Kanki.

Campos Vélez, Marcelo. 2014. "La UFI pasa a tuición del Ministerio de Economía." *El Día*, April 16, 2014. https://www.eldia.com.bo/noticia.php?id=143190&id_cat=381.

El Deber. 2015. "Evo inaugura aeropuerto en antigua base de la DEA." October 17, 2015. https://eldeber.com.bo/bolivia/evo-inaugura-aeropuerto-en-antigua-base-de-la-dea _115019.

Erbol. 2017. "Gobierno plantea elaborar Código de Ética efectivo contra microcorrupción." February 1, 2017. https://anteriorportal.erbol.com.bo/noticia/politica/01022017/ gobierno_plantea_elaborar_codigo_de_etica_efectivo_contra_microcorrupcion.

Fundación Construir. 2012. *Reforma procesal penal y detención preventiva en Bolivia*, coordinated by Ramiro Orias, Susana Saavedra, and Claudia V. Alarcón. La Paz: Fundación Construir.

Fundación La Paz. 2016. *Balance de la implementación de las políticas anti-trata en Bolivia.* Fundación La Paz, 84. http://www.vuelalibre.info/descargas/85610761292 cdf755afdd- 7bea817cfa1.pdf.

Herrera, William. 2013.. *El Estado de la justicia boliviana*. Santa Cruz: Editorial Kipus.

Laserna, Roberto. 2011a. *El fracaso del prohibicionismo*. La Paz: Fundación Pazos Kanki. La Paz.

———. 2011b. *La trampa del rentismo... y cómo salir de ella*. La Paz: Fundación Milenio.

Ledebour, Kathryn. 2002. "Coca and Conflict in the Chapare. Wola, Drug War Monitor. Washington Office on Latin America." https://www.wola.org/sites/default/files/ downloadable/Drug%20Policy/past/ddhr_bolivia_brief.pdf.

Los Tiempos. 2011. "Lavado: 835 denuncias y 44 casos procesados en 4 años en Bolivia." November 6, 2011. https://eju.tv/2011/11/lavado-835-denuncias-y-44-casos -procesados-en-4-aos-en-bolivia/.

Molina Céspedes, Tomás. 2013. *Realidad carcelaria Cifras y Fotografías*. Bolivia.

Morales Luján, Armando. 2008. "Bolivia sin ATPDEA por no cooperar en la lucha antidrogas." *La Razón*, November 27, 2008. https://eju.tv/2008/11/bolivia-sin-atpdea-por-no-cooperar-en-la-lucha-antidrogas/.

Oporto, Henry. 2014. "La justicia se nos muere." In *Bolivia: Encrucijadas en el siglo XXI: Visiones e ideas para una agenda de país*, edited by Henry Oporto, 17–73. La Paz: Plural.

Pacheco, Napoleón. 2004. *En defensa de la racionalidad*. La Paz: Fundación Milenio.

Página Siete. 2015. "En Bolivia sólo 12 de 1.340 casos de trata y tráfico tienen sentencia." July 31, 2015. https://eju.tv/2015/07/en-bolivia-solo-12-de-1-340-casos-de-trata-y-trafico-tienen-sentencia/.

PIEB. 2012. "Retardación de Justicia por la Ley 1008." http://bit.ly/Pij1ZH.

TNI. 2010. "Leyes de drogas y cárceles en Bolivia" https://www.tni.org/my/node/16677.

United States Department of State. 2014. "Bolivia" In *2014 International Narcotics Control Strategy Report*.

United States International Trade Comission. 2009. "Decisions of the United States Court of International Trade." January 30, 2009. https://www.cbp.gov/bulletins/43slip16.pdf.

UNODC. n.d. "UNODC: Son legales 12.000 ha de coca, mientras no cambien la ley." https://www.unodc.org/bolivia/es/stories/unodc_son-legales_12000_ha_de_coca.html.

———. 2013. "UNODC recibió el Estudio Integral de la Hoja de Coca." December 6, 2013. https://www.unodc.org/bolivia/es/press/presentacion_resultados_estudio_coca_a_unodc.html.

———. 2014. *World Drug Report 2014*. Vienna: UNODC.

———. 2015. *Bolivia: Monitoreo de cultivos de coca 2014*, August. La Paz: Estado Plurinacional de Bolivia.

———. 2016. *Global Report on Trafficking in Persons 2016*. Vienna: UNODC.

Wickberg, Sofia. 2012. "Overview of corruption and anti-corruption in Bolivia. U4 Expert Answer." https://knowledgehub.transparency.org/assets/uploads/helpdesk/346_Overview_of_corruption_in_Bolivia.pdf.

Youngers, Coletta A., and Kathryn Ledebur. 2015. *Building on Progress Bolivia Consolidates Achievements in Reducing Coca and Looks to Reform Decades-Old Drug Law*. Cochabamba, Bolivia: WOLA (Washington Office on Latin America) and Andean Information Network.

Part 4
Balance

6 The Border Subsystem from Illegal Drug Markets

The research began from the concept of the border system and the way it has evolved in the last decades, marked by the strong penetration of globalization. From this perspective, the history of borders and their reflection in the practice of policy and academic research explain, in part, the slow path to understand an important dimension of Bolivia's insertion as a subsystem in the region's border system. Faced with the concept of the border as a binational dividing line, the modern concept of the system of relations is gaining ground in political, economic, and cultural practice. This issue is not very palpable, because there is no discussion about it in the country. The concept of the border line persists, given the historical development of Bolivia's borders.

On the Integration of Illegal Sectors

The study has tried to highlight the main aspects to understand the dominant role of the illegal markets in the border subsystem and their overwhelming impact on bilateral trading relations, which has reached a new height not only in terms of contraband goods but also in terms of drug trafficking. Furthermore, some of the consequences of this role of illegal markets on the policies and life of the country have been noted.

The importance of this general framework for the real understanding of the conditions under which the most important sectors of the illegal markets operate is generally not well considered. They are usually analyzed in a sectoral way, isolating the implications of the mutual relationship between all of them. There are studies on drug trafficking that tend to be reduced to the coca leaf, trafficking in coca paste and, casuistically, the production of cocaine hydrochloride. Trafficking and smuggling are analyzed from the perspective of each of the sectors, as if they could exist independently of the corruption and informality that prevail.

The contribution of the study's approach, which does not exclude the necessary depth of sectoral studies, is to mark the conceptual and political added value of their intersectoral and global relationship that deploys the importance of the role of each of them as pieces that cannot be ignored in the construction of the subsystem. We know that drug trafficking is linked to human trafficking, smuggling, money laundering, hitmen networks, and the corruption that so deeply

DOI: 10.4324/9781003203117-11

168 *Balance*

conditions the justice system, police forces, and other levels of the system. All these institutional levels are linked and condition each other. This global vision is usually a variable, by which we understand the functioning of each one of them and, particularly, their policies.

In this sense, we sought to incorporate into the book all the elements of an overall framework that is provided by the concept of the border system. We have not been able to develop the ways in which this global structure works, and, above all, the organizing role of drug trafficking. This should be the objective of other studies based on the hypotheses that this research offered. The interpretation that results of the research on drug trafficking, smuggling, and contraband – though each issue is important in itself and should be studied in the depth of its own specificity – makes sense when understood from an integral relationship and by the interrelationship that exists between them.

Finally, it is necessary to interpret the illegal markets from the perspective of Bolivia's relationship with the world. Each of the different markets functions in a set of intersectoral relations, and, at the same time, this set articulates a system of global relations. Thus, it will be possible to understand why a policy does not work from the logic of the sector and its institutions, nor from the institutional system of the country, but from the determinations of the global system of which the borderlines are part.

Figure 6.1 illustrates the lines of interaction that are necessary to consider in the elaboration and implementation of comprehensive policies at the national level.

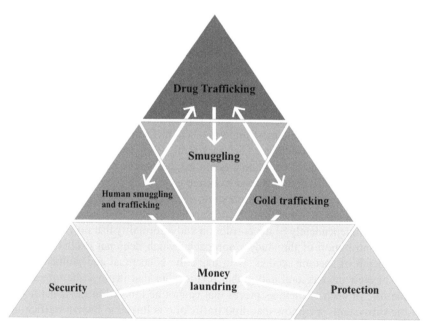

Figure 6.1 Framework of Interaction of the Main Illegal Sectors. Figure by the author.

The Border Subsystem from Illegal Drug Markets 169

Obviously, these sectoral areas are not homogeneous, but rather stratified. In them, there are power domes and very important base armies, such as the smugglers army, informal sellers, coca leaf producers, small-scale miners, police and hired killers, employees in the exploitation sites, goods traffickers, and human traffickers. In addition, there are actors who function as pieces of a global system of crime. Within the illegal markets, we consider one of them to be predominant and to instill orientation and preponderant conditions in the rest: drug trafficking, not only because of its volume, but also because of its capacity to influence others within a generalized framework of informality. This market is the axis that drives globalized crime.

An analysis of the socioeconomic environment that surrounds, sustains, conditions, and facilitates the growth and strength of the coca-cocaine complex in Bolivia emphasizes the fundamental role played by informality with illegal drug trafficking markets and other related criminal practices, such as money laundering and, to a lesser extent, the illegal sale of arms and human trafficking.

Informality, Smuggling, and Drug Trafficking

In Bolivia there is a system of interaction between informality, smuggling, and drug trafficking. Openly criminal businesses feed and deepen the informal behavior of the economy, especially in the internal and external trade sectors. This is facilitated by the absence of State presence at borders, the weakness of border control institutions (Customs, Migration, Police), the permissiveness with smuggling, and the lack of action by the administration of justice.

Drug trafficking operates under the control of criminal groups (national and foreign), but its dynamics transcend these, spreading to a group of people and economic agents; many of them act in the border areas, but not exclusively. This is also the reason for the complexity of the criminal world that operates in Bolivia, immersed in a dense social fabric, with a dislocated presence in the national territory and connections in other countries. The mafias connected to drug trafficking are also related to other criminal activities: kidnapping, human trafficking, organ and arms trafficking, and gold smuggling.

Figure 6.1 shows how the triangle of informality, smuggling, and drug trafficking connects all the illegal sectors, including productive sectors such as services, defense, and support. The triangle is also key in the understanding of the multiple possibilities for legitimizing money, in an economy where thousands of small traders and informal producers operate and in multiple other criminal services and public corruption, forming fertile ground for the insertion of illegal flows into the circuits of circulation of money and other assets. Certainly, the density of the phenomenon of informality and its cross-cutting nature to many economic sectors are especially conducive to the transformation of money, initially, into small-scale goods, such as merchandise, then into legal financial assets, such as small savings accounts, and return flows that add up and derive in real assets of greater magnitude, also legal and subject to property records, finally, in legal businesses that consolidate the integration of activities (Ramírez Romero 1996, 13).

170 *Balance*

These conditions help to understand the innumerable loopholes in the penetration of drug trafficking into the Police, Justice, and other official bodies, as well as the proliferation of links between the State apparatus and illegal markets, the protection of influential political interests that stifle the State's ability to tackle illicit trafficking, and the action of criminal groups.

Scenarios of Conflict and Violence

It is striking that a generalized panorama of informality and criminality does not generate large-scale conflicts as in Mexico. Why? This is a question that is frequently asked; however, this type of conflicts might represent one of Bolivia's foreseeable futures.

> InSight Crime does not believe that Bolivia has been taken over by transnational organized crime, or even that it is close to it. Nevertheless, the country is vulnerable, and, currently, the opportunities and profit potential of drug trafficking are too high for international criminal groups to ignore.
>
> (McDermott 2014, 10)

Although it is predicted that Santa Cruz, where crime is on the rise, could turn into the epicenter for negotiating the purchase and transport of drugs, making the city an attractive place to live, "If the large drug traffickers begin to live there, this will not only accelerate the process of corruption of Police and Judicial institutions, but they will most likely also seek to influence the political arena" (McDermott 2014, 10) and, consequently, increase the activity of insecurity and violence similar to conflict environments in other countries.

A new political phenomenon in Bolivia, compared to Colombia and Peru, is the reciprocity pact with the coca growers' movement, whereby the government allows and respects coca crops and not only traditional crops, but also surpluses. Coca growers, for their part, respect not advancing in the expansion of the agricultural border of coca and even agree to "rationalize" their family and community crops. This situation has made it possible to pacify the coca-growing areas and to avoid the lack of control of the cultivation areas. At the same time, the government can show the result of a gradual and concerted decrease and show the world that it is a government that fulfills its commitment to reduce the surplus crops, without giving up its preaching in defense of the coca leaf. The strategy of rationalization and concerted reduction of coca crops has allowed the continuity of several of the alternative development programs in the coca-producing areas, although under the name of "integral development."

Whether of its own volition or forced by international pressure, the government of Evo Morales has remained within the policy of controlled substances outlined by Law 1008. Despite political and diplomatic disagreements with the U.S. government, with mutual accusations and recriminations about the results of the anti-drug problem, the Bolivian government has been able to overcome the situation and show progress, even more than it can objectively demonstrate.

If this policy has made it possible to lower the level of conflict in the coca leaf production phase, it is the policy of ease and weakness in the attack on drug trafficking that would explain, although partially, the relatively low level of conflict. The State faces institutional, police, and judicial limitations, as well as the technical and financial resources needed to wage a relentless and successful fight against drug trafficking and to prevent its further expansion. Society itself, or sectors of it, seem to have accepted a status quo of coexistence with drug trafficking. Even though opinion polls show citizen concern about drugs and drug trafficking, and the widespread perception is of a close connection between drug trafficking, crime, and public insecurity, there is no citizen pressure and movement capable of altering the tolerant and permissive social climate with the crime.

> The Bolivian Minister of the Interior acknowledged at a regional summit that many border crossings remain vulnerable to criminal activity, which recalls the role of the Andean nation as a regional center for the drug trade. At a meeting of the Southern Cone countries this week in Brasilia, Bolivian Interior Minister Carlos Romero said that 34 points on the border of their country are vulnerable to drug trafficking.
>
> (Farfán 2016)

Despite continued reports of an increasing number of operations and seizures by the FELCN, there are indications that drug trafficking has continued to grow, and that against it, all the repressive action of the State is insufficient and ineffective because it fails to contain its progress.

Perspectives and Future Scenarios

By recapitulating the main findings of the research, some prospective scenarios can be tested on the position that Bolivia maintains with respect to illegal markets, in particular, with respect to international drug trafficking. At the same time, it is necessary to understand the factors that can impulse changes in the Bolivian situation. Bolivia is a subsidiary actor in the global system of illicit trafficking, and there is little chance that this will change in the future. On the other hand, the coca-cocaine complex is a consolidated economic reality with a specific weight in the national economy; its penetration in the society is growing, as well as its influence on the political, police, judicial, and administrative structures of the State. It has developed important links with smuggling and, in general, with the informal sector, which is at the heart of the popular economy. So, what alternatives does Bolivia have to redefine its terms of insertion and participation in the global drug market? Let's look at some scenarios.

172　*Balance*

Scenario A: Bolivia Seeks to Disconnect from the Drug Trafficking Circuit

Is this scenario a realistic and viable option? Everything indicates that it is not, at least not on a predictable horizon. The fundamental reason of this lies in the following: there is a dynamic and expansive illegal drug market, and, as long as the force of transnational organized crime remains intact, the stimuli for production and trafficking in and from Bolivia will surely continue to be more powerful than any repressive strategy or action from the State, even more so because of the interactions between informality, contraband, and drug trafficking, which have taken root and tend to reproduce and operate under their own dynamics.

Scenario B: Bolivia Positions Itself as the Regional Epicenter of Drug Trafficking

According to McDermott (2014, 9), this is something that some analysts believe. However, some others do not consider this scenario to be possible, at least not from a self-sustaining position. The country's geographical barriers and its landlocked status, the fact that transnational criminal organizations operating on a global scale have not taken root here, and the overwhelming dependence on neighboring countries as markets[1] and as platforms for exporting cocaine to overseas markets are apparently insurmountable obstacles to Bolivian drug trafficking substantially strengthening its international position and enabling it to play a vigorous role. This would eventually displace the production and trafficking generated in the other Andean basin countries.

Scenario C: The Situation Remains Unchanged: Bolivia as a Relevant Actor

This scenario implies that Bolivia remains a relevant actor, but in a subsidiary position in the global drug market, with its economy trapped in the networks of illegality and informality, its institutions weakened and vulnerable to corruption, corporate pressures, and the penetration of drug trafficking and with multiple links between the State apparatus and illegal markets. This would seem to be the most likely scenario, thus drawing a vicious circle of inertial growth of drug trafficking and, with it, of the underground economy superimposed on informality.

But to what extent can Bolivian society live with phenomena such as these, of enormous dissociative influence, without being plunged into political, institutional, economic, social, and ethical decomposition, and without eroding the capacity and authority of the State and undermining the foundations of peaceful coexistence?

Recently, the Conferencia Episcopal Boliviana, in a direct, forceful, and unambiguous pronouncement, warned about the threats hanging over the country. They stated that drug trafficking threatens not only the State institutions, but also the peaceful coexistence and the sovereignty of the State and the development of the country (2016, 22). This situation raises a feeling of frustration and mistrust among the population toward the judicial administration.

> As it is in the public domain, drug trafficking, in its strategy of expansion and impunity, even penetrates State structures and forces of law and order, buying consciences. Corruption has undermined the credibility of authorities of various ranks in charge of the fight against drug trafficking, both in the present and in the past.
>
> (Conferencia Episcopal Boliviana 2016, 22)

It was once said that, in Bolivia, it has been possible to get around explosive situations of criminal violence and recurrent and horrendous confrontations between criminal gangs, as has happened in other countries. But can one always avoid such extremes?

That Bolivia and its borders are not "hot spots" of criminal geopolitics in the region does not mean that they are safe from this threat since the circumstances that contain or buffer violence within certain limits could eventually change, due to both internal and external factors. For example, an eventual hardening of the repression of drug trafficking and smuggling at the borders by neighboring governments, together with greater international pressure to control these activities (including coca production), has the potential to turn internal and border areas of the national territory into scenarios of violent confrontation, especially if the Bolivian government is forced to mobilize police and military forces for a frontal fight against criminal groups, which in turn could increase disputes between the mafias.

Opportunities and Great Challenges

Certainly, an analysis of the different scenarios does not inspire optimism; however, not everything points toward immobility. Fortunately, winds of change are blowing internationally, especially from the side of national and State policies. There is already a willingness in the international community to debate anti-drug policies, considering the evident failure of the war on drugs; this paradigm has for many years permeated anti-drug strategies in Latin America and in Bolivia. In this sense, it is necessary to raise the voices of former presidents, academics, and other personalities, who are increasingly critical of repressive policies and who advocate the adoption of a new global drug strategy, based on principles of public health, reduction of the impacts created by illicit markets, properly monitored regulatory experimentation, a strong commitment to human rights, etc. The determination of the OAS to open the discussion and explore possible scenarios for other alternatives is also a prominent milestone. Added to all this, there are the experiences of drug market regulations in European countries and, also, in some states of the United States – especially for recreational and medicinal consumption of marijuana – and, now, the neighboring country of Uruguay, although these are extremely small aspects in relation to the enormous volume of

174 *Balance*

drug trafficking. Marijuana consumption cannot be compared to drug trafficking and its associated businesses. Bolivia, as one of the main coca leaf and cocaine producing countries, is directly concerned by a discussion of great importance, but which would necessarily remain in the field of coca leaf policy, but nothing beyond that; the most important aspect of drug trafficking will hardly be made more flexible.

The first of the country's major challenges has to do with transforming the coca-cocaine complex, promoting the consolidation of a diversified family and business economy in the coca-growing regions, with profitable alternative crops and less dependence on income from coca leaf and its illicit derivatives.

As José Carlos Campero points out, in view of the progress and maturation of the alternative development process, especially in the Chapare, where the convergent results of technical and financial assistance to producers, investment in infrastructure, social projects, the intervention of municipal governments, and even the contribution of private investment are already perceptible, alternative development and the diversification of local economies are now more clearly visible as possible goals, although much remains to be done, especially by removing political and union controls that restrict the freedom and initiative of producers, but also by generating other incentives to reduce the diversion of coca leaf to illicit cocaine production (2014).

From that point of view, the most valuable incentive is probably the industrialization of coca; a process that, if developed to its full potential, has the capacity to generate an economic return for peasant families, perhaps even higher than what they perceive by selling their coca production on the illegal market. Until now, the issue of industrialization has been no more than rhetoric and has been deprived of the necessary scientific knowledge and technological innovations, as well as of the entrepreneurial and institutional capacities that are indispensable for economically viable ventures. In other words, a serious, effective, and far-reaching policy of industrialization of the coca leaf must go beyond the products derived from it, such as tea, flour, jellies, syrups, ointments, and others, which are currently made, but with little projection and competitive advantages. The real demand is to open a new productive border, using the coca leaf, for example, as a "biological bank," and, thus, generate products with high added value in the food, medicinal, and recreational industries.

Today, the innovations developed by Coca Cola, Red Bull, and other large companies, using decocainized coca extract in their products, are already well known. One should consider that the coca leaf contains 14 alkaloids. Those can potentially be industrialized and put under chemical-industrial processes to obtain inputs and a great variety of consumer products.[2]

Comprehensive policy approach is the second major national challenge. A renewed vision of the drug problem is required. This vision would have to be broad and take into account: issues such as new facets of crime, including the interrelationships between drug trafficking, money laundering, and other related crimes; the issue of citizen security, the administration of justice and the prison system; border control; the role of the police and public forces; programs for

The Border Subsystem from Illegal Drug Markets   175

critical scenarios that are closely related to crime; and, of course, socioeconomic dimensions.

From the Bolivian experience, it is clear that unilateral, unrelated, and intermittent efforts are ultimately ineffective and even counterproductive, with the overall result that drug trafficking and criminality are always several steps ahead. Consequently, nowadays, replacing Law 1008 has become less urgent than having good studies and diagnoses of the criminal and delinquency scene in the country, and a modern and efficient system of police information and crime statistics, which can produce accurate and reliable data. In the absence of these basic tools, public policies continue to move blindly, improvising responses, and often wasting scarce State resources. The legislative proposals being worked on in the Executive Branch, such as the General Coca Law project, which replaces the current Law 1008, suffer from these same flaws.

In the meantime, serious problems have been forgotten, such as those in the justice and prison systems, which have practically collapsed due, among other things, to the excessively punitive nature of criminal and anti-drug justice – particularly against small-scale traffickers and occasional suppliers – and, in general, to the reductionist approaches, legal fetishism, and punitive populism that permeate Bolivian laws.[3]

The same happens with the institutional crisis of the Police and the well-known practices of corruption within it, its incompetence and lack of professionalism, but whose solutions are postponed *ad eternum*, because no government or authority dares to address the real problem. Part of it is the lack of a modern system of police information and crime statistics, as well as the lack of an adequately professional intelligence apparatus for the investigation and prosecution of major crimes and criminal organizations, and, in short, the absence of a criminal policy that articulates the various components, instruments, and resources used in the fight against crime. Legislative reforms are justified only if they contribute to improving institutions, rather than weakening them, as it is often the case. The country does not need more laws that will not be even enforced, but it does need good policies and strategies based on experience, information, knowledge, and, above all, institutional capacities and qualified human resources.

Depoliticizing the fight against money laundering is another challenge to achieve a true State policy on drugs. Part of the comprehensive, long-term approach of an effective and more legitimate anti-drug policy is the requirement to completely depoliticize the Financial Information Unit (FIU), in order to control and monitor all financial operations and other services that may be used to convey spurious and suspicious acts. It is true that important steps have been taken to establish norms and control mechanisms in the financial system and to adjust its development to international standards in prevention measures, risk identification, transparency, and availability of information generated in the system. However, there are many other equally critical areas for detecting, curbing, and dismantling the various operations of money laundering and legitimization of illicit profits – among them, those in border areas – and in which the capacity for intervention is practically nonexistent. In addition, the overwhelming weight

176 *Balance*

of the informal sector, where legality and illegality overlap, generating multiple interstices for money laundering and other concomitant crimes, cannot be ignored.

A new era of international cooperation is the fourth challenge, which has to do with how Bolivia is going to redefine its relations with the international community and, above all, with neighboring countries, in order to tackle the problems of drugs, crime, and illegal markets, after several years in which the dominant trend has been to renounce international cooperation, confronting the power of the north, distancing oneself from one's neighbors, isolating oneself and becoming absorbed in one's own convictions, falsely deluding oneself with the idea of absolute sovereignty, and all this more for ideological and political reasons than for a realistic assessment of national possibilities and the factors of power at play. Today, it is absolutely clear that Bolivia, like other countries in a similar position, not only cannot turn its back on the international community but cannot do without intense and effective cooperation and external assistance.

The regional environment becomes very challenging for Bolivia for two reasons: First, the problems of drug trafficking, smuggling, illegal mining, illegal migration, human trafficking, and others criminal activities in border areas do not cease to grow and become more and more complex, surpassing any unilateral effort by Bolivia or its neighbors to solve or contain them. Second, and as a consequence of the above, the pressures from other governments are intensifying, so that the Bolivian government redoubles its efforts and intensifies its repressive actions and control over illegal activities and, above all, over the drug trafficking that is generated or circulates through Bolivian territory.

In fact, these are issues that are on Bolivia's diplomatic agendas with its neighbors, in some cases with some progress, in others with little or no progress, but, in general, the Bolivian government's policy is moving in the direction of achieving bilateral and tripartite agreements, for more effective collaboration.

This is a great opportunity to promote collaboration at the bilateral, subregional, and regional levels, with a broad and comprehensive perspective. This is the most important thing of all: to move from punctual, occasional, and somehow limited cooperation to strategic cooperation that goes far beyond sharing information and coordinating. It would complement actions, since it necessarily implies generating and integrating capacities, working with supranational plans, monitoring, and evaluating results, negotiating joint cooperation agreements with the United States and Europe, in short, developing a frank and open dialogue on the different realities and requirements of each country that must be taken into account to set cooperation objectives, in a framework of solidarity and mutual commitments.

Local Border Policies

It is time to address decentralization programs that facilitate municipalities to address border issues more directly related to the main critical scenarios such as gender, human trafficking and smuggling of persons, youth, police, and prisons. Special attention to indigenous populations that are often victims of drug trafficking and smuggling must be put. Of course, true territorial development must be multilevel, but generally what is observed is a very strong oscillation between the isolation and oblivion of borders and the centralism of border programs with direct actions from the central government.

The current challenges can be used to generate national awareness of the role that borders play in anchoring the country in the international order that invades us all the time. The municipalities should be able to structure cooperation programs with the municipalities in the neighboring country and facilitate the functioning of the Latin American and Caribbean Organization of Border Cities (OLACCIF), along with other forms of cooperation between border cities.

Spaces for Political Action Are Required

Certain scenarios are particularly critical and affect the especially vulnerable population. Concrete studies are required to make these scenarios visible, since the forms of attention to these spaces will have to be differentiated. As Boris Miranda mentions,

> [I]n Bolivia, and, of course, throughout Latin America, there are segments of the population that are more vulnerable to being colluded, forced, or co-opted by drug trafficking and organized crime. These segments require special attention, not only from legislation, but from the planning of lines of action, strategies, plans, and programs. The protection of society from the territorial networks of illegal economies must be differentiated and segmented.
>
> (2016, 39)

This is a path in which time and resources need to be invested. It particularly refers to territories that require special treatments, such as strengthening local police, provincial observatories, border areas for horizontal cooperation, and local development approaches.

By critical scenarios, we will then understand a concept that allows us to approach places and situations in which the drug business has different levels and forms of influence. There are areas in Bolivia where the combination and concentration of different illicit activities build up territorial scenarios that are especially serious for the population and especially for some very specific populations: young people, adolescents, the elderly, women, and indigenous people. Miranda concludes his work by proposing a subject for future study and mentioning that "Much field work and research is needed to make an approach that encompasses places and situations more broadly" (2016, 46–47). This statement also applies for this research.

Notes

1 Based on the research carried out by InSight Crime, McDermott states that only 5% of the cocaine seized in the United States comes from Bolivia (2014, 9).

178 *Balance*

2 On this topic, see Campero (2014, 269).

3 UNODC Bolivia recommends targeting the new law on controlled substances, on first instance, against the large drug trafficking networks, rather than the weakest links in the drug trafficking chain, such as consumers, small farmers, minor distributors, "mules and swallowers," considering the socioeconomic factors of the population most vulnerable to drug consumption, production, supply, and transport. It also recommends that the project be part of a comprehensive reform of the penal system, as well as medium- and long-term policies and programs for education, health, employment and housing, and social reinsertion and prevention of recidivism (UNODC 2015).

References

Campero, José Carlos. 2014. "Los retos para Bolivia ante un nuevo marco mundial de política de drogas." In *Bolivia: Encrucijadas en el siglo XXI. Ideas y visiones para una agenda de país*, edited by Henry Oporto, 583–633. La Paz: Fundación Pazos Kanki.

Conferencia Episcopal Boliviana. 2016. "Hoy pongo ante ti la vida o la muerte." In *Carta Pastoral sobre Narcotráfico y Drogadicción*. La Paz: Obispos de Bolivia.

Farfán, Williams. 2016. "Gobierno identifica 34 zonas vulnerables al narcotráfico." *La Razón*, November 18, 2016. https://www.la-razon.com/lr-article/gobierno-identifica -34-zonas-vulnerables-al-narcotrafico/.

McDermott, Jeremy. 2014. "El desafío de Evo: Bolivia, el epicentro de la droga." *InSight Crime*, October 2014. https://insightcrime.org/wp-content/uploads/2019/10/Desafio _Evo_Bolivia_epicentro_droga.pdf.

Miranda, Boris. 2016. "Etnografía de la Vulnerabilidad: Escenarios Críticos del Narcotráfico en Bolivia." In *Seguridad Regional en América Latina y el Caribe. Anuario 2015*, edited by Catalina Niño Guarnizo, 38–40. Bogotá: Frederich Ebert Stiftung.

Ramírez Romero, Juan Ramón. 1996. "El lavado de dinero y la economia en Bolivia." *Revista de Análisis Económico* 16 (7): 195–2013. http://www.udape.gob.bo/portales _html/AnalisisEconomico/analisis/vol16/art07.pdf.

UNODC. 2015. "UNODC comparte estándares internacionales, buenas prácticas y lecciones aprendidas sobre normativas de drogas." September 17, 2015. https:// www.unodc.org/bolivia/es/normativa-drogas/UNODC-comparte-estandares-sobre -normativas-de-drogas.html.

Index

1961 Single Convention on Narcotic Drugs 140
1961 United Nations Conventions on Narcotic Drugs *see* Vienna Convention
2001 census 49
40 recomendaciones 158

Acre War 18
Act No. 004 159
Act No. 170 159
Act No. 262 159
Act No. 263 150
Act No. 3325 149
acullico 88; *see also* National Acullico Day
Africa 53; people from 117–118
Agencia para el desarrollo de las zonas fronterizas (ADEMAF) 22, 27, 29
Agrarian Reform 54
agriculture 20–21, 34, 63, 105, 117
Aguarague mountain 55
Aguas Blancas 54–55
air routes 61–62
alcohol 56
alcoholic beverages 58, 109
alkaloids 81, 102, 174
Altiplano 39, 46, 56
Altmann 123
Alto Paraguay 51
Aluvión de fuego 23
Amazon 61–62; Bolivian 46–47; East 19–20
Amazonian haciendas 47; products 7
Americas, the 160
ammunition 154–155
Andean: countries 80, 143; governments 143; people 89; products 160; region 141–142

Andean Trade Preferences Act (ATPA) 142
Andean Trade Preferences and Drug Eradication Act (ATPDEA) 142–143, 160
Andes 8, 20, 40, 75, 79, 81, 88
Aniceto Arce de Tarija 55
ant: smuggling 132, 138; trade 55, 57
anti-drug 143; agencies 161; justice 175; legislation 135; policy 140; problem 171; strategy 142, 148, 173–175
anti-narcotics 143; agreements 161; control 124; force 100; police 48, 57
anti-trafficking 152
Arequipa 35
Argentina 15, 18–23, 43, 51, 61–64, 80, 88, 95, 107–109, 118, 154; border 117; currency 55; smuggled products from 109
Argentine Republic *see* Argentina
Arica 37, 45, 57, 59–61, 107–108, 138
Armed Forces 27, 29, 32, 136–138, 141, 151, 155
arms 2, 61, 71, 74, 110, 137, 140, 154–155, 169
Article 185 (bis) 159; (ter) 159
Article 281bis 149–150
Asia 7, 21, 24, 34, 57–58; markets 10, 88; people of 117–118
asymmetries 7–8, 13, 27, 45; complementary 6, 21
asynchorinies 49, 53
Atlantic 19, 23–24, 35, 46, 56
Aymara territory 35

bagalleros 55–56
Bagalleros 27; de mayo 63
bagayeros see bagalleros
Bahía Negra 33
ballon effect 11, 34

180 *Index*

bank secrecy 158
Banzer, Hugo 29, 142–143, 161
Barbie, Klaus 123
Bárometro Global de Corrupcíon de
  Transparencia Internacional 160
bazuco market 123
Beni 20, 33, 38, 46, 61, 85, 88, 114
Beni River 33, 114
Bermejo 33, 35, 53, 55–56
Bermejo River 55
bilateral 146, 176; lines 17; relations 6,
  148, 167; synchronies 139; trade 51, 167
binational 1, 6, 8, 22, 35, 133; bridge 47;
  lines 62, 167
black market 34, 53
Bolivia: biodiversity 140; border with
  Argentina 33–35, 52–57; border with
  Brazil 33–35, 43–49; border with Chile
  33–35, 57–61, 138, 153; border with
  Paraguay 33–35, 49–52; border with
  Peru 33–35, 38, 119; communication
  routes 23–24, 44; exporter country 7;
  global flows 1–2, 7–10, 20, 24–28,
  80; illegal markets 2, 5, 25, 69, 75,
  86; landlocked country 6, 17, 23; Port
  Capital of 49
Bolivian: cocaine 44; economy 21, 51, 97,
  106, 115, 139, 145; exports 46, 113;
  government 23, 55, 62, 83, 90, 102,
  140, 143, 160, 171, 173, 176; laws 175;
  subsystem 8, 89, 102; territory 79, 85,
  112, 122, 176
Bolivian Constitution 140
Bolivian Criminal Code 84
Bolivian East 46
Bolivian Institute of Foreign Trade 21
Bolivian Pantanal 48
Bolivian Pocitos 63
Bolpebra 33, 38–39, 45
border: areas 27–28, 39, 177; cities 35;
  concept 11, 22; evolution 17, 21, 23;
  physical 6, 12, 17–18, 21, 28–29,
  62; population 28, 39, 53, 139, 153;
  posts 8, 24, 38, 45, 71, 139; *see also*
  border crossings; programs 27–28,
  177; subsystem 10, 21, 32, 69, 89, 131,
  167; system 5, 10–15, 23–26, 33–35,
  62, 70, 85, 131, 137, 167–168; towns
  43, 48, 56; trade 9, 12, 21, 53–55, 137;
  transformation 12; violence 13, 39,
  60, 116
border crossings 8–10, 15, 27, 32–39, 45,
  53, 57, 64, 136–138, 171; clandestine 64

borderline 43, 63, 168
border posts 8, 24, 38, 45, 71, 139; *see
  also* border crossings
Brasiléia 33
Brazil 9, 15, 18–23, 33, 38–39, 43–56,
  60–63, 79, 88, 107–109, 117, 154, 161;
  smuggled products from 109
Buenos Aires 19–21, 35, 46, 52, 56, 88
Bush, George H. W. 142
Bush, George W. 143
Butcher of Lyon *see* Altmann

Cáceres 33, 37, 47
Cáceres, Felipe 123
Cáceres Lagoon 48–49
caciques 27
Campero, José Carlos 24, 46, 82–84, 104,
  122, 160, 174, 178
Carabineros de Chile 64
cargachos 90
Carrión, Fernando 13–14
Carrión, Fernando and Federico Alagna
  86
cartel 8, 61, 79, 83–88, 104; drug 141;
  system 43, 81
cartelization 86
Casa Suárez 20
casinos 119
cato 79, 97, 122, 145, 147, 160
cattlemen 48
Central Axis 20
centralism 24, 26–27, 131, 138, 177
centralist 2, 138; agenda 28; nature 131;
  orientation 27; perspective 32
Cerrito Jara 33
Cerro Cuatro Hermanos 33
Cerro Malpaso 33
Cerro Panizo 33
Cerro Ustares 33
Cerro Zapaleri 33
Cerruto, Oscar 23
Céspedes, Augusto 23
chaco 97
Chaco 34, 49, 55; region 18
Chaco oil war *see* Chaco War
Chaco War 17–18, 22, 54
Chapare 79, 82, 92–93, 122, 144–148, 160,
  174; area 52; farmers 144
Charagua 49
Charaña 15, 57, 61
chemists 103
chestnut 7, 46–47, 117
child pornography 117, 154

Index 181

Chile 9, 15, 17, 23, 46, 51, 63, 88,
105, 108–109, 117, 154; ports of 19;
smuggled products from 109–110
Chilean: authorities 109; border 59–60;
expansion 18; police 59; ports 58, 107;
posts 49
Chimoré International Airport 161
China 7, 10, 24, 105
Chiquitano 49
Choquecota 33
Chungará 61
Chungará Lagoon 61
chuto 64
Ciudad del Este 44, 51
clandestine crossings 8, 55, 62, 64;
economy 10, 110; gold 39, 45, 114;
roads 10; routes 32, 61; runways 61, 88;
trade 95
Clinton, Bill 143
Cobija 33–39, 44–46, 63; illegal markets
and insecurity 45
coca: basin 8; crops 83, 142–147, 170;
cultivation 79–81; eradication 97;
eradicators 63; growers 79, 97, 139–
140, 170; leaves 53, 102, 135; market
82; plantations 124, 141; policies 139;
producers 75, 133, 144–145; production
zones 90; seizures 100;trade 83
Coca and Controlled Substances Regime
Law 123, 160
coca-cocaine: chain 104; complex 7, 73,
81, 167, 171, 174; economy 142
Coca Cola 174
coca fields 92; colonization 39; cultivation
46
coca growers 79, 85, 139–145, federations
97; movement 170; organizations 83;
unions 147, 161
coca-growing: areas 83, 93, 103, 161;
basin 79; regions 148, 174
cocaine 15, 43, 51, 61–63; base 8, 84,
103, 123; base paste 53, 104, 124; basin
75; coup 123, export 10; hydrochloride
73, 167; market 89; producing countries
174; production 77, 80, 102; pure 53,
122; refined 85; routes 79; seized 177;
trafficking 39, 47
Cocaine King 85; book 123; *see also* Pablo
Escobar
coca leaf 8, 53, 89, 96–104, 139–144, 167,
174; commercialization 93; consumers
146; market 82; plantations 81; prices
93; producers 39, 169; production 25,
52, 75, 82–83, 90, 123

coca leaf chewing 140; *see also* pijcheo
cocalero movement 140, 147
coca-narcotics 84
Cochabamba 20, 52, 79, 90–101, 134
Cochabamba Tropics 92–94, 100, 123, 161
cockroach effect 87–88
Colchane 60
collective consciousness 22; imagination 17
Colombia 15, 44, 75, 79–88, 136, 170
Colombian cartels 85–86, 88
Colombian Method 103–104
colonial period 46, 115
Comando Vermelho 84, 123
communication: channels 20, 23; land 20;
networks 18, 26; nodes 48, routes 44,
49, technologies 74
Comprehensive Law against Trafficking
and Smuggling of Persons *see* Law 263
Conferencia Episcopal Boliviana 173
Consejo Nacional de Lucha contra el
Tráfico Ilícito de Drogas 25
Consejo Plurinacional contra la Trata y el
Tráfico de Personas 152
consumer 120, 178; American 142; centers
6; goods 106; market 26; products 174;
regional 34, 53, 89; sectors 118
contraband 10, 21, 34, 38–39, 53, 70, 105,
137, 172
contrabandista 12
Convergencia Nacional 103
Copacabana 33, 39
Córdoba 52
corruption 24, 28, 62, 71, 114, 135–137,
155, 173; public 169
criminal: activities 14, 60, 122, 150;
clans 122; codes 136; economy 25;
gangs 32, 85, 123, 173; groups 71,
133; informality 87; networks 69;
organizations 84, 135, 172; sectors 72;
violence 173
Criminal Code 84, 149, 159
criminality 28, 72, 116, 170
criminalization 135
Crónicas heroicas de una guerra estúpida
23
cross-border: economic activity 105; flows
112; forces 10; region 14; trade 21
crystallization 79–80; laboratories 47–48,
123
Cuzco 35

decentralization 6, 24, 26–29, 54; policies
27; programs 176; reforms of the 1990's
45, 47

182 *Index*

Desaguadero 33, 35, 38, 119
development strategy 26
Dignity Plan 141–145, 160
Di Leo, Antonino 102
Dirandro 88, 103–104, 124
Dirección Antidrogas de Perú 88; *see also*
  Dirandro
Dorado, Luis Felipe 103
Drug Enforcement Administration 148
drugs 61, 80, 104; commercialization of
  84; synthetic 57; war on 141
drug trafficking 25, 44, 53, 75, 89, 132,
  141, 169; in Bolivia 84–85, 121, 148;
  cartel 43; circuit 172; in the Economy
  104–105; international 171; in Latin
  America 80; market 90, 103; products
  75; sector 74

economy 21, 119; border 28, 53;
  extractivist 20, 105; formal 53, 72, 87;
  illegal 20, 46, 69, 87; Latin American
  12; legal 12, 60, 159; mining 20;
  national 106, 133, 171; underground 61,
  172; world 12
Ecuador 15, 142, 160
El Alto international airport 161
El Día 123
Empresa Nacional de Coca (ENACO)
  82–83, 122
eradication 97, 124, 143–145, 160
Erbol 162
Esmeralda 33, 51
Europe 19–21, 34, 47, 53, 88, 123–124, 176
European countries 173
European Union 102, 124, 145–149
Evia, José Luis 70
Excelsior 123
explosives 154–155
exports 18, 142, 160; gold 114, 122;
  legal 113
extension zone 108
extortion 12–13, 57, 62, 70, 116, 135
extractivism 7

Federación Especial de Trabajadores
  Gremiales 63; *see also vivanderas*
Ferrufino, Rubén 110–111
Financial Action Task Force 156
Financial Investigations Unit (FIU)
  156–159, 162, 175
Florida 86
flows: aerial 51; border 20; cocaine 161;
  cross-border 112; economic 17; global

1–2, 6–8, 10, 75; illegal 119, 169;
  migrant of 32; Pacific 23
force fields 6, 11–12
formal trade: from Argentina 51
Fortín Campero 33
Fortín d'Orbigny 33
Fortín Manoa 33
foundational border 22
free trade 57, 63, 107, 143
free trade agreement (FTA) 143
Free Zone of Iquique *see* Iquique Free
  Zone (ZOFRI)
free zones 57; Arica 138; Iquique *see*
  Iquique Free Zone (ZOFRI)
Fuerza de Tarea Conjunta 144
Fuerza Especial de Lucha contra el
  Narcotráfico 88, 123
Fundación La Paz 115, 149, 151
Fundación Milenio 124

García Linera, Álvaro 104
gender-based violence 149
General Coca Law 175
General Customs Law 64
global border system 5, 11, 14–15, 25, 33,
  70, 85
globalization 1, 5, 9, 15, 25, 86, 167;
  flows 22
Golberg, Philip 148
gold 10, 25, 33, 38–39, 72; clandestine
  extraction of 45; exploitation 47; export
  59; Peruvian 61, 114; smuggling 74,
  111, 122; trafficking 45
Golfo cartel 86
Gran Chaco 49, 51, 53
Gravetal 49, 63
Great Depression 18
Guajará-Mirim 44, 46–48
guano 18
Guatemala 15
Guayamerín 44, 46–47
Gun Control Act 154–155

Herrera, William 160
hitmen 12–13; networks 167
hot spots 34, 45, 173
human trafficking 38, 53, 55, 71, 74, 115,
  136, 149, 152–154, 176
hydrocarbons 5, 54, 104; industry 56
hydrochloride 61–62, 73, 81, 102, 104,
  120, 167; crystallization laboratories
  47–48; flows of 51; manufacture 33;
  production 8

Index 183

illegal adoptions 153–154
illegal earnings 159
illegal markets 12, 14, 21, 25, 63, 69, 72–73, 111, 137, 167; in Bolivia 114; cartelization of 86; in Cobija 45; Internet 13
illegal trade 63, 69–70, 93
imports 20, 26, 55, 106, 160; gold 122; smuggled 72, 111
indigenous: communities 9; organizations 133; people 22, 177; populations 60, 154, 176; women 117
informal economy 39, 62, 119, 121, 158; unregulated sector 74; urban informal sector 69
informality 2, 25, 62, 70, 86, 110, 120, 153, 167; criminal 87; institutional 28; triangle of 132–133, 169
informal markets 8, 120; *see also* informal economy
informal trade 70, 72; in Tarija 53
informal workers 120
InSight Crime 167
insitutionality 122, 131–132
institutionalization 45
Integrated Information and Statistics System 116
Integration of Regional Infrastructure in South America 24
Inter-American Drug Abuse Control Commission 156
International Court of Justice 23
International Narcotics Control Strategy 123, 161
International Organization for Migration 117
international trade: dynamics 24–25
Iquique Free Zone (ZOFRI) 57, 59–60, 107; smuggled products from 110
Isiboro Sécure and Carrasco National Parks 93
Italy 21

Japan 7, 47
Jiménez Guachalla, Diego Ernesto 153
Jorge Chávez airport 61, 112
Katanas case 118
laboratories 47, 80, 85, 123
labor exploitation 115–119, 150, 153–154
La Gaiba 33
Lake Titicaca 33, 35, 62
land borders 9, 27, 32, 38, 61–62
land routes 61, 86

La Paz 26, 35, 37–41, 43, 57, 60, 79, 83, 88–99, 115, 118, 123, 161
La Quiaca 56, 118
La Rinconada 119
Larrea, Freddy 121
Latin America 112, 119, 141, 154, 161, 173, 177; border system 10; global border system 14–15, 70; legal economy 12; trafficking in 80
Latin American and Caribbean Organization of Border Cities 177
Lauca River 33, 59
law 27, 59, 71, 78, 131, 136, 139–140, 155, 173; development of 2, 64, 133
Law 263 116–117, 149
Law 1008 134–135, 139–140, 146–147, 160, 170, 175
Law 1178 92
Law 1990 *see* General Customs Law
Law 3467 64
Law of Administrative Decentralization 27
Law on Amendments to the Criminal Code No. 1768 159
Law on the Control of Arms, Ammunition, Explosives, and Other Related Materials 154
Ledebur, Kathryn 143
Libro del mar 23
Licancabur volcano 33
Línea Roja 93
local border policies 176
Los Tiempos 121

Machicado 26
macro-corruption 138
macro-regions 29
Madera River 33
Madre de Dios River 33, 45
mafias 71, 160, 169, 173
Malaysia 105
Mamoré River 33, 47
Manaus 45
Mandioré 33
marijuana 34; consumption 173–174; destination routes 51; trafficking 51
marriage 150
McDermott, Jeremy 87–88
Medellín Cartel 85–86
Méndez, Armando 162
Mendoza 52
Mercosur 55
mercury 115
Mesa, Carlos 160

184 *Index*

Mexican cartels 85–86
microeconomics 81–82
migrant 49, 52, 153; flows of 32, 55;
 trafficking in 117–119
migration 8, 14, 21, 39, 45, 52, 57, 61, 71,
 169, 176
militarization 14, 144, 160
mineral fuels 110
mining 22, 71, 119; activities 46;
 cooperatives 133; gold 112; illegal 74,
 105, 111, 176
Ministry of the Environment and Water
 92
Ministry of the Presidency 27
Miranda, Boris 177
mirror cities 46
Modesto Omiste 56
Molina Céspedes, Tomás 134
money laundering 14, 24, 33, 53, 72, 74,
 114, 119, 121, 137, 156, 158, 175
Morales, Evo 102, 139, 141, 146, 154,
 161, 170
mules 55, 178
municipalization 9, 24, 27–28
murder 39, 46, 70
Mutún Iron Reserve 49
Mutún iron route 49

narcos 83, 123, 131–132; Bolivian 85, 103
National Acullico Day 160
National Committee against Illicit
 Firearms Trafficking 154
National Council for the Revaluation,
 Production, Commercialization, and
 Industrialization of the Coca Leaf
 (CONCOCA) 147, 161
National Customs 28, 111, 138
National Fund for Alternative
 Development (FONADAL) 146–148,
 161
National Institute of Agrarian Reform 93
National Institute of Statistics 32, 118, 151
nationalism 23
National Plan 151, 153
National Plan to Combat Trafficking in
 Persons 2015–2019 151
National Police 28
National Protected Areas Service 92
National Resource Governance Institute
 160
National Revolution 54
National Service for Registration and
 Marketing of Minerals 123

national subsystems 14
National Treasury 146
native palm hearts 47
Northern Border Plan 108
North Valley Cartel 84

Obama, Barack 161
Oceania 80
offshore logic 12
oil 5, 7, 55–56, 110, 160; crude 63
Ojo Público 112
Ollagüe volcano 33
Oporto, Henry 160
Organization of American States (OAS)
 117–118, 156, 173
organs 154; sale of 153
organ trafficking 169
Oruro 16, 35, 60, 153

Pablo Escobar 85, 123
Pacheco, Napoleón 70
Pacific flows 23
Painter, James 104
Palermo Protocol 149
Palmar de las Islas 33
Panamá City 135
Pando 20, 38, 44–46, 59
Paraguay 9, 18, 20, 33–35, 44, 49, 61, 88,
 110; smuggled products from 110
Paraguay River 33, 48
Paraná River 19, 49
Pastoral de Movilidad Humana 150–151
Payachata hills 33
Paz Estenssoro, Víctor 143
Paz Zamora, Jaime 143
penal codes 14–15
Peru 15, 33, 75, 80, 96, 114, 119, 141, 154,
 170; smuggled products from 110
Peruvian cocaine 46, 62, 105, 109, 161
phenacetin 103–104
physical borders 18, 21, 28, 62
pijcheo 146, 161
Pilcomayo River 33
pimping 117, 152, 154
pisacocas 104
Pisiga 57, 59, 107, 138
Plan Colombia 141–142
Plan Decenal 29
Plan de desarrollo 1984–1987 de Hernán
 Siles Suazo 29
Plan de todos de Gonzalo Sánchez de
 Lozada 29
Plan nacional de desarrollo 2006–2011 29

Plan quinquenal de Hugo Banzer Suárez 29
Plurinational Council against Trafficking and Smuggling in Persons 150
Pocitos 51, 63, 107
policies 132, 139, 153; anti-drug 156; anti-smuggling 137; border 14, 131; coca 139; comprehensive 168; definition 132; development 20, 45; eradication 78; import 120; local 63, 176; monetary 21; national security 14; prohibitionist 82–83; public 24, 131, 151, 175; sectoral 137; State 79, 173
policy: self-regulation of 145; anti-drug 140; plurinational 150
Polígono 7 93
Political Constitution of the State 149; reform 27
politicization 28, 159
Pontón, Daniel 72, 119
Popular Particiaption Law 27
porters *see bagalleros*
ports: Chilean 107; Pacific 19, 24
Porvernir 44
Potosí 38, 52–53, 56, 64, 95, 118
Primeiro Comando da Capital 84
prisoners 134
prisons 134, 136, 160, 176
privatization 74
Protocol against the Smuggling of Migrants by Land, Sea and Air *see* Palermo Protocol
Protocol to Prevent, Suppress, and Punish Trafficking in Persons, Especially Women and Children 149
Puerto Aguirre 19, 35, 48
Puerto Evo 44, 63–64
Puerto Gutiérrez Guerra 33
Puerto Quijarro 19, 44, 48–50
Puerto Suárez 19, 35, 44, 47–48, 61
Puno 35, 43, 88, 119

Quechua territory 35
Quezada, Gonzalo 123
quinine 18, 46
quintals 56, 64

rail network 57
rationalization 97, 124, 141–145, 170
raw materials 6, 22, 33, 81
recidivism 161, 178
Red Bull 174
red press 116

red zones 24
Regional Development Corporation of Tarija 54
Resolution No.003/2015 151
Revolutionary Armed Forces of Colombia (FARC) 39, 43, 46, 79, 84
Richard, Nicolás 23
Richmond Levering Co. 55
Rio Branco 23
Rio Negro 33
Ríos, Susana 121–122
Romero, Carlos 171
Rosario 52
rubber 5, 46–47, 109; cultivation 22; extraction 19–20
rural populations 60, 117
Russian mafia 84

Salinas, Siles 23
saltpeter 18
Salvador Mazza 53
Sanabria, René 135
Sánchez de Lozada, Gonzalo 143
San Ignacio 48
San José de Chiquitos 48
San José de Pocitos 63
San Matías 33
Santa Cruz 20, 38, 44, 47, 88, 118, 131, 170
Santa Fé 52
Santos, port of 19
São Paulo 21, 62, 88
Sauzal 54
sectoral studies 15, 167
Sendero guerrillas *see* Sendero luminoso
Sendero luminoso 39, 43, 46, 79; *see also* Shining Path
sex tourism 150
sex trade 115, 117
sexual exploitation 117–118, 150, 154; *see also* sex work
sex work 119
Shining Path 84, 124
Sinaloa Cartel 84
smuggling 153; adults 153; gold of 46, 71, 74, 111–114, 122, 169; goods 45; minors 153; persons 119, 149, 176; wood 46
Social and Economic Policy Analysis Unit 72
Socioeconomic Development Strategy 20
South America 24, 74, 105, 117–118, 123
Southern Common Market *see* Mercosur

186 *Index*

Spain 21, 117, 154
Special Force to Fight Crime 117
Standard Oil 55
sterile protectionism 139
Suárez, Roberto 123
sugar: factories 10; industry 55–56
sugarcane: crops 55; harvest 52, 117; industry 56
Supreme Decree 24771 159
Supreme Decree No. 1486 150
surplus crops 97, 143–144, 146, 170
swallowers 178

Tacna 107
Tambo Quemado 15, 57, 60, 138
Tamengo Channel 48–49
Tarija 38, 49, 52–57, 118, 131
technological innovations 174
terrorism 154, 156, 158
textiles 110, 138
tobacco 110
Torlot, Timothy 102
Torres Cuzcano, Víctor 112–114
traders 9, 57, 119, 133; micro- 120; small 169
transnational cartels 84; crime 14; criminal networks 69; organized crime 88, 170, 172
transparency 147, 158, 160
transport 55, 62; air 61; infrastructure 34; minerals 56
transportation 39, 55, 80
Treaty of 1904 18
Treaty of Peace and Friendship 23, 33
Treaty of Petrópolis 18
tripartite border 33; Argentina, Bolivia, and Paraguay 51
Tropic of Cochabamba 83, 90, 97, 144–145, 147; *see also* Cochabamba Tropics
Túpac Amaru Revolutionary Movement 84
Tuyuyú Channel 49
twin cities 44, 49, 60

U.S. Embassy's Anti-Narcotics Division 148
undocumented *see chuto*
United Nations 25, 83, 149, 160

United Nations Convention against Transnational Organized Crime 149
United Nations Office on Drugs and Crime (UNODC) 25, 83, 89, 90, 96, 102, 123, 135, 145, 149
United States 7, 21, 39, 47, 61, 86, 88, 103, 122–124, 141–148, 176
United States Agency for International Development (USAID) 146–148
United States Trade Commission 142
urbanization 34–35
urban sector 70
Uru Chipaya 60
Uruguay 49, 173

Valle de los ríos Apurímac, Ene y Mantaro 79–80
value added tax (VAT) 120
Vienna Convention 102, 140
vigilante justice 134
Villa Bella 33
Villamontes 51
Villazón 33, 35, 46, 56, 118
violence: border 13, 39, 60, 116; criminal 173; gender 13, 28; modern 13; traditional 13; urban 13; youth 14
Virreira, Mario 112
Visión Mundial Bolivia 151
Visviri 33, 60–61
vivanderas 63

Wall Street Journal 104
War for Oil *see* Chaco War
War of the Pacific 18, 23
war on drugs 141–142, 173
Washington Consensus 27
Washington Office on Latin America 143
West Africa 80, 161
Western Altiplano 56
White House 148
women 57, 115, 117, 135, 153, 177

Yacuiba 33, 35, 51, 53–55, 63
young people 119, 153, 177

Zapaleri 33
Zetas 84